CHILD RIGHTS
(ICDS Programme)

CHILD RIGHTS
(ICDS Programme)

By
Dr. T. Mamatha
&
Dr. D. Sarada

DISCOVERY PUBLISHING HOUSE PVT. LTD.
NEW DELHI-110 002

First Published – 2009

Reprinted – 2025

ISBN: 978-81-8356-429-8

Child Rights (ICDS Programme)

Published by:

DISCOVERY PUBLISHING HOUSE
4383/4B, Ansari Road, Darya Ganj
New Delhi-110 002 (India)
Phone: +91-11-23279245; 23253475; 43596065
Mobile: +91 9811179893 / +91 9871656464
E-mail: discoverybooksindia@gmaii.com
orderdphbooks@gmail.com
namitwasan9@gmail.com
web: www.discoverypublishinggroup.com

Printed at:
Infinity Imaging Systems
Delhi (INDIA)

Dedicated
to my
Beloved Husband

Contents

Foreword

Child Development in India has been planned to be achieved through a range of programmes and by different institutions both in the government and NGO sector. The development of children has occupied a prime position in the country and has been an integral part of its developmental planning since 1951. Tracing the historical development in this sector since then, provides evidence to increased governmental involvement with a marked shift from welfare to development. This shift has recorded the expansion of child welfare services to health, education and nutrition sectors with the launch of ICDS in 1975. ICDS still continues to be the country's largest and prime child development programme in India. An analysis of the recent trends and review of the child development programmes suggest that the country's perspective is considerably influenced by the UN convention on the rights of Children. However, the next paradigm shift from a development, needs based approach to a rights approach remains to be achieved.

The present research on "Reflection of Child Rights in the ICDS" aimed at studying the coverage of Child Rights in the ICDS programme is rightly timed and the observations would serve as an important source for policy makers and administrators to facilitate the shift towards a right based approach. The study not only assesses the coverage of child rights in the ICDS programme but also attempts to assess the knowledge, attitudes and practices of mothers and anganwadi workers towards child rights.

The research suggests the adoption of scientific approach through the development and use of appropriate scales to assess knowledge, attitudes and practices. What the 200 Mothers and equal number of anganwadi workers have shared is far from encouraging but indicates a good beginning in the derived direction. A large number of teachers/workers think that the anganwadi, to them, is a major source of knowledge about the child rights. This is an indication of the important role of this grass root level institution in making child rights a reality. Age, educational status, marital status and place of residence do not make a difference to the knowledge, attitudes and practices of the anganwadi workers. However, job experience records a significant difference to the child right's practice. The contribution of training to positive attitudes to child rights is well established in the study. However large gaps in practice are recorded. It is also interesting to note that these is no association between educational status and the child rights knowledge, attitude and practices of anganwadi workers. Building on the long years of experience of the anganwadi workers coupled with intensive trainings appears to be the path to be adopted by all those interested in adopting a rights approach to child development services. These workers then can work towards enhancing the mother's knowledge, Attitudes and Practices towards child rights, which now is far from satisfactory. Anganwadi emerges to be the non-negotiable institutional medium to protect the rights of the thousands of children in the country, the poor and the unreachable is particular.

To any one interested in child development, I commend to you the significance of this work. What can be more important than promoting child rights. While congratulating the authors for their work and contribution to the field of child rights. I request all concerned, academicians, practitioners, policy makers and administrators to read, reflect and respond and hope that it will lead to suitable action.

Prof. Uma Vennam

Dean; School of Social Sciences, Law and Management;
And Lead Qualitative Researcher
Young Lives Project
SPMVV - Tirupati.

Acknowledgement

In the preparation of this thesis, I have received help, advice and guidance from several quarters. My profound thanks and deep sense of gratitude to Dr. (Mrs.) D. Sarada, Associate Professor, Department of Human Development and Family Studies, SPMVV, Tirupati under whose meticulous care and guidance this research was completed. Her probing supervision, constructive and valuable suggestions, expert guidance and continuous inspiration made it possible for me to complete this enormous research with ease.

I am extremely grateful to Dr. (Mrs.) E. Manjuvani, Professor, Department of Human Development and Family Studies, SPMVV, Tirupati; Dr. (Mrs.) A. Violet, Professor, SPMVV, Tirupati for their advice and valuable suggestions.

I am indebted for the patient efforts of Dr. (Mrs.) Lavanya, Lecturer, Department of Statistics, S.P.W College, Tirupati in seeing me through with the statistical analysis.

I am also grateful to the Librarians of Sri Padmavathi Mahila Visvavidyalayam Library, Tirupati; Sri Venkateswara University Library, Tirupati; Middle Level Training Centre Library, S.V. University, Tirupati; National Institute of Public Co-operation and Child Development Library, New Delhi, for their co-operation in carrying out this enormous task, permitting me to utilise the library facilities.

I owe much for the completion of this study to Smt. Padmaja, CDPO, Puttur, Dr. Mrityanjaya Rao, MO, RASS, Tirupati, Supervisors, Anganwadi workers of Puttur, Ramachandrapuram, Vadamalapeta, Tirupati Rural and Urban Mandals and anganwadi children and their mothers for their co-operation in data.

I acknowledge with thanks for the help of Mrs. Bujji, Mr. Kumaresan and staff of M/s Students Xerox, Tirupati, for their promptness and expertise in computer work.

My indebtedness is beyond words to my brother-in-law Mr. B. Ravindra Babu for helping me in collecting data, my sister B. Rajeswari and my parents for their co-operation in caring my baby during this marvellous task.

Words are inadequate to express my appreciation and admiration to my husband Mr. A. Kiran Kumar for his co-operation and encouragement in this pursuit at this task.

T. MAMATHA

Abbreviations

AH	Anganwadi Helper
AIDS	Acquired Immuno Deficiency Syndrome
AIIMS	All Indian Institute of Medical Sciences
ANC	Anti-Natal Care
ANMs	Auxiliary Nurse Midwife
ANOVA	Analysis of Variance
ANP	Applied Nutrition Programme
AWC	Anganwadi Centre
AWW	Anganwadi Worker
BDO's	Block Development Officers
BMI	Body Mass Index
BNP	Balwadi Nutrition Programme
BPNI	Breastfeeding Promotion Network of India.
CAAS	Children Affected with AIDS
CBR	Crude Birth Rate
CDPOs	Child Development Project Officers
CHCs	Community Health Centres
CIAS	Children Infected with AIDS
CMR	Child Mortality Rate
CSSM	Child Survival and Safe Motherhood

CSWB	Central Social Welfare Board
CTC	Central Technical Committee
ECCE	Early Childhood Care and Education
ECOSOC	Economic and Social Council
FW	Family Welfare
GO	Government Organisation
HIV	Human Immuno Virus
IAP	Indian Academy of Paediatrics
IAP	Indian Academy of Paediatrics
ICDS	Integrated Child Development Services
ICMR	Indian Council for Medical Research
IDD	Iodine Deficiency Disorder
IFA	Iron Folic Acid tablets
IFTU	International Federation of Trade Unions
IMR	Infant Mortality Rate
INGO	International Non-governmental Organisation
IUCW	International Union Council of Women
IUCW	International Union for Child Welfare
IYC	International Year of the Child
LBW	Low Birth Weight
LHV	Lady Health Visitor
MCH	Maternal and Child Health
MDM	Midday Meal Programme
MLTCs	Middle Level Training Centres
MMR	Monthly Monitoring Report
MOs	Medical Officers

MUAC	Mid Upper Arm Circumference
NCHS	National Centre for Health Statistics
NFHS	National Family Health Survey
NGO	Non Government Organisation
NHP	National Health Policy
NIPCCD	National Institute of Public Co-operation and Child Development
NNFPD	National Neonatology Forum Perinatal Database
NNMB	National Nutrition Monitoring Bureau
NNMR	Neonatal Mortality Rate
NPC	National Policy on Children
ORS	Oral Rehydration Salt
ORT	Oral Rehydration Therapy
PEM	Protein Energy Malnutrition
PEO	Programme Evaluation Organisation
PHC	Primary Health Centre
PSE	Pre School Education
RASS	Rastriya Seva Samithi
RCH	Reproductive and Child Health
RTI	Reproductive Tract Infections
SCIU	Save the Children International Union
SNP	Supplementary Nutrition Programme
STD	Sexually Transmitted Diseases
TBA	Traditional Birth Attendants
TINP	Tamil Nadu Integrated Nutrition Programme
UN	United Nations

UNDP	United Nations Development Programme
UNESCO	United Nations, Education, Scientific and Cultural Organisation
UNICEF	United Nations Children's Education Fund
WNP	Wheat-based Supplementary Nutrition Programme

1

Introduction

"There shall be peace on earth, but not until
Each child shall daily eat his fill,
So warmly clad against the winter wind
And learn his lessons with a tranquil mind.
And thus released from hunger, fear and need,
Regardless of his colour, race or creed,
Look upwards, smiling to the skies,
His faith in man reflected in his eyes".

—***Dorothy Right*** (1999)

The child not only inherits but also transmits the human culture and civilisation, human values and ethos. The child is the greatest human asset and most valuable wealth, which has to be nourished with all love and care and protected from all kinds of evils and exploitation, so the human beings, will be happy and the world will prosper.

Children are considered as a gift of God by all cultures around the world. India's commitment to the cause of children is as old as its civilisation. Ancient texts like vedas, epics and religious scriptures provided the details of upbringing children and prescribed the roles and responsibilities of parents, families and societies towards children. These ancient texts are highly valued and respected by majority of Indians. Yet they are commented and criticised for the discrimination shown towards female children, indigenous populations, socially backward and the poor. The discrimination was prominent in accessing resources, education, health and nutrition. Over the years as a result of several social movements notable reforms were brought to eliminate discriminations and legislations were made to effect the reforms. (Pandey, 1993).

Government and Non-government organisations have made considerable efforts to improve the state of children in India. That is for the welfare of children policies was made, legislation frameworks were developed and programmes were organised. All these programmes failed miserably, due to lack of political will, lack of commitment in the administrators and lack of awareness among public/people. Though some of the welfare projects undertaken by the committed individuals and institutions for the development of children could achieve notable results. Majority of child welfare and development projects have failed in reaching the needy groups and leaving the state of children to deteriorate.

In addition, the current socio-economic and cultural changes have affected Indian families and brought changes in its structure, functions, roles and responsibilities and livelihood opportunities. These changes are more drastic among the rural and tribal populations, who are forced to migrate in search of livelihood opportunities. These changed situations placed rural, tribal and urban families, where they are unable to take care of their children and are exploited by the middle men, anti-social elements, traffickers etc. Thus the code of child centeredness got replaced by neglect, abuse and deprivation. Particularly in the poverty afflicted sections. (Sarada, 1999).

The plight and sufferings of millions of children the world over, particularly in the underdeveloped and in the developed countries has awakened the conscience of the people. The International Community has expressed its concern at the infant mortality, child labour, child abuse and in human exploitation of innocent human beings. The concern found its formal expression in the 10th December convention on the rights of child, drafted by United Nations Commission on Human Rights, and adopted by the General Assembly of the United Nation on 20th November 1989, is a set of International standards and measures intended to protect and promote the well-being of children in society, convention on children's rights came into force on 2nd September, 1990. The convention recognises the exceptional vulnerability of children, and proclaims that childhood is entitled to special care and assistance. It is guided by the principle of a "First Call for children" a principle that the essential needs of children should be given highest priority in the allocation of resources at all times. It obligates the states to respect and ensure that children get a fair and equitable deal in society. It emphasises the importance of the family and the need to create an environment that is conducive to the healthy growth and development of children. It advocates concerted public action by all individuals and agencies, government as well as non-governmental, at local, regional, national and international levels to promote the rights of children. The convention in a sense, is a means of empowering children, creating an environment in which all children are able to live securely and realise their full potential in life. (UNICEF, 1997)

The convention on the rights of the child speaks of four sets of civil, political, social, economic and cultural rights of every child. They are:

The Right to Survival: Which includes the right to life, the highest attainable standard of health, nutrition, and adequate standards of living. It also includes the right to a name and a nationality.

The Right to Protection: Which includes freedom from all forms of exploitation, abuse, inhuman or degrading treatment and neglect including the right to special protection in situations of emergency and armed conflicts.

The Right to Development: Which includes the right to education, support for early childhood development and care, social security, and the right to leisure, recreation and cultural activities.

The Right to Participation: Which includes respect for the views of the child, freedom of expression, access to appropriate information, and freedom of thought, conscience and religion (UNICEF, 2003).

This conviction, expressed as the convention on the rights entered into international law on 2 September 1990, nine months after the convention's adoption by the United Nations General Assembly. Since then the convention has been ratified (as of mid-September 1996) by all countries except the Cook Islands, Oman, Somalia. Switzerland, the United Arab Emirates and the United States, making it the most widely ratified Human Rights treaty in history.

The convention has produced a profound change that is already beginning to have substantive effects on the world's attitude towards its children. Once a country ratifies, it is obliged in law to undertake all appropriate measures to assist parents and other responsible parties in fulfilling their obligations to children under the convention. Now, 96 per cent of the world's children live in states that are legally obligated to protect child rights.

These rights are comprehensive. The convention defines children as people below the age of 18 (Article—1) whose "best interest" must be taken into account in all situations (Article—3). It protects children's rights to survive and development (Article—6) to their full potential, among its provisions are those affirming children's right to the highest attainable standards of care (Article—24), and to express views (Article—12) and receive information (Article—13). Children have a right to be registered immediately after birth and to have a name and nationality (Article—7), a right to play (Article—31) and to protection from all forms of sexual exploitation and sexual abuse (Article—34).

The convention recognises that not all governments have the sources necessary to ensure all economic, social and cultural rights immediately. But it commits them to make those rights a priority and to ensure them to the maximum extent of available resources. Fulfilling their obligations sometimes requires States to make fundamental changes in national laws, institutions, plans, policies and practices to bring them into line with the principles of the convention (UNICEF, 1997).

A statement of child rights is a statement of adult responsibilities. It is the responsibility of all adults. of governments and the International community, to create and maintain the circumstances in which families themselves can protect the rights of the child. Child rights needs to be understood by one and all, for which the information on child rights should be made available in all languages in the form of booklets, pamphlets, brochures, handouts etc. Any attempt to help children to utilise rights requires education of adults on child rights. Adults include parents, teachers, administrations, professionals, elders and all those who are involved in development of children with families and without families (UNICEF, 1987).

Child rights education demands appraisal of existing levels of knowledge, attitudes and practises of child rights by various sections of people and the stake holders of child welfare and development programmes. Basing on these appraisals need based child rights education programmes have to be developed using appropriate participatory methodologies. Such programmes receive greater attention, participation and commitment from the people for whom it is intended.

Several Child Welfare Programmes launched at different intervals highlight the priority and importance of young child's right to survival and development. Which is the responsibility of the State. National Policy on Children (NPC) 1974 directed the "State to provide adequate services to children, both before and after birth and throughout the period of growth—to ensure their full physical, mental and social development". A study team constituted by the Planning Commission in 1972 suggested comprehensive plan of action to meet the needs of children. As a result of the recommendation of the study team, along with the national policy of children in 1974, the Integrated Child Development Services (ICDS) project was started in 1975. In the initial stages ICDS was implemented in 33 selected community development blocks. Young children are most vulnerable, because the foundation for the life long learning and human development is laid in the early years, therefore the ICDS Programme has been designed to promote and facilitate total development of the child, through different components *viz.*, health, nutrition, pre-school education etc. (Lakshmi Devi, 1999)

The main aim of the programme is to reach every child from disadvantaged groups belonging to poor sections of our population. The main objectives of the ICDS Programmes are:

(a) To improve the nutritional and health status of children in the age group of 0-6 years;

(b) To lay the foundation for the proper psychological, physical and social development of the child;

(c) To reduce the incidence of mortality, morbidity, malnutrition and school drop-outs;

(d) To achieve effective coordination of policy and implementation among various departments to promote child development;

(e) To enhance the capability of the mother to look after the normal health and nutritional needs of the child through proper nutrition and health education.

ICDS programme launched in 1975-76 has already completed two successful decades of its services and has entered the third decade of its existence and is moving towards universalisation by the turn of the century. The year 1995-96 was a landmark when ICDS projects achieved 40 per cent universalisation. ICDS has emerged as a most powerful project for its holistic approach, empowering communities and families through trained local community-based women anganwadi workers (AWW) (Naswa, 1999). ICDS is the only major national programme that addresses the needs of children under six. It seeks to provide young children with an integrated package of services relating to nutrition, health and pre-school education. Because the needs of a child cannot be addressed in isolation from those of his or her mother, the programme also extends to pregnant women, nursing mothers and adolescent girls.

Basic ICDS services include supplementary nutrition, immunisation, health check-up, nutrition and health education, referral services and pre-school education. These services are provided through a vast network of ICDS centres, better known as "anganwadis". Each anganwadi is managed by an anganwadi worker (AWW), assisted by an anganwadi helper (AH). An anganwadi is supposed to cover a population of about 1,000 persons—roughly 200 families. The coverage of ICDS has steadily expanded since its inception in 1975. Currently, the programme is operational in almost every block, and the country has more than seven lakh anganwadis. However, the effective coverage of ICDS remains quite limited: barely one-fourth of all children under six are covered under the supplementary nutrition component. (Dreze, 2006)

As mentioned earlier, the basic premise of the demand for umversalisation of ICDS is that all children have a right to nutrition, health, pre-school education and related opportunities. The anganwadi is an institutional medium to protect these rights, or at least to bring them within the realm of possibility.

Despite the remarkable progress of the ICDS, some shortcomings have also been noticed in various evaluation reports. The major share of the project is absorbed in supplementary nutrition as already stated in the universalisation of ICDS. The maximum beneficiaries in 1996-97 were the children under Supplementary Nutrition Programme (SNP) on the contrary the beneficiaries of preschool education (PSE) were quite low. Though ICDS emphasises the importance to relieve girls from the burden of sibling care to enable them to participate in primary education, still the dropout figures are quite alarming. It has been observed that coordination among the Block Development Officers (BDO's), Child Development Project Officers (CDPO's) Medical Officers (MOs) etc. is sometimes not satisfactory. Coordination at the grassroot-level is very important for the successful implementation of the project. Similarly proper supervision and timely evaluations have also an important role to play. (Sinha, 2006)

The ICDS programme launched well before the declaration of the Child Right's and the international year of the child encompasses the most important child rights: Health (Article 23), Nutrition (Article 27 and 6), Education (Article 28 and 29) and also parental responsibilities (Article 18). The child rights' perspective to ICDS needs to be added and incorporated in these services and training of personnel.

ICDS aims at providing basic needs to the children of India. Basic needs of children have been included in the UN declaration of child rights as rights of children. So the needs of children have become the rights of children, fulfillment of which is a responsibility of families, societies, and the State. Hence it is become necessary to assess the child welfare programmes in view of child rights and their coverage. As ICDS is the largest and chief child development programme in India, the investigator made an attempt to study the reflection of child rights especially the health, nutrition and education rights in the ICDS programme.

STATEMENT OF THE PROBLEM

Integrated Child Development Services (ICDS) is India's response to the challenge of meeting the holistic needs of the children, launched initially in 33 blocks (33 Projects), on October 2, 1975.

The programme provides an integrated approach for converging basic services for improved child care, early stimulation and learning, health and nutrition, water and environmental sanitation—targeting young children, expectant and nursing mothers and adolescent girls groups. They are reached through nearly 300,000 trained community structures/women's groups—through anganwadi centres, the health system and the community.

As ICDS it stands at the threshold of the universal coverage by the turn of the century. It is the reality of today, on which our vision for tomorrow is founded. Thus. ICDS has covered 4,200 projects covering nearly 75 per cent community development blocks and 273 urban slum blocks. ICDS reaches out to 4.8 million expectant and nursing mothers and 22.9 million children (under 6 years of age) of disadvantage groups, of these 12.5 million children (3 to 6 years of age) participate in centre based pre-school education activities.

ICDS has several important characteristics which can be summarised as follows:

(i) It seeks to achieve the aim of child development through health, nutrition and early childhood education services;

(ii) It has the village centre as the focal point for the delivery of services to ensure maximum participation of pre-school children, pregnant mothers and lactating mothers;

(iii) It started in the most backward areas and expanded to cover more and more of such areas on priority basis;

(iv) It took conscious decision to create a minimum new staff structure focused on better utilisation of the existing infrastructure of primary health centres, medical institutions and other organisations;

(v) For the first time in any national programme the local women has been identified as a key functionary at the anganwadi centre for delivery of the mother care and child development services;

(vi) It has the unique feature of a very large number of honorary functionaries. This includes the anganwadi workers, health and paramedical staff and academicians;

(vii) It has established a systematic and well planned optimal cost of monitoring. training and evaluation system from the very beginning;

(viii) It has started the process of co-ordinations and team work amongst administrators. health staff, academicians and voluntary workers.

Well beyond the stage of experimentation, ICDS is here to stay and today it stands out as the world's largest programmes reaching the most disadvantaged and vulnerable sections of the society.

Well before the declaration of child rights by the United Nations, the National policy for children enunciated in August 1994 declared children as "a supremely important asset of the Nation, whose nurture and solicitude are the responsibility of the nation. The policy also recognised that it is in early childhood that the foundations for physical, psychological and social development are laid and that provisions of early childhood services especially, the child development services were need based, with the declaration of child rights by United Nations. The earlier approaches welfare, need based have changed to rights approach. Fulfillment of child needs by parents, family and State is no longer a choice, as they are rights of the child. Hence it is necessary to revisit the ICDS in the context of child rights in order to equip the service providers to deliver the services more effectively and also educate, empower the beneficiaries to access the services in order to make ICDS units more functional.

The rights approach to child development emphasis provision of quality services to all the children with greater accountability on the part of the service providers / ICDS functionaries.

Statement of the Problem

Reflection of child rights in the Integrated Child Development Service (ICDS) Programme.

Aim

To study the coverage of child rights in ICDS programme.

OBJECTIVES

1. To assess the coverage of child rights in the ICDS programme.
2. To assess the knowledge of anganwadi workers and mothers on child rights.
3. To assess the attitudes of anganwadi workers and mothers towards child rights.
4. To assess the practise of child rights by the anganwadi workers and mothers.
5. To assess the coverage of child rights component in the anganwadi workers training programme.
6. To assess the participation of mothers in the ICDS programme.
7. To know the relationship between the personal and service profile of anganwadi workers and their knowledge, attitudes and practise of child rights.
8. To know the relationship between personal and family profile of the mothers of anganwadi children on their knowledge, attitude and practise of child rights.
9. To know the difference between urban and rural anganwadi workers and mothers with regard to their knowledge, attitude, practise on child rights and participation.

HYPOTHESES

1. The coverage of child rights in ICDS programme is inadequate.

2. The child rights knowledge of anganwadi workers is low.
3. The child rights knowledge of mothers of anganwadi children is low.
4. The attitudes of anganwadi workers towards child rights is low.
5. The attitudes of mothers of anganwadi children towards child rights is low.
6. The practise of child rights by anganwadi workers is not adequate.
7. The practise of child rights by mothers of anganwadi children is not adequate.
8. The child rights component is not covered in the anganwadi workers training programme.
9. The participation of mothers in the ICDS programme is not adequate.
10. There is no relationship between personal and service profile of anganwadi workers and their knowledge, attitude and practice on child rights.
11. There is no relationship between personal and family profile of mothers and their knowledge, attitude and practise on child rights and participation anganwadi activities.
12. There is no difference between anganwadi workers of government organisation and non-governmental organisation managed ICDS projects with regard to their knowledge, attitude and practise on child rights.
13. There is no difference beriveen mothers of children attending anganwadi centres run by government organisation and non-governmental organisations management with regard to their child rights knowledge, attitude and practise.
14. There is no relationship between child rights knowledge, attitudes, practise of anganwadi workers and mothers.

2

Review of Relevant Literature

The concept of child rights added another dimension to child development, emphasising the need to view the existing child development programmes from the child rights perspective. Prior to 1975 the development programmes adopted welfare perspective, later came the need based approach which was followed by development perspective. The current approach to child development is rights approach with the declaration of child rights and India being signatory to it, there is every need to view our child development programmes from rights perspective.

The conceptual and theoretical issues relevant to the research topic "Reflection of Child Rights (Health, Nutrition and Education) in the Integrated child development services" was collected from various sources, books, journals reports and documents of government and other agencies, literature was reviewed in order to identify the gaps in literature, understand the research topic and formulate more appropriate research design.

The literature available on the research topic is presented under the following heads:

- Child—Definition and Concept
- Situational Analysis of Women and Children in India
- Early Childhood and Development Tasks
- Child Rights Declaration and Convention

- Child Rights and Indian Constitution
- Welfare Programmes for Child Development
- Integrated Child Development Services (ICDS)
- Integrated Child Development Service—Government Initiative for Voluntary Organisation.
- Theoretical and Empirical Issues on ICDS and Child Rights.

CHILD DEFINITION AND CONCEPT

"Child" is Human Offspring: Male or female passing through infancy, toddlerhood and childhood. Although infancy and childhood occupy only a small fraction of life span they are the most crucial years in determining and influencing the personality of adulthood. The needs of children have to be fulfilled at the right time as the childhood is for today and it cannot be made to wait till tomorrow (Mistral, 2002). The following poem of Gabriel Mistral well explains the urgency of children's needs fulfillment:

We are guilty of many errors and faults. But our worst crime is abandoning the children, neglecting the foundation of life, many of the things we need can wait the child cannot,

Right now is the time his bones are being formed,

His blood is being made

And his senses are being developed

To him we cannot answer "Tomorrow "

His name is Today.................

Dare we answer "Tomorrow"?

The child development professionals and scientists defined "child" in various ways, based on the care, needs, developmental tasks and roles of the child. Some of them are as follows:

"Child" one who has not reached maturity. Depending on the nature of the reference, the term may signify an individual between birth and puberty or one between infancy and puberty (Chaplin J.P. 1985)

"Child" a young boy or girl. Until the 17th century, there were no children in western cultures in fact, there was not even a word for "Child" in the English language (or in German or French). Children, after infancy, were simply small and inferior adults, sharing the then more limited adult world, also dressing and speaking like adults and the word child referred to kinship rather than age. (Medieval paintings depicted even neonates, including the infant Jesus, with adult features and adult head-to-body proportions). It was only with the evolution of the modern concepts of individuality and personality that children were seen apart from adults, and that the reality of child development and the need for child education became recognised (Goldenson, 1984).

"Child": What is a child? A thinking feeling entity? An organism shaped by parental constrictions? A possession of his or her family, of the government or of him or herself? A being in transis to adulthood? We see children as all of these, and more. We see children and their developmental needs as the fundamental building blocks of a human society. A society that does well by its children and their parents is basically sound (Bronfenbrenner, 1970)

The way the child's society defines the child influences contemporary policy and practice, and this macro system effect has existed since the ancient geniuses, Plato and Aristotle began their efforts to develop a systematic conceptualisation of human development. Their concern was to define the child in relation to family and society. Plato believed that most parents, inbued with the moral decadence of contemporary Athenian society, were unfit to raise their own children. Even parents who gave every appearance of being capable were still not up to the challenge of creating the caretakers of some future ideal state, because parenting techniques differed so widely that their separate influences would create a "medley of incongruities" in character of the citizens. (Laxmidevi, 1998).

Children is the plural of child which refers to an off spring of either of sex of human parents, a son or a daughter. The concept of the role of "Children" as held by many children, is greatly influenced by parental concepts. If parents think of children as dependents, children will learn to think of this as the child's role. If parents wait on their children, children will believe that a child should be waited on by parents. (Raul, 1999)

"Child" the various enactments do not have a uniform definition of the term "Child". The Bombay Children Act, 1948 defines "Child" as a boy or girl who has not attained the age of sixteen years. The Madhya Pradesh, and Uttar Pradesh Children acts stipulate the upper age limit as sixteen years. The East Punjab (applicable to the states of Punjab and Haryana), Andhra Pradesh (Telangana area) children acts also prescribe sixteen years as the age limit but includes children who are in certified schools though they have attained the age of sixteen years. Under the Andhra Pradesh (Andhra Area) Children Act, 1920, a child means a person under fourteen years and when used with reference to a child sent to a certified school applies to that child during the whole period of detention not withstanding that the child attains the age of fourteen before the expiration of that period. The Saurashtra and West Bengal Children Acts define a "Child" to mean a person who has not attained the age of eighteen years. However, under the Central Children Act a "Child" means a boy who has not attained the age of eighteen years. Thus, we see that the Central Act, unlike the State Acts, has made a meaningful distinction between boys and girls as regards their upper age limit. (Jain, S.N. 1979)

SITUATIONAL ANALYSIS OF WOMEN AND CHILDREN IN INDIA

In the Indian context, for the poor, the safe delivery of a healthy child and the survival of both mother and child cannot be taken for granted. Absence of a normative framework that supports the well-being of women and children is bound to adversely impact the manner in which the state takes up its responsibility towards mothers and infants. The infant mortality rate in India is 67 per 1,000 live births; 47 per cent of children are malnourished; there are 60 million underweight children under the age of five; and 67 per cent of pre-school deaths are associated with malnutrition. In absolute numbers, there are as many as 2.42 million malnutrition deaths under the age of five each year (Arun Gupta, Jon E. Rohde, 2004). The maternal mortality rate is 540 per 1,00,000, which is unacceptable by any standards (Human Development Report, 2004). When the data are further disaggregated on the basis of birth, socio-economic status, caste and gender across the country, analysis reveals that several districts and blocks in the country have alarming statistics on infant and maternal mortality, almost on par, if not even worse, than countries in sub-Saharan Africa. Bangladesh fares better than India with regard to both infant mortality and maternal morality rates. (Shantha Sinha, (2006)

There is an urgent need for new approaches and priorities in the overall strategy to reduce under-five mortality. Such a need is clearly indicated by the near stagnation of infant and child mortality in the last few years, the relatively large share of neo natal mortality, and the regional variations and inequities in child survival and health outcomes. Some of the strategies that need to be adopted are as follows:

Policy and programme emphasis on interventions to address perinatal and neonatal mortality: Ante-natal care, safe delivery and quality new born care are key requirements for reduction of perinatal/neo-natal mortality. All Community Health Centres (CHCs) and Primary Health Centres (PHCs) should be fully equipped to handle institutional deliveries and basic newborn care, and to transport emergencies to the nearest referral hospital where a paediatrician is available.

- **Safe delivery and Newborn Care:** Institutional deliveries must be actively promoted. In districts where home delivery is high, focussed and intensive training of Auxiliary Nurse Midwife (ANMs), and anganwadi workers in clean deliveries, new born care and the management of infections must be taken up. Since the auxiliary nurse midwife (ANM) may not be immediately available for home deliveries, the anganwadi workers should also be specifically trained in first-day care of the new born, to ensure referral and transportation of babies weighing less than 2.2 kg and those suffering from hypothemia/fever/convulsions, or signs of asphyxia.

- **Addressing low birth weight effectively:** Screening and referral for low-weight foetuses by auxiliary nurse midwife and primary health centre doctors must receive focus. Staff should be trained, and guidelines and treatment protocols developed to address low-birth weight babies for every level of care.

- **Timely medical interventions to control infections of the new born:** That this plays a major role in reducing Neonatal Mortality Rate (NNMR) is borne out by an intervention implemented in a district of Maharashtra during 1993-98. The most important medical causes of neonatal mortality rate were found to be sepsis, meningitis, and penumonia. A home-based package was designed to manage these infections ($5.3 per neonate), administered through village-based, trained health workers. The study results are phenomenal, with a reduction in the neonatal mortality rate by 50 per cent. The female health worker is the key in the delivery of the planned action. The Indian Council for Medical Research (ICMR) is undertaking operational research to explore the possibilities of replicating this experiment, if replicable, the current Reproductive and Child Health (RCH) programme must make provision for this intervention in high Infant Mortality Rate (IMR) districts. The anganwadi worker could also be trained to deliver this package with an extra remuneration per case.

- **Improve Immunisation and Vitamin A coverage levels:** Given the unsatisfactory immunisation coverage levels, the post-neonatal components of the child survival programme provide cause of concern. Andhra Pradesh has initiated a pilot computerised name-based registry system for monitoring immunisation coverage. The system will track each child by vaccine and by due date, information will be available on line, from the PHC upto the state directorate and secretariat. The system can be expanded to cover other intervention for Maternal and Child Health (MCH). Another key to improved immunisation coverage levels is the convergence of services between lCDS and health personnel, and a fixed-day programme for outreach services. Given the low coverage of vitamin-A and iron prophylaxis, a campaign mode on the lines of the pulse polio immunisation campaign could be considered. Orissa has implemented vitamin-A prophylaxis through a campaign mode every six months. To save on costs, one dose is given every year with the pulse polio campaign, and other after six months through an individual campaign. Wide publicity among the medical fraternity and the public must aim at concerted action to prevent this continuing tragedy.

- **Identify priority targets for health and the nutritional status of school children and plan interventions:** Data in micro studies reveal that school children are plagued by health and nutrition problems such as TB, helminthic infestations, parasitic worms, and deficiencies in iron, iodine and vitamin A. Health check-ups and supplements can be easily delivered in a school settings: in Gujarat, three million primary school children receive a mid-day meal which includes vitamin A, an iron supplement, and an anti-worm drug. The state reports coverage of over 90 per cent compared to the earlier 40 per cent. This effort has not yet been independently evaluated for coverage and cost-benefits, but it appears to be a good model for replication. (Sinha, 2006)

- **Define and implement specific prevention and treatment protocols for major causes of childhood death:** This applies to diarrhoea, measles, malaria in some areas and malnutrition, staff at each level of care must be trained to deliver services.
- **Monitor and check the misuse of technologies:** Although appropriate authorities have been formed, the prenatal diagnostic techniques, act to prevent and control misuse is a non-starter in most states.

India crossed the one billion population mark in May 2000. The second most populous country, India accounts for 16.7 per cent of the world's population and 2.4 per cent of the total world area. In the mid 1990s, the annual population growth declined below two per cent but because of the huge population base this translates into a net population gain of around 18 million a year. As per the 2001 census, children aged 0-6 years number around 158 million.

The Crude Birth Rate (CBR) has declined from 148.1 in 1911 to 26.1 in 1999. Similarly the CBR too has declined from 47.2 in 1911 to 8.7 in 1999. The expectation of life at birth which was 37.1 years for males and 36.1 for female in 1951 rose to 62.8 for males and 63.4 years for females in 1996-2001. Yet, in spite of these achievements, the country as a whole has not made many great strides in the last five and half decades. This is not due to lack of political or administrative will, but on account of magnitude of the problem, the size of the numbers involved, financial constraints, the complexity of the vicious cycle of poverty.

Infant Mortality Rate (IMR) an indicator of Human Development Index (HDI), even though has declined drastically from 204 in 1911 to 70 in 1999, it is still high. It is much higher for rural areas (77) than urban regions (45). There are vast variations (SRS, 1999) in different parts of the country with lowest in Kerala at 16 and highest in Orissa (98). IMR is found to be higher among females at 73 as compared to males at 70.

The health of women and that of children are closely linked and while looking for factors affecting infants and children, the analysis is incomplete unless the health of women is looked into, as well. However, for a better understanding of factors that has an impact on levels and trends of morbidity and mortality the discussion has been organised within an analytical framework using life cycle approach. Firstly affecting the fetus, newborn, neonate, infant young child and adolescent has been discussed then going on to motherhood. The socio-environmental factors have been dealt along with the different stages in life giving relevant data wherever possible.

Perinatal Period

The Perinatal period spans both the intr-auterine and extra uterine periods and emphasises the continuity of hazards in both. It is defined as the period that begins after twenty-eight weeks of intra-uterine life and extends upto 7 days after birth. A high perinatal death rate is an indication of poor supervision of maternal health, inadequate facilities during delivery and care of the baby after birth. The common causes of perinatal deaths that relate to mother include pregnancies under 18 years and over 35 years of age, high parity, spacing of less than two years, poor nutrition particularly anaemia, toxemia and diabetes; causes of perinatal deaths that relate to foetus are premature baby, low birth weight babies and twins; and common causes of perinatal death that relate to the infant include birth injuries, asphyxia neonatorum, infection including tetanus, hypothermia and congenital malformations. All these causes are preventable with proper care of newborn baby. At the national level perinatal mortality has been estimated to be 42 (SRS, 1998). It is higher in rural areas 45 as compared to urban areas 29.

Still birth rate (SRS, 1998) is estimated at 9 and ranges from 8 in urban areas to 9 in rural areas. Perinatal mortality is three times higher for Low Birth Weight (LBW) babies. Improving maternal nutrition and reducing the prevalence and severity of anaemia will help to improve birth weight.

Neonatal Mortality

The neonatal death rate is estimated at 45 (SRS, 1998) i.e. deaths within one month after birth per 1000 live births is also high and accounts for 63 per cent of infant deaths. The causes of neonatal mortality include low birth weight, asphyxia, infection, sequelae of birth trauma and congenital malformation. Infections are often related to unhygienic delivery practices. Tetanus neonatorum still remains a significant cause of death, though the incidence has came down greatly because of tetanus toxoid during pregnancy and improved delivery practices. Strict hygiene during delivery observing the 5Cs (clean surface, clean hands, cutting the cord with sterilen blades, sterile cord and no application on the cord stump) and administration of two doses of TT to the mother during pregnancy can totally eliminate the infection-tetanus neonatorum.

Childhood Diseases

About 12.4 million children under the age of 5 years die every year in developing countries. The main causes of death are infections (*viz* ARI, diarrhoea, measles and malaria) often combined with malnutrition. Countries in South East Asia Region (SEAR) contribute to nearly 40 per cent of these deaths. More than 9 out of 10 of those deaths occur in five countries of the region which include Bangladesh, India Indonesia, Myanmar and Nepal. In India, of the 25 million children born every year, approximately 2.7 million die before completing five years of age. Of these, nearly two-thirds, close to two million die before reaching the age of one. Of these almost 60 per cent die before reaching the age of one month. India also has the unfortunate distinction of having 75 million (63%) of malnourished children under five. Compared with the risks facing a well nourished child, the risk of death from common childhood diseases is doubled for a mildly malnourished child and may be eight times for a severely malnourished child.

Causes of Infant Deaths

Prematurity remained top killer among the ten top killer diseases of infants accounting for 29.9 per cent deaths of the total reported 70 per cent deaths due to ten specific cause-groups such as—prematurity; pneumonia; respiratory infection of newborn; congenital malformation; anaemia, diarrhoea of newborn; tetanus neonatorum; birth injury; typhoid and paratyphoid; and bronchitis and asthma.

Morbidity Status

Respiratory infections together with diarrhoea are the most common causes of morbidity and mortality in childhood. These range from the simplest form—the common cold and cough to pneumonia. Most children with cough need simple home care and no antibiotics. A child with cough and cold need to be given extra fluid and her nostril to be cleaned so that she has no problem in having breastfeeds. Two key signs of pneumonia that parents and caregivers need to watch for are fast breathing and chest indrawing. In such a case a child has to be taken to a health facility but unfortunately due to lack of awareness on the parts of parents or caregivers, usually a life is lost. National Family Health Survey (NFHS-II) (1998-99) found that 19 per cent of children under age three in India suffered from ARI. About 64 per cent of children received some advice or treatment from a health facility or health provider when ill with ARI. This percentage was low for children whose mothers are illiterates, who live in household with low standards of living. Boys, urban children and children of birth order one were taken to a health facility or provider for advice or treatment than their counterparts.

Diarrhoea is a common childhood morbidity. Most under privileged children have 4 to 5 episodes of diarrhoea in a year. Diarrhoea is the cause of death of one in four deaths among children. Dehydration usually is the main cause of death and it is easy to prevent such death. Rehydration is the key to saving life which can be done by giving Oral Rehydration Salt (ORS) a low cost technology.

However, data received from NFHS-II (1998-99) is not very encouraging. NFHS II (1998-99) found that 19 per cent children under three had diarrhoea. Only 62 per cent mothers knew about ORS packets. Knowledge of ORS packets was somewhat lower among mothers aged 15-19 and among mothers age 35 years or older than among mothers in the middle age groups. Knowledge was considerably higher among urban mothers 76 per cent than rural mothers 59 per cent and among more educated mothers especially literate mothers as compared with illiterate mothers.

Immunisation Status

Immunisation is a born to developing countries in particular and the world in general. It is one major strategy for bringing down mortality and promoting life of children. However, according to NFHS-II (1998-99) only 42 per cent of children aged 12-23 months had primary immunisation and 14 per cent had not received any vaccination according to NFHS II. More boys 43 per cent were fully vaccinated than girls 41 per cent. Only 28 per cent of children of illiterate mothers were fully vaccinated as compared to 73 per cent of mothers who have at least completed high school.

Infant Feeding Practices

Infant feeding practices have significant effects on both mothers and children. Mothers are affected through the influence of breastfeeding on the period of postpartum infertility and hence on fertility levels and length of birth interval. These effects vary by both the duration and intensity of breastfeeding. Proper infant feeding, starting from time of birth is important for the physical and mental development of the child. Breastfeeding improves the nutritional status of young children and reduces morbidity and mortality. Breast milk not only provides important nutrients but also protects the child against infection. The timing and type of supplementary foods introduced in a child's diet also have significant effect on child's nutritional status.

According to NFHS II (1989-99) only 16 per cent of children began breastfeeding within one hour and 37 per cent within one day. Nearly two-thirds of women discarded colostrum rich in antibodies. Also some mothers give prelacteal feeds such as fresh milk or powdered milk in the belief that there is no milk, this practice may give infection to the child as also the infant may not want to suck again leading to problems. Only 55 per cent children received exclusive breastfeeding only 35 per cent breastfed children received solid and mushy foods. Also median duration of breastfeeding is two months shorter for girls than for boys showing preference for boys over girls. The median of breastfeeding of children in rural areas was five months longer than in urban areas.

Nutritional Status of Children

Nutritional status is a major determinant of the health and well being of children. Inadequate or unbalanced diets and chronic illnesses are associated with poor nutrition among children. Infections causes undernutrition, because it reduces food intake (child may not be hungry or mother may reduce food quantity), but increases the body's need for nutrients. If a child does not eat much during illness and does not eat enough during recovery to regain the weight lost nutrients, she becomes malnourished. Three indices weight-for-age, height-for-age, and weight-for-height were used to ascertain the nutritional status in NFHS-II (1998-99) and the data revealed that almost half of children under three years of age were underweight and a similar percentage 46 per cent were stunted. Wasting affected 16 per cent of children under-three.

The nutritional status of children strongly related to maternal nutritional status. Undernutrition was more common for children of mother whose height was less than 145 cm or whose body mass index was below 18.5. Children from households with low standard of living were twice as likely to be under-nourished as compared to children from households with a high standard of living.

Anaemia

Anaemia too is a serious concern for young children because it can result in impaired growth and development as also increase morbidity from infections and diseases. According to NFHS-II (1998-99) nearly three-quarter of children between 6 months-3 years had some anaemia including 23 per cent who were mildly anaemic, 46 per cent moderately anaemic and 5 per cent who were severely anaemic.

Gender Bias in Nutrition and Health

A large number of deaths in early childhood account for most of the skewedness in the overall sex ratio. Malnutrition is a significant underlying factor in many of these deaths. Nutritional status and growth are influenced not only by the adequacy of food intake but illness episodes, severity and duration of illness, treatment received and feeding and care during and after illness episode also exercise an interrelated effect on the child's growth profile. There is abundant research to indicate that gender bias in allocation of food and health care is widely prevalent.

Because of undernourishment, girls are likely to take longer time to recover from illness. This combined with a lack of appropriate medical attention during the vulnerable years of childhood accounts for the considerably higher morbidity in childhood. It is a grave indictment of the cultural norms and perceptions that defeats the biological head start with which the female is endowed. Given equivalent environmental factors *viz.* exposure to the risks of health impairment and provision of health care, fewer females than males should die of infection and malnutrition. Delayed inadequate or no health care during illness accounts for the abysmally low sex ratio in India. Girl's environment disadvantage far outweighs their genetic advantage.

Female Foeticide and Declining Sex Ratio

In India since the beginning of the century male to female ratio has been worsening. In 1901 there were 972 females for 1000 males and it has declined to 933 in 2001. There is ample data on discrimination against the female sex starting even before birth and going on till death. Sex preselection is gaining more and more popularity, while the States of Andhra Pradesh, Maharashtra and Rajasthan have imposed legal ban on the practice, it continues to increase in other parts of the country especially the States of Haryana and Uttar Pradesh. Infact, Rohtak District in Haryana is called the fulcrum of female foeticide. Every year thousands of healthy female fetuses are being aborted. It was estimated that in the period 1979-83, alone 75,000 such abortions took place.

Adolescence

Adolescence represents a period of active growth. According to data from national surveys, during adolescence, girls of poor rural communities gain over 5 cm in height and nearly 6.8 kg. in body weight. The adolescent growth support represents a second opportunity to make even the mal-affects of childhood undernourishment. Studies have shown that if fed adequately during this period, girls are likely to experience catch-up growth and achieve adult size comparable to better nourished children.

Majority of girls low income families reach adolescence about 12-15 cm shorter than their well-do peers in the same society. The National Nutrition Monitoring Bureau (NNMB's) data on Indian women's height and weight shows that 12 to 23 per cent of 20-24 year old women in different states surveyed were less than 145 cm tall and between 15 to 29 per cent were below 38 kg in weight (NIPCCD, 2004).

Age at Marriage

Age at marriage is an important indicator to determine the health of women and her child. The percentage of women who got effectively married before the age of 18 years is 17.8 at the national level and varies from 1.6 in Himachal Pradesh to 58.9 in Andhra Pradesh. Unless girls are allowed to develop to their full potential before taking on reproductive role, we would be loosing them and the infant. Hence, enforcement machinery to be strengthened to adhere to the legal age of marriage for girls and boys to help them become responsible parents.

Birth Spacing

A major hazard for both children and mothers are pregnancies that are too early (under 18 years), too late after (35 years), too many (more than three or four) and too frequent (spacing less than two years). At the national level 2.8 per cent live births occur within one year from the previous live births. The number of children a women has along with birth interval is one of the key factor that determines not only her health but also her child's health. The level varies considerably with level of education. Hence, improving levels of education as well as improving family planning services is key to bringing down the fertility rates.

Maternal Mortality

Maternal mortality is estimated at 437 per 100,000 live births and the main causes are anaemia, haemorrhage, sepsis and toxaemia. It is estimated that India has only about 15 per cent of the world's population, at least 25 per cent of the world's maternal mortality occur in India. There is a direct correlation between maternal and infant deaths, through the period of adolescence to womenhood. According to NFHS II (1998-99) the mean Body Mass Index (BMI) for women in India is 20.3 (chronic energy deficiency is usually indicated by a BMI of less than 18.5) and more than one-third of (36%) of women have BMI below 18.5. The BMI was lower for rural women, illiterate women, SC and ST women and women who live in households with low standards of living.

Anaemia among Women

Anaemia is widely prevalent and almost 80-90 per cent of women during the third trimester of pregnancy have a haemoglobin level of less than 11 gm/dl. The anaemia prophylaxis programme under RCH has not made the desired impact due to many reasons; lack of complacence among women, poor quality of tablets, lack of awareness about the importance of tablets, long waiting time, etc. According to NFHS-II (1998-99) overall 52 per cent women have some degree of anaemia, a 35 per cent are mildly anaemic, 15 per cent are moderately anaemic and 2 per cent severely anaemic.

Diet during Pregnancy

A woman needs extra calories during pregnancy to build up her own tissues to build fat stores, to make breast milk and for growth of the fetus and placenta. According to the estimates of ICMR her dietary requirement is 2500 Kcal/day. However, most women do not eat extra food even if it is available at home because of fear of large baby leading to difficult delivery. Many beliefs and taboos too exist regarding pregnant women's diet, several foods are considered bad. All these factors compound leading to a calorie gap of 500 to 600 Kcal a day (25 to 35 per cent of requirement). Poor dietary intake during pregnancy, hard physical work and anaemia result in poor weight gain during pregnancy. Underprivileged poor women gain only 3 to 5 kg weight during pregnancy as opposed to 10 to 12 kg which better socio-economic group women do. Of this weight gain of 10 kg about half is contributed by the weight of fetus, placenta and amniotic fluid and to other half by the deposition of fat which provides a store that can be used during lactation.

About 15 per cent deaths among women of reproductive age are pregnancy related. Illegal abortion is a major cause of maternal deaths. Even though the Medical Termination of Pregnancy Act (MTPA) was passed in 1971, a large number of abortions estimated at over 6 lakhs annually continue to be carried out illegally.

Children of anaemic mothers tend to have low birth weight which increase their risk of illness and death. Perinatal mortality increases 2 to 3 fold when maternal haemoglobin levels fall below 5g/dl.

Antenatal Care

Ideally antenatal care should monitor a pregnancy for signs of complications, detect and treat preexisting and concurrent problems of pregnancy and provide advice and counselling on preventive care, diet during pregnancy, delivery care, postnatal care and related issues. The Reproductive Child Health (RCH) programme recommends that as part of antenatal care women should have a minimum of three antenatal check-ups, receive two doses of tetanus toxoid vaccine, adequate amount of iron and folic acid tablets or syrup to prevent and treat to detect pregnancy complications.

According to National Family Health Survey NFHS-II (1998-99) percentage of women who had:

Atleast one antenatal check-up	65.4
Atleast three or more anti-natal (AN) check-ups	43.8
Received and anti-natal care (ANC) in the first trimester of pregnancy	33.0
Received two or more doses of tetanus toxoid injection	66.8
Received iron folic acid (IFA) tablets	57.6
Received 3 months supply of IFA tables	47.5

Nutritional Status of Women

Since the mother has to nurture the foetus, her nutrition and health have a direct relationship with birth weight and foetal stores of iron, vitamin-A and nutrients. A majority of women are underweight and anaemia, and this malnutrition sets in childhood.

Maternal Nutrition and Low Birth Weight Babies

Inadequate weight gains results in low birth weight (less than 2.5 kg) of the baby. National Neonatology Forum Perinatal Database (1994) from 14 large hospitals from 9 States spanning 24,410 live births showed prevalence of low birth weight to be 30 per cent. The proportion of LBW babies reflects the condition of women, and particularly their health and nutrition not only during pregnancy but over the whole of their childhood and young lives. Early marriage, repeated pregnancies and short inter pregnancy intervals are contributing factors not only among LBW babies, and these small babies grow up to be small adults and in the case of girls, small mothers who in turn give birth to LBW babies perpetuating the intergenerational malnutrion cycle.

Type of Medical Attention Received at Birth

Ideally a delivery should be conducted by such trained personnel as Traditional Birth Attendants (TBA) or ANM or any other trained health personnel. A significant reduction in maternal and infant mortality can be achieved by this strategy. Institutional deliveries should be encouraged for better health of mother and child. However, at the national level more than 25 per cent of births were institutional i.e. attended by medical personnel in institutions and about 29 per cent were attended by trained medical professionals. Nearly 42 per cent of the births were attended by traditional birth attendants. More than 4 per cent of births were attended by relatives and others.

Postnatal Care

The health of a mother and her newborn child depends not only on the health care she receive during her pregnancy and delivery, but also on the care she and the infant receives during the first few weeks after delivery. Only 17 per cent of non-institutional births were followed by a check-up within two months of the delivery.

Female literacy is considered to be one of the most sensitive indices of social development. The education of girls is a worthy objective in itself and needs no further justification. Nonetheless the 'second order' affects of female literacy with respect to promoting social development in general, make the objective doubly worthy of pursuit. Social development has significant beneficial consequences for women, men and children. Some of these consequences include lower fertility rates, lower IMR and child mortality rate, lower population growth and greater participation of women in different sectors of the country.

The overall mortality rate declines sharply with increasing education of mothers ranging from a high or 87 deaths per 1000 liver births for illiterate mothers to a low of 33 deaths per 1000 births, for mother who have atleast completed high school. Similar figure for neonatal mortality rate is 55 deaths per 1000 live births for illiterate mothers to 24 deaths per 1000 live births for mothers who have atleast completed high school. An educated mother make better use of health services, provide better child care including feeding, have more hygienic households, have better knowledge of appropriate child rearing practices and are more assertive and more likely to change their beliefs. Education contributes in delaying age at marriage and contributes a small family norms—all contributing to better health and nutrition. Also women's autonomy and status and her control over what she earns also correlates with better nutrition of the child.

School Attendance

In the country as a whole 79 per cent of children 6-14 years are attending school according to NFHS-II (1998-99) as against 68 per cent in NFHS-I. The attendance rate drops off sharply to 49 per cent at age 15-17 years. For the age group 6-17 years, the attendance rate is 78 per cent for males 66 per cent for females, and 72 per cent for India as a whole. In urban areas attendance rates for males and females differ by less than 5 percentage points for every age group. In rural areas, however, attendance rates are considerably higher for males than for females at every age, and the gap widens with increasing age. For both males and females schools attendance rates are much higher in urban areas than the rural areas in every age group.

The gap between the participation rates of boys and girls in elementary education is the biggest single gap that needs to be filled by universalisation. Gender disparity in participation rates reflect the discriminatory social attitude with respect to the girl child. While the solution for this problem does not lie entirely in the education system, education can and should play a positive role in the improvement of women's status by fostering the development of new values through redesigned curricular textbooks as well as the training and orientation of teachers, decision-makers and administrators as the most critical educational institution in an individual's life, the school can provide exposure to a counter-culture that engenders self esteem, confidence and decision making skills in girls. This would have far reaching implications for the status of women and children in the next and succeeding generations.

EARLY CHILDHOOD AND DEVELOPMENTAL TASKS

Most people think of childhood as a fairly long period in the life span—a time when the individual is relatively helpless and dependent on others.

Although the foundations of some of the developmental tasks young children are expected to master before they enter school are laid in babyhood, much remains to be learned in the relatively short four-year span of early childhood. When babyhood ends, all normal babies have learned to walk, though with varying degrees of proficiency; have learned to take solid foods; and have achieved a reasonable degree of physiological stability. The major task of learning to control the elimination of body wastes has been almost completed and will be fully mastered within another year or two. While most babies have built up a useful vocabulary, have reasonably correct pronunciation of the words they use, can comprehend the meaning of simple statements and commands and can put together several words into meaningful sentences, their ability to communicate with others and to comprehend what others say to them is still on a low level. Much remains to be mastered before they enter school.

Similarly, they have some simple concepts of social and physical realities, but far too few to meet their needs as their social horizons broaden and as their physical environment expands.

Few babies know more than the most elementary facts about sex differences and even fewer understand the meaning of sexual modesty. It is questionable whether any babies, as they enter early childhood, actually know what is sex-appropriate in appearance, and they have only the most rudimentary understanding of sex appropriate behaviour. This is equally true of concepts of right and wrong. What knowledge they have is limited to home situations and must be broadened to include concepts of right and wrong in their relationships with people outside the home, especially in the neighbourhood, in school, and on the playground.

Even more important, young children must lay the foundations for a conscience as a guide to right and wrong behaviour. The conscience serves as a source of motivation for children to do what they know is right and to avoid doing what they know is wrong when they are too old to have the watchful eye of a parent or a parent substitute constantly focussed on them. One of the most important and, for many young children, one of the most difficult of the developmental tasks of early childhood, is learning to relate emotionally to parents, siblings, and other people. The emotional relationships, which existed during babyhood must be replaced by more mature ones. The reason for this is that relationships to others in babyhood are based on babyish dependence on others to meet their emotional needs especially their need for affection. Young children, however, must learn to give as well as to receive affection. In short, they must learn to be outer bound instead of self bound.

Physical Development

Growth during early childhood proceeds at a slow rate as compared with the rapid rate of growth in babyhood. Early childhood is a time of relatively even growth, though there are seasonal variations; July to mid-December is the most favourable time for increases in weight, and April to mid-August is most favourable for height increases.

Physical Development in Early Childhood

Height: The average annual increase in height is three inches. By the age of six, the average child measures 46.6 inches.

Weight: The average annual increase in weight is 3 to 5 pounds. At age six, children should weigh approximately seven times as much as they did at birth. The average girl weighs 48.5 pounds, and the average boy weighs 49 pounds.

Body proportions: Body proportions change markedly, and the "baby look" disappears. Facial features remain small but the chin becomes more pronounced and the neck elongates. There is a gradual decrease in the stockiness of the trunk, and the body tends to become cone-shaped, with a flattened abdomen, a broader and flatter chest, and shoulders that are broader and squarer. The arms and legs lengthen and may become spindly, and the hands and feet grow bigger.

Body-Build: Differences in body build become apparent for the first time in early childhood. Some children have an endomorphic or flabby, fat body build, some have a mesomorphic or sturdy, muscular body build, and some have an ectomorphic or relatively thin body build.

Bones and Muscles: The bones ossify at different rates in different parts of the body, following the laws of developmental direction. The muscles become larger, stronger, and heavier, with the result that children look thinner as early childhood progresses, even though they weigh more.

Fat: Children who tend toward endomorphy have more adipose than muscular tissue; those who tend toward mesomorphy have more muscular than adipose tissue, and those with an ectomorphic build have both small muscles and little adipose tissue.

Teeth: During the first four to six months of early childhood, the last four baby teeth—the back molars erupt. During the last half year of early childhood, the baby teeth begin to be replaced by permanent teeth. The first to come out are the front central incisors—the first baby teeth to appear. When early childhood ends, the child generally has one or two permanent teeth in front and some gaps where permanent teeth will eventually erupt.

Emotions of Early Childhood

Emotions are especially intense during early childhood. This is a time of disequilibrium when children are "out of focus" in the sense that they are easily aroused to emotional outbursts and, as a result, are difficult to live with and guide. While this is true of the major part of early childhood, it is especially true of children aged 2½ to 3½ and 5½ to 6½.

Although any emotion may be "heightened" in the sense that it occurs more frequently and more intensely than is normal for that particular individual, heightened emotionality in early childhood is characterized by tempertantrums, intense fears, and unreasonable outbursts of jealousy. Part of the intense emotionality of children at this age may be traced to fatigue due to strenuous and prolonged play, rebellion against taking naps, and the fact that they may eat too little. Much of the heightened emotionality characteristic of this age is psychological rather than physiological in origin. Most young children feel that they are capable of doing more than their parents will permit them to do and revolt against the restrictions placed upon them. In addition, they become angry when they find they are incapable of doing what they think they can do easily and successfully. Even more important, children whose parents expect them to measure up to unrealistically high standards will experience more emotional tension than children whose parents are more realistic in their expectations.

Socialisation in Early Childhood

One of the important developmental tasks of early childhood is acquiring the preliminary training and experience needed to become a member of a "gang" in late childhood. Thus early childhood is often called the pre-gang-age. The foundations for socialisation are laid as the number of contacts young children have with their peers increases with each passing year. Not only do they play more with other children, but they also talk more with them.

The kind of social contacts young children have is more important than the number of such contacts. If young children enjoy their contacts with others, even if they are only occasional, their attitudes towards future social contacts will be more favourable than if they have more frequent social contacts of a less favourable kind. Children who prefer interacting with people to interacting with objects develop more social know-how and, as a result, are more popular than those who have limited social interactions.

Moral Development in Early Childhood

Moral development in early childhood is on a low level. The reason for this is that young children's intellectual development has not yet reached the point where they can learn or apply abstract principles of right and wrong.

Neither do they have the necessary motivation to adhere to rules and regulations because they do not understand how these benefit them as well members of the social group. Because of their inability to comprehend the why and where forces of moral standards, young children must learn moral behaviour in specific situations. They merely learn how to act without knowing why they do so. And because the retention of young children, even those who are very bright, tends to be poor, learning how to behave in a socially approved way is a long, difficult process. Children may be told not to do something one day but, by the next day or even the day after that, they may have forgotten what they were told not to do. Thus what may appear to adults to be willful disobedience is often only a case of forgetting.

Childhood Misdemeanors

Misdemeanors—mild forms of breaking of rules or misbehaviour—are very common during the pre-school years. This is one of the reasons why young children are regarded as "troublesome" and why they are said to be in states of disequilibrium. There are three common causes of misdemeanors during the early childhood years.

First, young children may misbehave due to ignorance of the fact that their behaviour is disapproved by the social group. They may have been told what a rule is but they may have forgotten it or they may not understand all the different situations the rule applies to. They may, for example, understand that it is wrong to take the material possessions of others—toys, candy, money etc., but they do not associate cheating taking another person's work as a form of stealing;

Second, many young children learn that willful disobedience of a minor sort will generally bring them more attention than good behaviour. Thus, children who feel that they are being ignored may misbehave in the hopes of gaining the attention of others; and

Third, boredom may be responsible for much misbehaviour during the years of early childhood. It is a case of "idle hands getting into mischief".

When young children have too little to occupy their time and attention, they want to "Stir up some excitement", just as bored teenagers often do. Or they may want to test adult authority to see how much they can get away with without being punished. While young children engage in every conceivable kind of misdemeanor, the most common forms are capriciousness ("Orneriness"), thumb-sucking, bed-wetting, boisterous attempts to get attention, tempertantrums, lying, destructiveness, cheating in games, and dawdling. Most of these are associated with immaturity and appearless and less frequently as the child grows older.

Family Relationships in Early Childhood

Even when young children begin to play with other children outside the home, the family remains the most important socialising influence. Not only are there more contacts with family members than with other people, but the contacts are closer, warmer, and more emotionally tinged than contacts with those outside the home. These close family relationships exert a greater influence over the child than do any other social influences. However, how much influence different family members have depends on their individual relationship with the child. In general, young children's attitudes toward people, things, and life in general are patterned by their home life. Although no one method of child training can guarantee good or poor adjustments, whether personal or social, there is evidence that children brought up in democratic homes generally make better adjustments to outsiders than children from permissive or authoritarian homes. The ordinal position of the child likewise influences the type of adjustments the child will make first-borns usually make better social adjustments than their later-born siblings, though not necessarily better personal adjustments. Perhaps the most important condition influencing the kind of adjustments young children will make, both personal and social, is the type of parent–child relationship there is during the early childhood years. Of less significance are sibling relationships and relationships with relatives, especially grand parents. The influence comes from the closeness of the relationship the child has with a specific family member. When, for example, young children feel closer to one parent than to the other, they imitate the attitudes, emotions and behaviour patterns of that parent.

The common interests of early childhood include interest in religion, in the human body, in self, in sex, and in clothes. Early childhood is often referred to as the critical age in sex-role typing because, at this time, the important aspects of sex-role typing are mastered, especially learning the meaning of sex-role stereotypes and accepting and playing the sex-role approved for members of their sex. Different family relationships parent child, siblings and relationship with relatives play roles of different degree of importance in the socialisation of young children and in their developing self-concepts. The important physical hazards of early childhood include mortality, illnesses, accidents, unattractiveness, obesity, and left-handedness. Among the most important psychological hazards of early childhood are unsocial content of speech, inability to establish the empathic complex, failure to learn social adjustments due to lack of guidance, preference for imaginary companions or pets, too much emphasis on amusements and too little on active play, unfavourable emotional weighting of concepts, inconsistent discipline or discipline that relies too much on punishment, failure to be sex-role typed in accordance with the approved pattern of the social group, deterioration in family relationships, and unfavourable self-concepts, Happiness in early childhood depends more on what happens to children in the home than outside the home.

CHILD RIGHTS DECLARATION AND CONVENTION

I am the child
All the world waits for my coming
All the earth watches with interest to see what
I shall become
Civilisation hangs in balance
For what I am, the world of tomorrow may be
I am the child
You hold in your hand my destiny
You determine, largely, whether I shall succeed or fail
Give me, I pray these things that make for happiness
Train me. I bed you that
I may be a blessing to that world

(Cole, 1999)

At a personal level, we often justify our actions in relation to our children by saying "We save for our children", we want to guarantee a good education for our children", we want the best health services for our children. Many of our personal actions actually affect our children positively or negatively. By choosing one course of action or another at the personal level we influence the future of our children. But our children's welfare does not only depend on the actions we make individually. Much of their condition depends on our collective attitudes and actions. With courage and dignity and with utmost innocence, they challenge us to abandon our antiquated conceptions and embrace a new vision—a vision of a united world, a world at peace, a world of harmony and prosperity. Children have a disarming way of telling the truth. Their proposals may sound unrealistic or native. But we can all benefit from their creativity which coupled with wholesome education and conviction that this is truly the age that will experience the coming of age of the human race. Indeed, the children have often provided inspiring glimpses of what the world, can learn to cooperate in building an environmentally sustainable, ecologically sound, physically healthy, socially happy and spiritually elevating future.

In the year 1923, the need to set down principles of child protection to meet the situation obtaining at that time had been felt. A project for children's charter was being studied by the Save the children's fund, London; a very detailed charter had been promulgated in summer 1922 by the International Union Council of Women in Oslo; there were some international conventions relating to child labour and, in the same field, the International Union of Young Workers, the International Association of Socialist Youth and the International Federation of Trade Unions, published in 1922 a socialist charter governing the work of adolescents. Herbert Hoover had also endeavoured to condense the duties of mankind towards the child into a few phrases. Some of the texts quoted were very detailed, but they were programmes setting out minimum requirements rather than the statement of fundamental principles, whereas others were very restricted. At the Save the Children International Union (SCIU) the importance of establishing a charter of the rights of the child, thus laying the basis of child welfare was realised, such a charted had, first of all, to be easy to translate into all languages, and such, that it could be reproduced by the press and above all readily understood and adopted by all countries. Aimed at attracting the attention of all and bringing about a legislative change, and a revision of customs, a charter is a valuable instrument of propaganda. The rights of child need to be proclaimed, but also and first of all the duties of adults towards children. How could these two concepts best be conciliated and united? Eglantine Jebb suggested that a short title should be adopted. "Declaration of Geneva" followed by explanatory preamble laying down the principles of the Rights and Duties.

The drafting proved long and laborious. Finally, on 17th May 1923, the Executive Board selected two drafts, one of which consisted of seven articles and the others five. The latter was adopted, the choice being unanimously approved by the General Council, the Sovereign Authority of the SCIU. A ceremony was held on 28th February, 1924 in Geneva, at the Art and History Museums in the presence of representatives of the authorities of the communes and canton of Geneva, the University, the technical and medical corps, the Swiss International Press, the League of Nations, the International Labour Office, the Red Cross etc., at which the Declaration of Geneva was solemnly presented by Georges Werner, who had helped to draft it to the archive of the Republic and canton of Geneva. The Declaration of Geneva met with almost unanimous approval by all sides and among the first to sign it were the Swedish Minister of Social Affairs, Prince Waldemer of Denmark and Elizabeth Queen of Belgium.

League of Nations Adopted the Declaration of Geneva

At its plenary session of 26th September 1924, the Fifth Assembly of the League of Nations unanimously adopted the following resolutions: "The Assembly endorse the Declaration of the Rights of the Child, commonly known as the Declaration of Geneva, and invites the States, Members of the league to be guided by its principles in the work of child welfare". In endorsing the Declaration of Geneva, the Assembly of the League of Nations consecrated it as the "world child welfare charter".

A copy of the Declaration which was originally written in French was translated in 37 languages and sent out to all members of the Assembly and many representatives. The Declaration of Geneva was read from the radiostation on the Eiffel Tower, other countries also used their radios to proclaim the Declaration and make it better known. The communique sent to press were widely published.

Declaration of Geneva

1. The child must be given the means requisite for its normal development, both materially and spiritually.
2. The child that is hungry must be fed; the child that is sick must be nursed; the child that is backward must be helped; the delinquent child must be reclaimed and the orphan and the waif must be sheltered and succoured.
3. The child must be the first to receive relief in terms of distress.
4. The child must be put in a position to earn a livelihood, and must be protected against every form of exploitation.
5. The child must be brought up in the consciousness that its talents must be devoted to the services of its fellowmen.

But unfortunately in 1939, world war broke out once again, and rendered the league powerless. Its declaration became mere "Scraps of papers".

Preparation for the Declaration of the Rights of the Child

In the aftermath of the second world war, in 1946 a year after the United Nations was formed and it was recommended to the Economic and Social Council of the United Nations (ECOSOC) that the Declaration of Geneva be revived to "bind the people of the world today as firmly as it did in 1924". Two years later, in 1948, the United Nations General Assembly approved the adoption of a Universal Declaration of Human Rights. In this Declaration the freedom and rights of children were implicitly included, but it was thought that this was not enough, the special needs of children justified an additional separate document. Therefore, in 1949, it drew up a preliminary draft of a new declaration of children's rights.

In 1948, the General Council of International Union for Child Welfare (IUCW) accepted the revised text counting seven points and including an additional clause on non-discrimination, based on race, nationality and religious faith-concept previously contained in the preamble and another implying the concept that the child should be helped with due respect for the integrity of his family. Some further specifications were also added, mainly relating to provisions for social welfare and security.

For the next few years however, further action was suspended, pending the formulation of this International convents on Human Rights—one on, Civil and Political Rights; one on Economic, Social and Culture Rights. It was not until 1959, a month after the adoption of the declaration of human rights by the United Nations General Assembly, that the latter adopted the new ten points. Declaration of the rights of child, which incorporates all the principles set out in the Declaration of Geneva and which is included in entirety in the first article of the statutes of IUCW.

In 1957, the Human Rights Commission of the Economic and Social Council took up the question of adopting a Declaration of the Rights of the child which would tie in with the Universal Declaration of Human Rights. After a preliminary discussion, this commission drafted a declaration which it submitted to its 21 member states, asking for their comments. Some of the member states said they would prefer a legally binding convention rather than a simple declaration, but the majority of the members favoured a brief declaration proclaiming general principles without providing methods of enforcing them.

The commission then redrafted the declaration and, on October 19, 1959, the Third Committee of the United Nations General Assembly (The Social, Humanitarian and Cultural Committee) approved this revised draft. The vote was 70 in favour, none against, with Cambodia and the Union of South Africa abstaining. On 20th November, 1959, the General Assembly with representatives of 78 countries meeting in plenary session—adopted the declaration of the rights of the child unanimously.

Preamble

Whereas the peoples of the United Nations' have, in the charter, reaffirmed their faith in fundamental human rights and in the dignity and worth of the human person, and have determined to promote social progress and better standards of life in larger freedom. Whereas the United Nations has, in the Universal Declaration of Human Rights, proclaimed that everyone is entitled to all the rights and freedoms setforth therein, without distinction of any kind, such as race, colour, sex, language, religion, political or other opinion, national or social origin, property, birth or other status. Whereas the child, by reason of his physical and mental immaturity, needs special safeguard and care, including appropriate legal protection, before as well as after birth.

Whereas the need for such special safeguards has been stated in the Geneva Declaration of Rights of the child and in the statutes of specialised agencies and international organisations concerned with the welfare of children, whereas mankind owes to the child the best it has to give. Now therefore,

The General Assembly

Proclaims this declaration of the rights of the child to the end that he may have a happy childhood and enjoy for his own good and the good of society the rights and freedom herein set forth, and calls upon parents, upon men and women as individuals and upon voluntary organisations, local authorities and national governments to recognise these rights and strive for their observance by legislative and other measures progressively taken in accordance with the following principles:

Principle 1: The child shall enjoy all the rights set-forth in this declaration. All children, without any exception whatsoever, shall be entitled to these rights, without distinction or discrimination on account of race, colour, sex, language, religion, political or other opinion, national or social origin, property, birth or other status, whether or himself or of his family.

Principle 2: The child shall enjoy special protection, and shall be given opportunities and facilities, by law and by other means, to enable him to develop physically, mentally, morally, spiritually and socially in a healthy and normal manner and in conditions of freedom and dignity. In the enactment of laws for this purpose the best interest of the child shall be the paramount consideration.

Principle 3: The child shall be entitle from his birth to a nationality.

Principle 4: The child shall enjoy the benefits of social security. He shall be entitled to grow and develop in health to this end, special care and protection shall be provided both to him and to his mother, including adequate prenatal and post-natal care. The child shall have the right to adequate nutrition, housing, recreation and medical services.

Principle 5: The child who is physically, mentally or socially handicapped shall be given the special treatment, education and care required by his particular condition.

Principle 6: The child, for the full and harmonious development of his personality, needs love and understanding. He shall, wherever possible, grow up in the care and under the responsibility of his parents, and in any case in an atmosphere of affection and of moral and material security; a child of tender years shall not, save in exceptional circumstances, be separated from his mother. Society and the public authorities shall have the duty to extend particular care to children without a family and to those without adequate means of support, payment of state and other assistance towards the maintenance of children of large families is desirable.

Principle 7: The child is entitled to receive education, which shall be free and compulsory, at least in the elementary stages. He shall be given an education which will promote his general culture and enable him on a basis of equal opportunity to develop his abilities, his individual judgement and his sense of moral and social responsibility, and to become a useful member of society. The best interests of the child shall be the guiding principle of those responsible for his education and guidance; that responsibility lies in the first place with his parents. The child shall have full opportunity for play and recreation which should be directed to the same purpose as educating society and the public authorities shall endeavour to promote the employment of the right.

Principle 8: The child shall in all circumstances be among the first to receive protection and relief.

Principle 9: The child shall be protected, against all forms of neglect, cruelty and exploitation. He shall not be the subject of traffic, in any form. The child shall not be admitted to employment before an appropriate minimum age; he shall in no case be caused or permitted to engage in any occupation or employment which would prejudice his health or education, or interfere with his physical, mental or moral development.

Principle 10: The child shall be protected from practices which may foster racial, religions and any other form of discrimination. He shall be brought up in the spirit of understanding, tolerance, friendship among peoples, peace and universal brotherhood and in full consciousness that his energy and talents should devoted to the services of his fellowmen.

The Significance of the Declaration

The Declaration of the Rights of the child is not a mere "Scrap of Paper", even though the rights it extols are not yet available to all—or even, unfortunately, to most children. The universal recognition that these rights exist is a very important first step in achieving them, and the fact that so many countries, of such diverse social conditions and cultural traditions, have agreed on the importance of these basic principles is an extremely encouraging omen of future progress.

Ancient, deep-rooted social problems and injustices die hard. There is an inevitable time lag between the recognition and acknowledgement of obligations and the ability to carry them out. But the unique value of every human being, even of the smallest and most helpless, is now officially acknowledged by almost every government in the world. All over the world it is now agreed that children need and deserve special assistance, and energetic efforts are, moreover, recognised as a duty of good government, not as an optional luxury.

In the modern world, with its highly, developed technology that makes possible destruction (and construction) on an unprecedented scale, peace is no longer a luxury either, but an increasingly urgent necessity. Children must be helped to enjoy the right to grow up healthy (physically, mentally, morally, spiritually and socially, in freedom and dignity as right 2 of the declaration asserts). If not, they will never be able to or willing to join together in helping to build a better world tomorrow, a safer and happier and more peaceful world, in which their children can enjoy their "rights".

When we protect and foster the rights of every child everywhere, we are protecting and fostering everyone's happiness and everyone's peace including our own, racial, religious and any other form of discrimination. He shall be brought up in a spirit of understanding, tolerance, friendship among people, peace and universal brotherhood and in full consciousness that his energy and talents should be devoted to the services of his fellow men.

Finally, the General Assembly resolved that governments, non-governmental organisations and individuals should give this Declaration the widest possible publicity as a means of encouraging its observance everywhere.

The Convention on the Rights of the Child

The question on the convention on the rights of the child was first proposed in 1978 by Government of Poland as one of the initiatives to be undertaken during International Year of the Child (IYC). The Economic and Social Council of the United Nations (ECOSOC), referred the proposal to the UN Commission on Human Rights, which created the "Open Ended Working Group" in 1979. This working group met annually since then.

On February 5, 1988 the open-ended working Group on the question of a convention on the rights of the child finished the first reading of the future UN convention on the rights of child. The proposed convention one of the most comprehensive international instruments since the Universal Declaration of Human Rights, addresses economic, social, cultural, political and civil rights and defines the obligations of adults towards children.

A agreement on these standards has been reached by international consensus—the result of 9 years of deliberations by representatives from more than 40 countries, supported by inter governmental agencies of Non-governmental Organisations (NGOs).

The draft convention was subjected to a technical review. The review group identified overlap and repetition within and between articles, compared the standards established by the convention with those in other human rights instruments, and check for the use of gender neutral language and inconsistency in the text. The group also had to make editorial suggestions as to how these problems can be corrected. One of the needs of this review was to renumber the articles, eliminating the terms, "bister, quarter etc", which were used as a drafting device when provisions were added to the original polish working document.

The chairman of the working group, Prof. Adam Lopatka of Poland, ensured that the technical review be completed by August 1988, so that there can be discussions of the recommendations and a formal second reading by the working group either later in 1988 or early 1989. Following the second reading, the proposed convention will be forwarded to ECOSOC for discussion in May 1989, and then to the General Assembly for consideration in November, 1989.

It was considered necessary and important to stress that special privileges and protection for children are included in many preceding international instruments. The novelty, however, was that the convention's attempt to codify under one title those provisions of International Law that pertain to children. So that the convention is an important and easily-understood advocacy tool for those who work for the benefit of the children.

It was also necessary to stress that the convention, was not initiated by UNICEF of NGOs. It was an action by Government for the benefit of their respective children. As internationalists, it was duty-bound to make the convention meaningful for all the children of the world.

Obviously and very clearly, the convention had an enormous potential for children throughout the world. When adopted by UN General Assembly and ratified by the requisite 20 member-states, the convention will provide a framework within which UNICEF and NGO's can more effectively define and promote their existing and future programmes and priorities. It will also assist in developing an alliance for action for the programmes of many diverse organisations—including UNICEF National Committee and Regional Offices, INGOs, other UN agencies and grassroot groups.

It was also important and crucial that public become aware of the conventions existence and the provisions it contains. A need was felt to develop a broad coalition to demand that governments support this critical initiative for children.

(a) Up-date Action and Follow-up

On 20th November 1989, more than 500 children from round the world were welcomed by United Nations to celebrate the 30th Anniversary of the United Nations declaration of the rights of children. The children presented petitions and made statements in support of the children's rights. Also on this date the General Assembly was scheduled to vote on the historic convention on the rights of child.

This convention modifies and consolidates the existing standards and introduced a range of relatively new issues of major importance. It is a comprehensive human rights convention drafted in full partnership between developing and developed countries, and, if and when adopted will represent the international community's first universal and binding policy statement on children's rights. The General Assembly's Social Committee began consideration of the convention on 9th November, 1989.

(b) Adoption of the Convention on the Rights of Child

The 54-Article convention was adopted by the General Assembly on 20th November 1989 and is the first comprehensive and binding human-rights instrument solely addressing the rights of children. On 26th January 1990, sixty countries signed the convention on the rights of child, in the signing ceremony at the headquarters in New York. Opening the signing ceremony, Jan Martenson, under Secretary General for Human Rights, said "the convention was an encouraging expression of the international community's faith in the future and a pledged to continue to strive for human world".

Mr. Martenson said "that the world community has to sincerely work and go quite for to make the world fit for children. It is so evident from the various problems affecting children, including the fact that the hundred million children had been abandoned by their families and left on the street to find their own ways, thus resorting to petty crimes and thefts, prostitution to beggary. Fifty million children round the world are forced to work under inhuman working conditions, and 3.5 million die each year from preventable diseases".

Mr.Martenson was convinced that the convention could only be successful as countries'. Institutions and individuals were willing to make it. He concluded by quoting the Secretary General Javier Perez de Cuellar, "that it was time to move on to make the principles embodied in the convention a reality for every living child".

Purpose: The purpose of the convention is to supplement and not replace the 1959 declaration.

The Rights of the Child

The preamble recalls the basic principles of the United Nations and specific provisions of certain relevant human rights treaties and proclamations; reaffirms the fact that children, because of their vulnerability, need special care and protection; and places special emphasis on the primary caring and protective responsibility of the family, the need for the legal and other protection of the child before and after birth, the importance of respect for the cultural values of the child's community, and the vital role of international co-operation in achieving the realisation of children's rights.

Ariticle-1

Definition of Child: All persons under 18, unless by law majority is attained at an earlier age.

Article-2

Non-discrimination: The principle that all rights apply to all children without exception, and the State's obligation to protect children from any form of discrimination. The States must not violate any right, and must take positive action to promote them all.

Article-3

Best interest of the Child: All the actions concerning the child should take full account of his/her best interests. The state is to provide adequate care when parents or others responsible fail to do so.

Article-4

Implementation of Rights: The State's obligation to translate the rights in the convention into reality.

Article-5

Parental Guidance and the Child's Evolving Capacities: The State's duty to respect the rights and responsibilities of parents and the wider family to provide guidance appropriate to the child's evolving capacities.

Article-6

Survival and Development: The inherent right to life, and the State's obligation to ensure the child's survival and development.

Article-7

Name and Nationality: The right to have a name from birth and to be granted a nationality.

Article-8

Preservation of Identity: The State's obligation to protect and, if necessary, re-establish the basic aspects of a child's identity (name, nationality and family name).

Article-9

Separation from Parents: The child's right to live with his/her parents, unless this is deemed in compatible with his/her interests; the right to maintain contact with both parents if separated from one or both; the duties or States in cases where such separation results from State action.

Article-10

Family Reunification: The right of the children and the parents to leave any country and to enter their own in order to be reunited or to a maintain the child-parent relationship.

Aritcle-11

Illicit Transfer and Non-return: The State's obligation to try to prevent and remedy the kidnapping or retention of children abroad by parent or third party.

Article-12

The Child's Opinion: The child's right to express an opinion, and to have that opinion taken into account in any matter or procedure affecting the child.

Article-13

Freedom of Expression: The child's right to obtain and make known information, and to express his/her views, unless this would violate the rights of others.

Article-14

Freedom of Thought: Conscience and Religion: The child's right to freedom of thought, conscience and religion, subject to appropriate parental guidance and national law.

Article-15

Freedom of Association: The right of children to meet with others and to join or set up associations, unless the fact of doing so violates the rights of others.

Article-16

Protection of Privacy: The right to protection from interference with privacy, family, home and correspondence, and from libel/slander.

Article-17

Access to Appropriate Information: The role of the media in disseminating information to children that is consistent with moral well-being and knowledge and understanding among peoples, and respects the child's cultural backgrounds. The State is to take measures to encourage this and to protect the children from harmful materials.

Article-18

Parental Responsibilities: The principal that both parents have joint primary responsibility for bringing up their children, and that the State should support them in this risk.

Article-19

Protection from Abuse and Neglect: The State's obligation to protect children from all forms of maltreatment perpetrate by parents or others responsible for their care, and to undertake preventive and treatment programmes in this regard.

Article-20

Protection of Children without Families: The State's obligation to provide special protection for children deprived of their family environment and to ensure that appropriate alternative family care or institutional placement is made available to them, taking into account the child's cultural background.

Article-21

Adoption: In the countries where adoption is recognised and/or allowed, it shall one be carried out in the best interests to the child, with all necessary safeguards for given child and authorisation by the competent authorities.

Article-22

Refugee Children: Special protection to be granted to children who are refugees or seeking refugee status, and the State's obligation to cooperate with competent organisations providing such protection and assistance.

Article-23

Handicapped Children: The right of handicapped children to special care, education and training designed to help them to achieve the greatest possible self-reliance and to lead a full and active life in society.

Article-24

Health and Health Services: The right to the highest level of health possible and to access to health and medical services, with special emphasis on primary and preventive health care, public health education and the diminution of infant mortality. The State's obligation to work towards the abolition of harmful traditional practices. Emphasis is laid on the need for international cooperation to ensure this right.

Article-25

Periodic Review of Placement: The right of children placed by the State for reasons of care, protection or treatment to have all aspects of that placement evaluated regularly.

Article-26

Social Security: The right of children to benefit from social security.

Article-27

Standard of Living: The right of children to benefit from an adequate standard of living, the primary responsibility of parents to provide this, and the State's duty to ensure that this responsibility can be fulfilled, and then fulfil, where necessary through the recovery of maintenance.

Article-28

Education: The child's right to education, and the State's duty to ensure that primary education at least is made free and compulsory. Administration of school discipline is to reflect the child's human dignity. Emphasis is laid on the need for international cooperation to ensure this right.

Article-29

Aims of Education: The State's recognition that education be directed at developing the child's personality and talents, preparing the child for active life as an adult, fostering respect for basic human rights, and developing respect for the child's own cultural and national values and those of others.

Article-30

Children of Minorities or Indigenous Populations: The right of children of the minority communities and indigenous populations to enjoy their own culture and to practice their own religion and language.

Article-31

Leisure, Recreation and Cultural Activities: The right of children to leisure, play and participation in cultural, artistic activities.

Article-32

Child Labour: The State's obligation to protect children from engaging in work that constitutes a threat to their health, education or development, to set minimum ages for employment, and to regulate conditions for employment.

Article-33

Drug Abuse: The child's right to protect from the use of narcotic and psychotropic drugs and from being involved in their production or distribution.

Article-34

Sexual Exploitation: The child's right to protection from sexual exploitation and abuse, including prostitution and involvement in pronography.

Article-35

Sale, Trafficking and Abduction: The State's obligation to make every effort to prevent the sale, trafficking and abduction of children.

Article-36

Other Forms of Exploitation: The child's right to protection from all other forms of exploitation not covered in Articles-32, 33, 34 and 35.

Article-37

Torture and Deprivation of Liberty: The prohibition of torture, cruel treatment or punishment, capital punishment, life imprisonment, and unlawful arrest or deprivation of liberty. The principles of appropriate treatment, separation from detained adults, contact with family and to legal and other assistance.

Article-38

Armed Conflicts: The obligation of States to respect and ensure respect for humanitarian law as it applies to children. The Principle that no child under 15 takes a direct part in hostilities or be recruited into the armed forces, and that all children affected by armed conflict benefit from protection and care.

Article-39

Rehabilitative Care: The State's obligation to ensure that child victims of armed conflicts; torture, neglect, maltreatment or exploitation receive appropriate treatment for their recovery and social re-integration.

Article-40

Administration of Juvenile Justice: The rights of children alleged or recognised as having committed an offence to respect for their human rights and, in particular, to benefit from all aspects of the due process of law, including legal or other assistance in preparing and presenting their defence. The Principle that recourse to judicial proceedings and institutional placement should be avoided wherever possible and appropriate.

Article-41

Respect for existing standards: The principle that, if any standards set in national law or other applicable international instruments are higher than those of this conventions, it is the higher standard that applies.

Article 42-45

Implementation and Entry into Force: The provisions of Article 42-45 notably for see:

(i) The State's obligation to make the rights contained in this convention widely known to both adults and children.

(ii) The setting up of committee on the rights of child composed of ten experts, which will consider reports that State parties to the convention are to submit two years after ratification and every five years thereafter. The convention enters into force:

(iii) States parties are to make their reports widely available to the general public.

(iv) The committee may propose that special studies be undertaken on specific issues relating to the rights of the child, and may make its evaluation known to each State party concerned as well as to the UN General Assembly.

(v) In order to "foster the effective implementation of the convention and to encourage international cooperation" the specialised agencies of the UN (such as ILO, WHO, UNESCO) and UNICEF would be able to attend the meetings of the committee. Together with any other body recognised as "competent", including NGOs in consultative status with UN and UN organs such as UNHC, they can submit pertinent information to the committee and be asked to advice on the optimal implementation of convention.

The First World summit for children attended by world leaders represented a commitment at the highest level to build a world order that would guard the most precious resource of the human race—its children. The commitment also assured top priority to the welfare of children and mothers and ensured that their rights are not violated.

Convention on children's Rights came into force on 2nd September, 1990. With its entry into force, the convention becomes binding international law for those states that are party to it. Twentynine states ratified the convention, two states have acceded to it and one hundred and five states signed it.

The convention on the rights of the child is unique. One of the main doctrines of the convention is that the 'child' is not alone; it considers the basic role of the parents and family for the welfare, care and protection of the children, also the need for special protection of children, who are separated or are without families. It considers the role of community and State when required and the crucial contribution that can be made by international organisations and international co-operation. Moreover, the convention provides a framework within which the child can make the difficult transition from infancy to adulthood.

The document which has been signed provides ten point programme to protect the rights of child, to improve their lives and plans of action at national and international level by the year 2000. The national plan of course will depend on that particular country social and special need and requirements.

The document considers and urgently calls for action in:

1. Infant and maternal mortality to be reduced.
2. Completion of Primary education covering 80 per cent of primary school age children.
3. Improve protection of children.
4. Reduction of server and moderate malnutrition of children under age of five.
5. Universal access to safe drinking water.
6. Sanitary means of disposal of excreta.
7. Improving status of women which will lead to better child care.

8. Within a decade it envisages:

   (a) Global eradication of poliomyelities;

   (b) High level immunisation of children under one year old with a coverage of 90 per cent children;

   (c) Reduction by 95 per cent measles cases;

   (d) Reduce 50 per cent deaths in children under 5 years old due to diarrhoea;

   (e) Reduce 1/3 deaths due to respiratory infections in children under 5 years old.

9. Universal access to safe drinking water, sanitary conditions, reduction in pollution, protect of environment and increase in food production.

10. The convention also seeks to balance the rights of child with the rights and duties of parents and others who have responsibility or child survival, development and protection.

The 20th century will be recorded as an era of extraordinary change for children, and among those changes, the convention on the rights of the child holds perhaps the greatest potential. The angularly powerful and wide-ranging legal instrument promotes and protects the full spectrum of human rights for children.

The convention, which entered into force in 1990, reflects a watershed in the way our world looks at children. The work of a few decades has overturned traditions that date back millennia: children have been transformed in the realm of justice from powerless charges into human beings with legal rights of their own; form 'object' to 'subject' of the law; from chattel to person hold.

Emblematic of this sea-change in perception was the 1990 world summit for children at which 71 heads of the Government adopted specific goals to substantively improve the lives of children by the year 2000. That such a high level summit came together around the subject of children would have been unthinkable even a few years before.

As on December 1995, all but eight countries in the world had ratified this treaty—propelling it towards becoming the first Universal Law in History. Already its ratification by 185 nations at year end has surpassed the record for any other human rights treaty.

The promises made by the international community at the world summit for children have been strengthened by commitments made to fulfil the obligations of the convention. The ratification of the convention by each government adds the force of law to the principle that States have a requirement to act in the best interests of the children. Now the countries have to be reminded that putting children first is now a legal obligation, not simply a matter of charity and compassion.

The convention on the rights of the child recognises that not all governments have the resources necessary to ensure all economic, social and cultural rights immediately. But it commits them to make those rights a priority and to ensure them to the maximum extent of available resources. Fulling their obligations sometimes requires countries to make fundamental changes in national laws, institutions, plans, policies, and practices to bring them into line with the principles of the convention.

The first priority must be to generate the political will to do this. As the drafters of the convention recognised, real change in the lives of children will come about only when social attitudes and ethics progressively change to conform with laws and principles. And when, as actors in the processes, children themselves know enough about their rights to claim them.

Generally speaking, there appears to be a problem of inertia that is preventing society from making such a change in the Baha's view (1995) there is a "Paralysis of will" rooted in a "deep-seated conviction of the inevitable quarrelssomeness of mankind". In other words people suffer from the belief that they are flawed from birth by an egotistical nature, and therefore cannot develop the altruism and other qualities necessary to the problems. As for the implementation of the provisions of the convention, the official monitor of this process of change is the committee on the rights of the child. Governments are obliged to report to the committee within two years of ratification, and every five years thereafter, specifying the steps taken to change national laws and formulate policies and actions.

The committee, made up of 10 experts, gathers evidence from NGOs and inter governmental organisations including UNICEF, and these groups may prepare alternative reports to that of a government. The committee and the government then meet to discuss the country's child rights efforts and the steps necessary to overcome difficulties.

The reporting process has proved dynamic and constructive, with dialogue established helping to advance children's rights. Unfortunately, however, many countries have missed their reporting deadlines, 28 of them by as muds as three years, as of September, 1996.

The Government of India ratified the convention on the Rights of the child on 12 November 1992. Accordingly the Government took various initiatives to review the National and State legislations and bring it in line with the provisions of the convention, develop appropriate monitoring procedures to assess progress in implementing the convention, involve all relevant Government/Ministries, Departments, International agencies, Non-Governmental Organisations and the legal profession in the implementation and reporting process to publicise the convention and seek public inputs for the frank and transparent reporting. No matter how progressive and rosy the convention looks on paper and sounds fantastic, no matter how many countries have signed or ratified it, the change will depend how it is put into practice. Improvement in the daily life of children and their welfare will depend largely on how it is implemented.

CHILD RIGHTS AND INDIAN CONSTITUTION

Situation in India

The process of implementing the convention still remains in its infancy but, as noted, the International treaty for children is already beginning to make an impact. India has long displayed a remarkable potential to achieve what it sets out to do. 1997 marks the golden jubilee of Independent India, several positive achievements characterise the Indian economy, particularly in terms of commodity production. Between 1950 and 1994, per capita net national product [at 1980-81 prices], increased from Rs.1.127 to Rs.2.282, recording an average growth rate of 1.65 per cent per annum. Foodgrain production more than tripled from 51 million tonnes in 1951 to 171 million tonnes in 1990, and to 185 million tonnes in 1997. The Index of Industrial Production shows a twelve-fold increase between 1950 and 1996.

However, from a Child's perspective, the balance sheet of development looks some what mixed. Life expectancy at birth increased from 33 years at the time Independence to 61 years in 1992, and infant mortality declined from 146 per 1000 live births in 1961 to 74 in 1993. Remarkable progress has been achieved in immunising children and in the control and eradication of guinea worm. Yet, around 2 million infants die each year today, almost the same number as in 1960 and most of these deaths are available. Despite the fact that the country has built up a buffer stock of 30 million tonnes of foodgrains, and adequate administrative and managerial capabilities to cope with famines and droughts, some 63 per cent of Indian's children below the age of five years are undernourished. Literacy rates more than doubled from 24 per cent in 1961 to 52 per cent in 1991. Yet there are nearly 60 million more illiterate persons today than there were in 1961. Only 64 per cent of children in India reach grade V of primary schooling, and the proportion of girl children enrolling and completing primary schooling remains lower than that of boys, and of those completing grade V may cannot even read or write simple sentence.

India is one country, but inhabited by many peoples. National level analyses mask genuine advancements in different regions, and also conceal wide disparities. It is, therefore, not all surprising to find that conditions of children vary enormously across the country. Only 29 countries in the world and all of them by far richer reported infant mortality lower than Kerala's rate of 13 per 1,000 births in 1993. On the other hand, there were only 20 countries or so in the world and most of them poorer—that reported infant mortality higher than Orissa's rate of 110 per 1,000 births. The life expectancy of a girl born in Kerala today, around 74 years, is 20 years more than that of a girl born in Uttar Pradesh. There is as much to learn from the experiences of other countries that have recorded rapid improvements in the well-being of children as there is from the differential performance of states within India. For instance, while some states have been able to reduce the striking caste, class and gender differentials in the well-being of children, others have not been as successful. Children of parents belonging to socially and economically backward communities continue to face for greater deprivation than other children.

Whereas effective policy design requires good data, the Indian data-base on children has several limitations. Basic statistics on several quantifiable indicators relating to morbidity, education, nutritional well-being and so on, are not systematically collected and presented even at the state level. Data are often not available for the less populous states and Union Territories. As we move to the district or sub-district levels and focus on different socio-economic groups in society, reliability of available data is still less. Additionally, critical issues relating to quality, coverage, timing and relevance of data remain unresolved. The problem of unreliable, incomplete and inadequate data is not unique to India, most countries face a similar situation. However, in the Indian context, it seems that with each year that goes by, this weakness reflects less and less a lack of capacity and more and more a lack of priority.

India has accepted the challenges of meeting the goals for the year 2000 adopted by the 1990 world summit for children. As in the past, the task may look difficult, but with political commitment and popular support, India can succeed once again in accomplishing what it has set out to achieve. India should enter the 21st century, the next millennium, having eliminated the worst form of deprivation, and giving its 350 million children the start they need to shape their own future.

The convention on the rights of the child represents a universally accepted charter of rights for the child. Drafted by the UN commission on Human rights and adopted by the General Assembly of the United Nations on 20 November 1989, it is a set of international standards and measures intended to protect and promote the well being of children in society. All countries except two had either signed the convention or become states parties to it by ratification, accession or succession.

The convention recognises the exceptional vulnerability of children, and proclaims that childhood is entitled to special care and assistance, it is guided by the principle of a first call for children, a principle that the essential need of children should be given highest priority in the allocation of resources at all times. It obligates the state to respect and ensure that children get a fair and equitable deal in society. It emphasises the importance of the family and the need to create an environment that is conducive to the health growth and development of children. It advocates concerted publication by all individuals and agencies – government and other wise, to promote the rights of the child. In a sense, it is a means of empowering children, and creating an environment in which all children are able to live securely and realise their full potential in life.

The laws framed in the statute books on India broadly recognise the Rights of the child as proclaimed in the child rights convention (CRC). The statute books proclaim that the child is entitled to the equal protection of the laws, that the child shall not suffer from any discrimination, child labour is condemned; the desirability of the child having a healthy environment, nutrition, food and education is recognised. The rights of the child to citizenship, the humane treatment when the child violates the law is also recognised.

The constitution of India itself guarantees many rights to the child. This is two-fold the fundamental Rights and the directive principles. Fundamental rights enforceable against the state only through the High courts and the Supreme Court:

Articles 14-17	:	Right to equality
Articles 19-22	:	Right to freedom
Articles 23-24	:	Right against exploitation
Article 25	:	Right to freedom of religion
Article 29	:	Cultural and Educational Rights
Article 32	:	Right to constitutional remedies Directive Principles not Enforceable at all
Article 39	:	Ban on unsuitable work for children, opportunities and facilities for them
Article 42	:	Maternity relief just conditions of work
Article 45	:	Free and compulsory education for children till 14 years
Article 47	:	Right to nutrition and health.

Fundamental Rights

Articles 14

Equality of Law: The state shall not deny to any person equality before the law or the equal protection of the laws within the territory of India.

Article 15

Prohibition of discrimination

(i) The state shall not discriminate against any citizen on grounds of religion, race, caste, sex, place of birth or any of them.

(ii) No citizen shall, on grounds only of religion, race, caste, sex, place of birth or any of them be subject to any disability, liability, restriction or condition with regard to—

- access to shops, public restaurants, hotels and places of public entertainment; or
- use of wells, tanks, bathing ghats, roads and places of public resort, maintained wholly or partially out the state funds or dedicated to the use of the general public.

(iii) Nothing in this article shall prevent the state from making any special provision for women and children.

Article 16

Equality of opportunity in matters of public employment

(i) There shall be equality of opportunity for all citizens in matters related to employment or appointment to any office under the state;

(ii) No citizen shall, on grounds only of religion, race, caste, sex, descent, place of birth, residence or any of them be ineligible for, or discriminated against, in respect of any employment or office under the state.

Sec. 4 deals with the powers of the state to make reservations to backward class of citizens.

Article 17

Abolition of Untouchability: Untouchability is abolished and its practice in any from is forbidden. The enforcement of any disability arising out of untouchability shall be an offence punishable in accordance with law.

Article 19

Protection of certain rights regarding freedom of speech, etc: All citizens shall have the right.

- to freedom of speech and expression
- to assemble peaceably and without arms
- to form associations or unions
- to move freely throughout the territory of India
- to practice any profession, or to carry on any occupation, trade or business.

Article 21

Protection of life and personal liberty: No person shall be deprived of his life or personal liberty except according to procedure established by law. The Supreme Court has declared the right to education as part of the fundamental right to personal liberty, as without education, life cannot be lived with dignity.

Article 22

Protection against arrest and detention in certain cases:

(i) No person who is arrested shall be detained in custody without being informed, as soon as may be, of the grounds for such arrest, nor shall be he denied the right to consult, and be defended by a legal practitioner of his choice;

(ii) Every person who is arrested and detained in custody shall be produced before the nearest magistrate within a period of 24 hours of such arrest excluding the time necessary for the journey from the place of arrest to the court of the magistrate, and no such person shall be detained in custody beyond the said period without the authority of a magistrate. (Exceptions are aliens and detentions under any law providing for preventive detention).

Article 23

Prohibition of traffic in human beings and forced labour: Traffic in human beings and began and other similar forms of forced labour are prohibited and any contravention of this provision shall be an offence punishable in accordance with law.

Article 24

Prohibition of employment of children in factories, etc.: No child below the age of 14 years shall be employed to work in any factory or mine or engaged in any other hazardous employment.

Article 25

Freedom of conscience and free profession, practice and propagation of religion: Subject to public order, morality and health and to the other provisions of this part, all persons are equally entitled to freedom of conscience and the right freely to profess, practice and propagate religion.

Article 29(1)

Freedom to conserve their distinct language, script or culture.

Article 32

Remedies for enforcement of Rights conferred by this part. The right to move the Supreme Court by appropriate proceedings for the enforcement of the Rights conferred by this part is guaranteed.

Directive Principles

Article 37

The provisions in this part shall not be enforceable by any court, but the principles there in laid down are fundamental in the governance of the country, and it shall be the duty of the state to apply these principles in making laws.

Article 39(e)

The state shall ensure that the health and strength of workers, men and women, and the tender age of children are not abused, and that citizens are not forced by economic, necessity to enter avocations unsuited to their age or strength.

Article 39(f)

That children are given opportunities and facilities to develop in a healthy manner and in conditions of freedom and dignity and that childhood and youth are protected against exploitation and against moral and material abandonment.

Article 42

The state shall make provision for securing just and human conditions of work and for maternity relief.

Article 45

Provision for free and compulsory education for children. The state shall endeavour to provide for free and compulsory education for all children until they complete the age of 14 years.

Article 49

Duty of the state to raise the level of nutrition and the standard of living and to improve public health: The state shall regard the raising of the level of nutrition and the standard of living of its people and the improvement of public health as among its primary duties.

The rights perspective has practical implications for public policy on child development services. First, this perspective is the main foundation of the demand for "universal" child development services. Indeed, one implication of the rights approach is that all children are entitled to certain "opportunities and facilities" (as the constitution puts it) that do not have to be justified on a case-by-case basis, let alone submitted to cost benefit tests. The main role of ICDS is to act as an institutional medium for the provision of these facilities. Second, the rights perspective points to the need for strong monitoring and redressal mechanisms so that people are able to claim their entitlements (Dreze, 2006).

The Supreme Court has also issued orders that the ICDS should be universalised to cover all settlements in the country, reaching out to every child under six years of age, mother and adolescent girl with supplementary nutrition. Universalising ICDS in accordance with the Supreme Court directive would mean increasing the number of ICDS centres by almost three times from the present six lakh anganwadi centres to the required 17 lakhs. Public action alone would bring pressure on the state to concretise these obligations and also expose the lacunae in the details of such policy instruments (Shanta Sinha, 2006).

WELFARE PROGRAMMES FOR CHILD DEVELOPMENT

Childhood is a period of rapid growth and development and the child must get proper stimulation at this stage, so that he can attain optimum development—physically, emotionally, socially and intellectually.

The qualities a person imbibes as a child deepen as he grows and appear in several obvious and subtle ways in his conduct and character as an adult. Therefore, what affects the interests of the children affects the well-being of the entire group, of which the child is but one member on their welfare and satisfaction depends, not only the health and welfare of the community, but the claim of the nation to civilisation itself.

Changing Concept of 'Child Welfare' in the Government

Child welfare as distinct from other aspect of social welfare is an integral part of the Economic Plan. There is a difference in the concept of social welfare as applied to child welfare on one hand, and applied to adult on the others. Social welfare for an adult is a part of the expenditure, and for the child it is a part of investment.

Since independence in all the five years plan, unfortunately there was not a single group or body existing or working in a co-ordinated way for the different services of child welfare. The services were split up among the various central government ministries, several ministries were dealing with some identical programmes, which were operated through the state governments. Co-ordination was important and necessary and hence a new body called "co-ordination committee on child welfare" was formulated under a resolution.

Programmes relating to child welfare were scattered among Ministries of Community Development and Co-operation, Health Education and Home Affairs. Therefore, Ministry of Education which was concerned with child welfare programmes was given the administrative responsibility for child welfare and also co-ordination of the activities of other ministries and organisations in connection with child welfare.

Under the umbrella of social welfare, child welfare has gone from ministry to ministry like a ping pong ball till the International year of child, when at last a separate ministry of social welfare came into existence which unfortunately was again split in 1985. From 1958-1960, the social welfare was under Ministry of Education.

From 1960-1961, Child welfare was looked often by department of social security, which was under the Ministry of Law and Social Security. From 1961-1964, Child welfare was under the Ministry of Education and was known as the Ministry of Education, Social Welfare and Culture. From 1964-1966, it was again handled by the Ministry of Law and Social Security. From 1966-1969, it was under the Ministry of Planning and handled by the Department of Social Welfare. From 1969-1979, it was handled by the Department of Social Welfare under the Ministry of Education.

In 1979, the Ministry of Social Welfare was established as an independence ministry composing different units for women, children, handicap, research etc. In 1985 beginning it was renamed ministry for Human Resource and Development under a Cabinet Minister. Under this umbrella one State Minister looked after women, welfare and sports youth affairs and child development. Under another State Minister, Department of Education and Culture. Then there was ministry of welfare under a State Minister who looked after children totally and also the handicap, scheduled caste, scheduled tribe, backward class and welfare of the children.

Today child welfare and child development has gained importance and the government as well as public in general have become conscious and aware of its need and priority in planning for the future of our country.

In 1989—The Ministry of Human Resource and Development was under a Cabinet Minister with State Minister who looked for: (i) Youth and Sports; (ii) Culture and Art; and (iii) Education.

Ministry of Welfare was made independent under a Cabinet Minister with State Minister looking after totally "women and children" in every aspect.

Child Welfare in India

Prior to independence, there were only small groups of voluntary workers in India, who took care of feeding of needy children and educational facilities for the handicapped in 1920, Balkanji Bari, the first children's organisation was formed in Bombay. In 1924, The Guild of Service started its child welfare services in South India. In 1927, The Children's Aid Society took vagrant children in residential care at Bombay. It was only in 1952 that the Indian Council for Child Welfare was formed, the first national organisation to mobilise voluntary activities in favour of various aspects of children's needs. The Central Social Welfare Board (CSWB) was established in 1953. It was wholly supported by government finance with a small staff at the Centre and in the States and assisted by thousands of unpaid women workers. Childcare programmes and projects, such as, rural balwadis, holiday homes and grants to over 7,000 non-governmental agencies etc., were apart of its programme.

After Independence in 1947, as per the Directive Principles of State Policy in the constitution, the Government laid down its objectives. The Planning Commission was set up in 1950, under the chairmanship of Prime Minister Jawaharlal Nehru and the formulations of Five Year Plans began. The major responsibility for developing child welfare services was placed on voluntary agencies.

The First Plan recognised the need for strengthening of the infrastructure of various national level voluntary agencies working in the field of child development. Maternal and child health services were in the fore front of the health programme during the plan period.

The second plan laid greater stress on services for handicapped children through expansion of institutional programmes and creation of additional facilities like schools for deaf and blind children, scholarship for handicapped children and training teachers for physically and mentally handicapped school children.

The Third Plan stressed the importance of welfare services being community and family oriented. The ICCW started the demonstration projects for child development during this plan. The scheme of Balasevika Training (for running balwadis) was also introduced during this plan period.

The Fourth Plan accorded highest priority to Family Planning Programme, where the schemes for immunisation of children and mother were also implemented. Special funds were earmarked under this plan for institutional and non-institutional services for destitute children.

During the Fifth Plan, Health, Nutrition and Family Planning were integrated for best results and children being a vulnerable group, were provided special attention. During this plan and the subsequent ones, a lot of progress was made through the ICDS scheme.

The National Children's Policy

The National Policy for children adopted by the Government of India in August, 1974 describes children as "supremely important assets". It enjoins on the state the responsibility for their nurture and solicitude. It provides high priority to programmes related to health and nutrition. Under this policy, a National Children's Board was set up to plan, review and co-ordinate services to meet the needs of children. A National Children's Fund (NCF) was also set up in 1979 and it finances voluntary organisations for implementing child welfare programmes.

The National Policy for children, enunciated in August 1974, declares children as "a supremely important asset" of the nation, whose "nurture and solicitude" are the responsibility of the nation. It affirms that it shall be the policy of the state "to provide adequate services to children, both before and after birth through the period of growth, to ensure their full physical, mental and social development".

In pursuance of the National policy for children and recognising that it is in early childhood that the foundations for physical, psychological and social development are laid and that provisions of early childhood services, especially to the weaker and more vulnerable sections of the community, will help to prevent or minimise the wastages arising from infant mortality, morbidity, malnutrition and stagnation in schools. The Government of India started the ICDS scheme in 1975 in 33 pilot projects.

National Health Policy (NHP) 2002

National Health Policy is to achieve an acceptable standard of good health amongst the general population of the country. The approach would be to increase access to the decentralised public health system by establishing new infrastructure in deficient areas, and by upgrading the infrastructure in the existing institutions. Overriding importance would be given to ensuring a more equitable access to health services across the social and geographical expanse of the country. Emphasis will be given to increasing the aggregate public health investment through a substantially increased contribution by the Central Government.

It is expected that this initiative will strengthen the capacity of the public health administration at the State level to render effective service delivery. The contribution of the private sector in providing health services would be much enhanced, particularly for the population group which can afford to pay for services. Primacy will be given to preventive and first-line curative initiatives at the primary health level through increased sectoral share of allocation. Emphasis will be laid on rational use of drugs within the allopathic system. Increased access to tried and tested systems of traditional medicine will be ensured. Within these broad objectives, NHP-2002 will endeavour to achieve the time-bound goals mentioned in Box-IV.

Box-IV: Goals to be achieved by 2000-2015

Goal	Year
Eradicate Polio and Yaws	2005
Eliminate Leprosy	2005
Eliminate Kala Azar	2010
Eliminate Lymphatic Filariasis	2015
Achieve Zero level growth of HIV/AIDS	2007
Reduce Mortality by 50% on account of TB, Malaria and other vector and Water Borne diseases	2010
Reduce Prevalence of Blindness to 0.5%	2010
Reduce IMR to 30/1000 and MMR to 100/Lakh	2010
Increase Utilisation of Public health facilities from current level of <20 to >75%	2010
Establish an integrated system of surveillance, National Health Accounts and Health Statistics	2005
Increase health expenditure by Government as a per cent of GDP from the existing 0.9% to 2.0%	2010
Increase share of central grants to constitute at least 25% of total health spending	2010
Increase State Sector Health spending from 5.5% to 7% of the budget	2005
Further increase to 8%	2010

This policy broadly envisages a greater contribution from the Central Budget for the delivery of Public Health services at the State level. Adequate appropriations, steadily rising over the years, would need to be ensured. The possibility of ensuring this by imposing an earmarked health cess has been carefully examined. While it is recognised that the annual budget must accommodate the increasing resource needs of the social sectors, particularly in the health sector, this Policy does not specifically recommend an earmarked health cess, as that would have a tendency of reducing the space available to parliament in making appropriations looking to the circumstances prevailing from time to time.

The policy highlights the expected roles of different participating groups in the health sector. Further, it recognises the fact that, despite all that may be guaranteed by the Central Government for assisting public health programmes, public health services would actually need to be delivered by the State administration, NGOs and other institutions of civil society. The attainment of improved health levels would be significantly dependent on population stabilisation, as also on complementary efforts from other areas of the social sectors—like improved drinking water supply, basic sanitation, minimum nutrition, etc., to ensure that the exposure of the populace to health risks is minimised.

Any expectation of a significant improvement in the quality of health services, and the consequential improved health status of the citizenry, would depend not only on increased financial and material inputs, but also on a more empathetic and committed attitude in the service providers, whether in the private or public sectors. In some measure, this optimistic policy document is based on the understanding that the citizenry is increasingly demanding more by way of quality in health services, and the health delivery system, particularly in the public sector, is being pressed to respond. In this backdrop, it needs to be recognised that any policy in the social sector is critically dependent on the service providers treating their responsibility not as a commercial activity, but as a service, albeit a paid one. In the area of public health, an improved standard of governance is a prerequisite for the success of any health policy.

Reproductive and Child Health Programme

The National Family Planning Programme was started in 1951 as a purely demographic programme. Subsequently the element of public education and extension was included to facilitate outcome under the Family Planning Programme. During the seventies, the Family Planning Programme was focussed mainly on terminal methods and the programme received set back due to rigid implementation of a target based approach. The programme has, however, remained fully voluntary and the main effort of the government has been to provide services on the one hand and to encourage citizens by information, education and communication on the other to use such services.

The experiences gained, within the country and outside, had amply established that health of women in the reproductive age group and of small children (up to 5 years of age) is of crucial importance for effectively tackling the problem of growth of population which led to change in the approach from family planning to family welfare. Since the Seventh Plan implemented during 1984-89, the family welfare programmes have evolved with the focus on the health needs of the women in reproductive age group and of children below the age of 5 years as well as on providing contraceptives and spacing services to the desirous people. The main objective of the family welfare programme for the country has been to stabilise population at a level consistent with the needs of national development.

The Universal Immunisation Programme (UIP) aimed at reduction in mortality and morbidity among infants and younger children due to Vaccine Preventable Diseases, was started in 1985-86. The Oral Rehydration Therapy (ORT) was also started in view of the fact that Diarrhoea was a leading cause of deaths among children. Various other

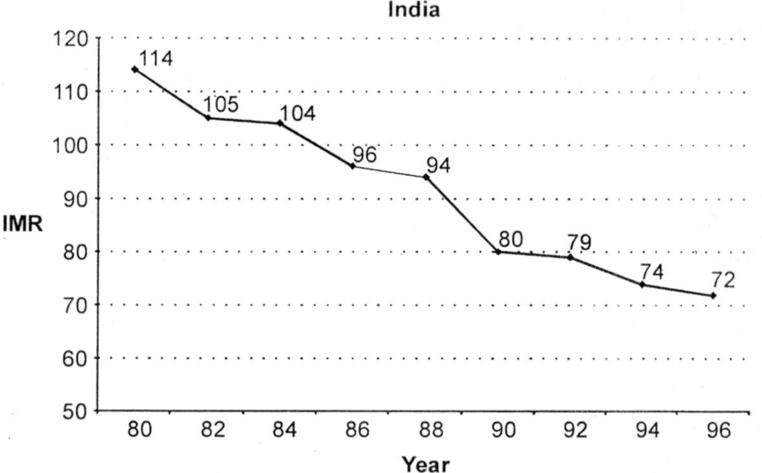

programmes under Maternal and Child Health (MCH) were also implemented during the 7th Plan.

The objectives of all these programmes were convergent and aimed at improving the health of the mothers and young children and to provide them facilities for prevention and treatment of major disease conditions. While these programmes did have a beneficial impact but the separate identity for each programme was causing problems in its effective management and this was also somewhat reducing the outcome. Therefore, in the 90s i.e., in the 8th Plan, these programmes were integrated under Child Survival and Safe Motherhood (CSSM) Programme which was implemented from 1992-93.

Progress made so far

Various programmes have led to substantial improvement in health indicators. The position with regard to some prominent health indicators is depicted in the table:

Indicator	***Past level***		***Current level***	
Crude Birth Rate	41.7	(1951-61)	27.4	(1996)
Crude Death Rate	22.8	(1951-61)	8.9	(1996)
Infant Mortality Rate	146.0	(1951-61)	72.0	(1996)
Maternal Mortality Rate		NA	4.37	(1991-92)
Life Expectancy at Birth (Years) Est.				
Male	37.1	(1951)	62.4	(1996-2001)
Female	36.1	(1951)	63.4	(1996-2001)
Total Fertility Rate	6.0	(1951)	3.5	(1994)
Effective Couple Protection Rate	10.4	(1970-71)	45.4	(31.3.97)
Immunisation Status* (% coverage) for Pregnant women				
TT	40.0	(1985-86)	80.0	(1997-98)
For Infant				
BCG	29.0	(1985-86)	96.0	(1997-98)
Measles	44.0	(1987-88)	83.0	(1997-98)
DPT	41.0	(1985-86)	90.0	(1997-98)
Polio	36.0	(1985-86)	90.0	(1997-98)

NA:Not available Relevant year in parentheses

* Universal Immunisation was started in (1985-86).

CRUDE BIRTH RATE: INDIA (Birth Rate Per 1000 Population)

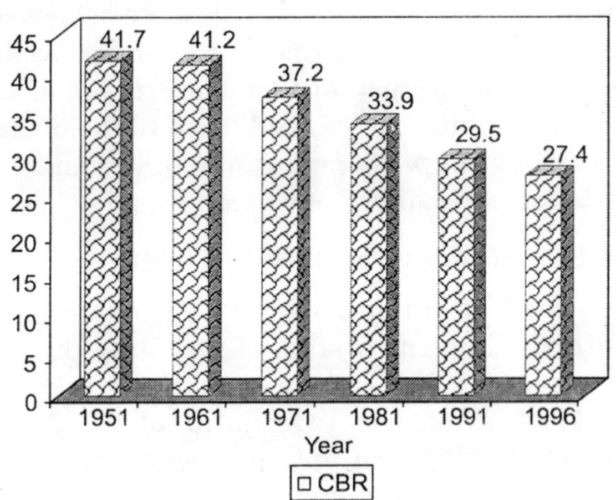

However, the position it not uniform all over the country. Whereas the States like Kerala, Tamil Nadu, Goa, Maharashtra and Punjab have achieved a considerably higher level, the States like Uttar Pradesh, Madhya Pradesh, Bihar, Rajasthan, Jharkand, Assam and Orissa are performing at levels much below the national level. This has been a matter of great concern because some of these States also happen to be very populous and unless performance in these States improve, the national performance will continue to remain depressed. The deficiencies in implementation of the maternal and child health services have been responsible for a high incidence of maternal mortality and child/infant mortality and low health status of women and children. Poor prospect of health and life of the children is one of the prominent factors leading to birth of more children per family.

The results at ground level are influenced by a number of factors like investment for the programme at National/ State level, efficiency of the State, health system and response of the people. Allocation for resources for Family Welfare Programme in the past has not been commensurate with the size of the job. This is a severe handicap particularly when it is noted that in almost all respects the health care system needs upgradation and that it needs to reach out to many more people for the national goals to be achieved. While there is a steady improvement due to economic development, spread of education/literacy and empowerment of citizens, substantial problems in regard to education/literacy particularly among the weak performing States and in regard to empowerment particularly of women remain.

Integrated Reproductive and Child Health

The process of integration of related programmes initiated with the implementation of the Child Survival and Safe Motherhood (CSSM) programme was taken a step further in 1994 when the International Conference on Population and Development in Cairo recommended that the participant countries should implement unified programmes for Reproduction and Child Health (RCH). The RCH approach has been defined as "People have the ability to reproduce and regulate their fertility, women are able to go through pregnancy and child birth safely, the outcome of pregnancies is successful in terms of maternal and infant survival and well being and couples are able to have sexual relations free of fear of pregnancy and of contracting diseases".

This concept is in keeping with the evolution of an integrated approach to the programmes aimed at improving the heath status of young women and children which has been going on in the country. It is obviously sensible that integrated RCH Programme, would help in reducing the cost of inputs to some extent because overlapping of expenditure would not longer be necessary and integrated implementation would optimise outcome at the field level. During the 9th Plan, the RCH programme accordingly, integrates all the related programmes of the 8th Plan. The concept of RCH is to provide need based, client centred, demand driven, high quality and integrated RCH services to the beneficiaries. The RCH Programme is a composite programme incorporating the inputs of the Government of India as well as funding support from external donor agencies including World Bank and the European Commission.

It is legitimate right of the citizen to be able to experience sound Reproductive and Child Health and therefore, the RCH Programme will seek to provide relevant services for assuring reproductive and child health to all citizens. However, RCH is even more relevant for obtaining the objective of stable population for the country. The overall objective since the beginning has been that the population of the country should be stabilised at a level consistent with the requirement of national development. It is now established that parents keep the family size small if they are assured about the health and longevity of the children and there is no better assurance of good health and longevity of children than health care for the mothers and for young children. Therefore, by ensuring small families RCH Programme also ensures stable population in the medium and long-term, though in the short-term, population is controlled by use of spacing methods and terminal methods for avoiding unwanted pregnancies. Therefore, the overall strategy of the Government of India (Department of Family Welfare) is to strive for obtaining reproductive and child health arrangements for the whole of the country's population and for simultaneously promoting and making contraceptive/terminal methods available for desirous couples. It also needs to be observed that the measures through the health system alone do not and cannot assure success in either ensuring reproductive and child health or in controlling population. These objectives are determined concurrently by the following:

1. Policy support expressed publicly by opinion leaders in different sectors of the national system and by the community at large. Without this kind of support, the receptivity of the people to make use of even available services cannot be ensured;

2. Adequate resources for making available Reproductive and Child Health services to all rural and urban communities in the country;

3. Accountability for performance among the health workers and efficiency of the health system. Without such efficiency the quality of services to citizens or even effective access to health services cannot be ensured; and

4. Literacy among women and educational status of families and similarly improvement in economic status of families. The educated and economically well-off families can more rationally assess the options before them and acquire capability/willingness to assess consequences of their present actions for future. Therefore, the effort of the Department of Family Welfare is to collaborate with the related Departments and Non-Governmental Organisations for seeking support of their Programmes

for the Family Welfare Programmes. This in turn will similarly improve the outcome of related Programmes of those departments as well.

The RCH programme for the 9th Plan is a very ambitious programme which aims to effectively bring all the reproductive and child health services within easy reach of the community. Almost all of the large outlay of Rs. 5112.23 crore for the programmes will be for improving facilities and services and the traditional items for creation of posts and construction of buildings will be only nominal. Therefore, the programme will require much greater management skill including a much more professional advanced management information System.

The RCH programme will make reproductive and child health services available at lower level of hospitals like specialist facilities for obstetric care will be available at Sub-divisional hospital level, medical termination of pregnancy services will be available at PHCs and general obstetric care facilities will be strengthened in PHCs. Simultaneously, the RCH programme will make available some new RCH services e.g., Specialist facility for Sexually Transmitted Diseases (STD) and Reproductive Tract Infections (RTI) (which have a high incidence) will be available in all district hospitals and in a fair number at sub-divisional hospitals. At another plane, the RCH programme will seek to broaden ownership of the community in the programme so that it does not remain a purely government programme which, unfortunately has been the situation so far. The non-government medical system will be prominently involved in providing many RCH facilities and Indian Systems of Medicine which are known to be efficacious, will be utilised in a substantial manner in providing RCH services. Certain prominent segments of population which have prominent RCH needs but which have not been adequately addressed in the past like the urban slum population, tribal population and the adolescents will be addressed through specially designed additional programmes. The Panchayati Raj functionaries at village, development block and district level will be involved in sensitisation and training along with health workers and workers of related Government Departments. The Panchayati Raj functionaries will have a central role in determining the need of the local population, for RCH services generally and for contraceptives particularly under the target free (Community Needs Assessment) approach. The Panchayat will also be the agency for implementing the programme and for extending financial and transport support to women from indigent families for taking them to specialist at Sub-divisional hospitals for deliveries.

The RCH programme incorporates the components relating to child survival and safe motherhood and includes two additional components, one relating to sexually transmitted diseases and other relating to reproductive tract infections. The main highlights of the RCH programme are:

1. The programme integrates all interventions of fertility regulation, maternal and child health with reproductive health of both men and women.
2. The services to be provided will be client centred, demand driven, of high quality and based on the needs of the community arrived at through decentralised participatory planning and the target free approach.
3. The programme envisages upgradation of the level of facilities of for providing various interventions and quality of care. The First Referral Units (FRUs), being set up at sub-district level will provide comprehensive emergency obstetric and new born care. Similarly RCH facilities in PHCs will be substantially upgraded.
4. It is proposed to improve facilities for obstetric care. MTP and IUD insertion in the PHCs, also for IUD, insertion in sub-centres.
5. The Programme aims at improving the outreach of services primarily for the vulnerable groups of population who have till now been effectively left out of the planning process e.g.—

- ❖ Special Programme will be taken up for urban slums, tribal population and adolescents.
- ❖ NGOs and Voluntary Organisations will be involved in a much larger way to improve outreach and make it the people's programme.
- ❖ Practitioners of Indian Systems of Medicine will be trained and research and development in Indian Systems of Medicine will be supported to improve the range of RCH services.
- ❖ Panchayati Raj System will have a greater role in planning, implementation and assessment of client satisfaction.

Intervention Programmes to Combat Malnutrition

(a) Integrated Child Development Services

The Government of India is making concerted efforts to reduce the prevalence of malnutrition in the country. In consonance with this, the scheme of Integrated Child Development Services (ICDS) was launched in 1975. This programme is implemented by the Nodal Department i.e., the Department of Women and Child Development. Starting with 33 experimental projects in 1975-76, the ICDS programme has been expanded to 2765 projects upto December 1992. This package of services provided to the beneficiaries of the programme are Supplementary Nutrition, Immunisation, Health check-up, Referral Services, Non-formal Pre-school Education and Nutrition and Health Education. Supplementary nutrition is one of the major components of the programmes.

The strategy adopted in ICDS is one of the Integrated delivery of early childhood services so that their synergistic effect will fulfill the objective of the programme. The beneficiaries of the programme are children below 6 years, pregnant and lactating mothers and women in the age group 15-44 years. This programme supplements the health, nutrition and family welfare activities with appropriate co-operation and co-ordination between functionaries of the Health Department and nodal department.

The other programmes in this direction are the Special Nutrition Programme, Balwadi Nutrition Programme, Wheat Based Supplementary Nutrition Programme, Tamil Nadu Integrated Nutrition Programme, Mid Day Meals Programme for school children and other intervention programmes for combating specific nutritional deficiency diseases such as Nutritional Anaemia Prophylaxis Programme, Goitre Control Programme and programme for prevention of Nutritional Blindness due to Vitamin A deficiency.

(b) Special Nutrition Programme

The Special Nutrition Programme (SNP) was launched in the country in 1970-71. It provides supplementary feeding to the extent of about 300 calories and 10 gm. of proteins to pre-school children and about 500 calories and 20 gm. of protein to expectant and nursing mothers for 300 days a year. At present SNP is operated, as a part of the Minimum Needs Programme in the various states. The nutrition component of the ICDS programme is funded by States and Union Territories from the SNP budget. At present about 21.5 million beneficiaries are covered under this programme.

(c) Balwadi Nutrition Programme

The Balwadi Nutrition Programme (BNP) is being implemented since 1970-71 through five national level voluntary organisations. The Central grant is given for supplementary feeding of children. It consists of 300 calories and 12.5 gm of protein every day per child in the age group 3-5 years. At present there are around 5641 Balwadis throughout the country benefiting 2.25 lakh children.

(d) Applied Nutrition Programme

Applied Nutrition Programme (1959): This is an educational Programme at the village and family level which aims to bring about changes in the choice of food and feeding practices that involve little or no extra expense for the family.

This programme directly concentrates on the feeding of the young child, both through the education of the mother and by channelling a part of the food produced under various schemes of the programme in the diet of the child.

(e) *Wheat Based Supplementary Nutrition Programme*

A centrally sponsored scheme called Wheat-based Supplementary Nutrition Programme (WNP) was introduced in 1986. This programme follows the norms of SNP or of the nutrition component of the ICDS. Central assistance for the programme consists of supply of free wheat and supportive costs for other ingredients, cooking, transport etc. At present around 3 million children and expectant and nursing mothers are covered under this programme. This scheme is now being transferred to the State Sector.

(f) *Tamil Nadu Integrated Nutrition Programme*

Tamil Nadu Integrated Nutrition Programme (TINP) is being implemented in the State of Tamil Nadu since 1981. Under this project nutritional surveillance and supplementary nutrition is being provided to children below six years and expectant and nursing mothers. The project is assisted by World Bank. The total outlay for the project is Rs.321 crores.

(g) *Mid Day Meal Programme*

In 1956 the erstwhile Madras State launched the mid-day meal programme of providing free meal to the elementary school children with a view to (a) enrolling poor children who generally remain outside the school due to poverty; and (b) giving one meal to the children attending the school. The MDM operates as a centrally sponsored scheme from 1962-63 in all the states. The objectives were (a) to improve nutritional status of the school children; and (b) to attract children to enroll themselves into school and to encourage regular attendance by providing supplementary nutrition.

(h) *Nutritional Anaemia Prophylaxis Programme*

Taking cognizance of this problem, the Government of India launched a Prophylaxis programme in 1970 to prevent nutritional anaemia in mothers and children. Under the programme, the expectant and nursing mothers as well as women acceptors of family planning are given one tablet of iron and folic acid containing 60 mg elemental iron (180 mg of ferrous sulphate and 0.5 mg of folic acid) and children in the age group 1- 5 years are given one tablet of iron containing 20 mg elemental iron (60 mg of ferrous sulphate and 0.1 mg folic acid) daily for a period of 100 days. This programme covered children and pregnant women with haemoglobin level less than 8 gm per cent and 10 gm per cent respectively.

There has been an increase in the number of beneficiaries under this programme from 3.52 million in 1975-76 to 41.20 million in 1988-89. About 30 million women and 50 million children have, however, been identified as eligible beneficiaries for the prophylaxis programme. During 1988-89, the programme envisaged to cover 22 million women and 30 million children.

Fortification of salt with iron, a universally consumed dietary article, has been identified as a measure to control anaemia. Efficacy of fortified salt in both rural and urban communities was assessed by a multicentric study and revealed that iron fortified salt when consumed over a period of 12-18 months reduced prevalence of anaemia significantly. Accordingly, fortification of salt with iron as a public health approach is piloted in Tamil Nadu and Rajasthan.

(i) Prophylaxis Programme Against Blindness, due to Vitamin A Deficiency

The programme was initiated by the Government in 1970. Under this programme children in age group 1-5 years are given an oral dose of 0.2 million I.U of Vitamin A in oil every 6 months. The number of beneficiaries covered under this programme has increased steadily from 4.48 million in 1975-76 to 30.12 million in 1986-87.

An interim evaluation in the States of Kerala and Karnataka after two years of implementation of the programme showed that the coverage was over 75 per cent and there was a 75 per cent reduction in the prevalence of conjunctival signs of Vitamin A deficiency. The evaluation also confirms the administrative feasibility of this approach within the existing health infrastructure.

During 1980, the Department of Food introduced a scheme of Fortification of Milk with Vitamin A to prevent nutritional blindness. At present there are 42 dairies in the country implementing this scheme. During 1988-89, the total quantity of milk fortified with Vitamin A through these dairies was 3.2 million litres per day.

MCH Division of the Ministry of Health and Family Welfare has been implementing the programmes on anaemia prophylaxis and prophylaxis against vitamin 'A' deficiency. These programmes were reviewed by two groups of experts and accordingly certain modifications have been made with concentrated efforts on all pregnant mothers receiving 100 tablets of iron folic acid and universalisation of vitamin 'A' to be provided to all children between 9 months and 3 years of age. The lactating women and those who have accepted certain family planning devices will continue to get the drugs as per earliest schedule. Suitable linkages have also been developed for these programmes with immunisation and arrangements have been made for regular monitoring through the same programme.

(j) Goitre Control Programme

A National Goitre Control Programme was initiated by the Government of India in 1962 to identify goitre endemic regions and to assess the impact of goitre control measures. The availability and production of iodized salt, strengthening of administrative machinery controlling the entry of non-iodized salt in the endemic regions have been recommended as measures to improve the implementation of the programme.

There is an increasing awareness about the broad spectrum of Iodine Deficiency Disorder (IDD) in the country. The Goitre Control Programme has gained momentum in recent years. The Government of India has started a scheme with effect from 1-4-1986 envisaging Universal Iodisation of Edible Salt in a phased manner to cover the whole country by 1992. It has liberalised production of iodized salt under the private sector by issuing licence to 700 salt manufacturers out of which 307 have commenced production. As a result thereof, the production of iodised salt in the country has steadily increased to 25.061akh M.T. in 1990-91 from 7.72 lakh M.T. in 1986-87. Since the inception of this programme in 19 States/Union Territories have so far established Goitre Control Cells in their State Health Directorates for effective implementation and monitoring of the programme.

(k) National Diarrhoeal Diseases Control Programme

The programme was launched in 1981 to reduce the mortality in children below five years due to diarrhoeal diseases through introduction of Oral Rehydration Therapy (ORT). The high priority accorded to the Programme is part of the package of services rendered under the MCH programme which was initiated during 1980-85 has now been strengthened extensively. The anganwadi centres of the ICDS Scheme have served as nucleus for the propagation of oral rehydration therapy which has been found to be an effective measure of preventing dehydration caused by diarrhoea.

(l) Education Related Programme

A number of committees and study groups were set-up from time to time suggest ways and means for preschool education families. All these groups emphasised the importance of preschool education but the recommendations remained mostly on paper. The Central Social Welfare Board (CSWB) initiated as a part of its welfare activities in the areas not covered hitherto, the scheme of Welfare Extension Projects. But most of the children education programms are integrated with the health and nutritional programme.

Welfare Extension Projects

This Scheme launched in 1958, provides for a programme of creches, Balwadis, Craft Education, Social Education for

Adult women, Recreational Activities for Youth, Maternity and Child Welfare Services etc. Each project benefits about 50 families.

Integrated Pre-school Project

This programme provides welfare services like education, health and recreation to the preschool children on an integrated basis. The main object of the programme is to provide all the basic amenities to a child necessary for his growth and mental development. This is particularly necessary in over crowded areas of low income group localities where there is poverty, lack of space etc.

Other Programmes

The Department of Education, Ministry of Human Resource Development, Government of India, is implementing a number of schemes for the development and welfare of children, namely.

1. Operation black board—It was started as a consequence of the New Education Policy and the purpose is to ensure minimum essential facilities in primary schools.
2. Non-formal Education.
3. Reimbursement - of Tuition Fee charged from girls in higher classes in States/Union Territories.
4. National Scholarships scheme.
5. National Loan Scholarships scheme.
6. Scheme for upgradation of merit of SC/ST students.
7. Scheme of Scholarships at secondary stage for talented children from rural areas.
8. Scholarship scheme for study in Approved residential schools.
9. Bal Bhavan society.

The Department of Rural Development runs two programmes which are related to child welfare as the well being and development of children is closely linked with the economic and nutritional status of the family, specially of women.

INTEGRATED CHILD DEVELOPMENT SERVICES

Thus the Indian constitution made primary efforts for the welfare of children well before the declaration of child rights by the United Nations. The Indian government launched several programmes for the welfare of children. Though many of the programmes could not achieve expected results the efforts show the concern of Indian government and policy makers. ICDS is one such ongoing programme which could sustain inspite some shortcomings, ICDS programme caters to the needs of rural, tribal, semi urban and slum children that is ICDS is one of the largest child welfare programme providing the rightful needs of children in India.

Integrated child development services is India's response to the challenge of meeting the holistic needs of the child. Today, the ICDS is one of the world's largest and most unique programmes for early childhood care and development.

Genesis: On the basis of eight inter-ministerial study teams set up by the planning commission, a scheme of ICDS was evolved. It is centrally sponsored scheme, 33 experimental projects were started in different parts of the country on 2, October 1975. During 1978-79, 67 new ICDS projects were started. Along with the ICDS project, adult women are given training in functional literacy which includes skills in childcare, home management, personal and environmental hygiene. Success of the scheme prompted expansion of ICDS to over 1000 blocks by the end of sixth plan (1984-85). During the seventh plan, programme is likely to expand to another 1000 blocks (Goel, S.L., 1980).

ICDS is a multi-sectoral programme and involves several departments, whose services are coordinated at the village, PHC project—district and state levels. The primary responsibility for the implementation of the programme lies with the department of women and child development, Ministry of Human Resource Development at the centre which may be Social Welfare, Rural Development, Tribal Welfare or Health and Family Welfare.

The ICDS beneficiaries are children below 6 years, pregnant and lactating women and women in the age group 15 to 44 years. The beneficiaries are to a large extent identical with those under the MCH and EPI programmes. The infrastructure of ICDS is an additional facility which can be profitably wed to supplement the health, nutrition and family welfare activities with appropriate co-operation and co-ordination between functionaries of the departments *viz.*, health and the nodal departments.

Objectives of ICDS are

1. To improve the nutritional and health status of children in the age group 0-6 years;
2. To lay the foundations for proper psychological physical and social development of the child;
3. To reduce the incidence of mortality, morbidity, malnutrition and school drop-outs;
4. To achieve effective co-ordination of policy and implementation amongst the various departments to promote child development; and
5. To enhance the capability of the mother to look after the normal health and nutritional needs through nutrition and health education.

Towards achieving these objectives, a package of services in rendered through the anganwadi worker at the village centre called anganwadi. The supportive supervision by the functionaries of the nodal department and health department is essential for the success of the programme. The social welfare functionaries have a primary responsibility of providing supplementary nutrition and non-formal education to the beneficiaries of the programme.

The ICDS has two components that is health component and social component. The inputs for the health component *viz.*, information, materials, training needs of personnel, identification of health services for the beneficiaries are looked after by the All India Institute of Medical Sciences (AIIMS), Delhi and the social component *viz.*, preschool education, nutritional aspects, materials, training needs of ICDS personnel are taken care of by the National Institute of Public Co-operation and Child Development (NIPCCD). Planning, monitoring and evaluation of social components is the responsibility of NIPCCD and the health component is AIIMS. The ICDS programme implementation is done through the Department of Women and Child Welfare that is the projects are either managed by the government department or allotted to a local non-government organisation. The inputs for the ICDS programme flow from NIPCCD and AIIMS through the government departments of; Women and Child Welfare and Medical and Health Services. Similarly feed back reports also flow back from the village level to the State and National level through the Department of Women and Child Welfare and Medical and Health Services.

ICDS Project Staff

District Programme Officer (DPO)

↓

Community Development Project Officer (CDPO)

↓

Supervisors

↓

Anganwadi Workers

↓

Helpers

The Training of Child Development Project Officers of ICDS programme is also undertaken by the NIPCCD at its regional centres located in Gauhati and Bangalore. The project level personnel or staff *viz.*, supervisors, anganwadi workers and helpers are given training at the middle level training centres. The middle level training centres (MLTCs) are allotted to Home Science Colleges/Departments or Social Work Colleges or Departments in various parts of India.

The ICDS was launched in 1975 soon after the formulation of the National Policy for Children. It was spurred by awareness that India exhibited some of the world's highest rates of infant mortality, morbidity, and malnutrition, and extremely high rates of maternal mortality during birth. According to the United Nations Development Programme (UNDP) Human Development Report for 2000, the infant mortality and under-five mortality rates are still 69 and 105 per cent thousand respectively, and the maternal mortality rate stands at 410 per 100,000.

The ICDS programme in anyone Block (a Block consisted of an administrative unit of approximately 100 villages) was considered a "project", and each project received funding independently. The structure of command of the ICDS bureaucracy at the District level was as follows: it was to be headed by a District Programme Officer (DPO). The Child Development Project Officers (CDPO), who heads the programme at the level of the Block, did reporting to the DPO. The CDPO was the head of the office. She was responsible for overseeing the work of the Supervisors (*Mukhya Sevikas*), the anganwadi workers in the block, and their helpers. The anganwadi worker is a key person in the ICDS programme and has multiple responsibilities for the development of women and children. The anganwadi workers were responsible for the day-to-day functioning of centers in villages, which especially targeted poor and low-caste women and children as beneficiaries. The anganwadi centers were supposed to operate every day from 9 a.m. to 1 p.m. Since it was not feasible for a single anganwadi worker to run a center, take care of as many as 45 children, teach the children, cook food for them, supervise their medical care, and maintain the records, the anganwadi worker was provided with a "Helper". The helper's duties included doing all the odd jobs associated with the anganwadi, including rounding up the children to attend the center, doing the cooking when the centers were supplied with food, and cleaning the "school" (Gupta, 2001).

Integrated Child Development Coverage and Outreach

It provides the framework for assigning priorities to different needs of children (both before and after birth), and for responding to them in an integrated manner, ICDS is India's response to the challenge of meeting the holistic needs of the child. Today, the ICDS is one of the world's largest and most unique outreach programmes for early childhood care and development, It symbolises India's commitment to its children. It is widely acknowledged that the young child is most vulnerable to malnutrition, morbidity, resultant disability and mortality. Recognising the early childhood development constitutes the foundation of human development, ICDS is designed to promote holistic development of children under six years, through the strengthened capacity of caregivers and communities and improved access to basic services, at the community level. The programme is specifically designed to reach disadvantaged and low income groups, for effective disparity reduction.

The programme provides an integrated approach for converging basic services for improved childcare, early stimulation and learning, health and nutrition, water and environmental sanitation targeting young children, expectant and nursing mothers and women's/adolescent girls' group. They are reached through nearly 300,000 trained community-based anganwadi workers and an equal number of helpers, supportive community structures/ women's groups—through the anganwadi centre, the health system and in the community. ICDS is a powerful outreach programme to help achieve major national nutrition and health goals, embodied in the National Plan of Action for Children, 1992. It also contributes to the national goal of universal primary education. ICDS provides increased opportunities for promoting early development, associated with improved enrollment and retention in the early primary stage and by releasing girls from the burden of sibling care, to enable them to participate in primary education.

ICDS, 2004 reaches out to 6.2 million expectant and nursing mothers and 33.2 million children (under six years of age) participate in centre-based pre school education activities. The ICDS programme was launched on October 2, 1975, the 106th birth anniversary of Mahatma Gandhi, The Father of the Nation. This signifies commitment to the Gandhian vision of addressing socio-economic inequities by reaching out to the most disadvantaged, undeserved and the most-vulnerable. As Gandhiji saw India's development in the empowerment of its people, so does ICDS seek to empower communities for the care and development of their children and women, to shape the country's present and future. All the ICDS services are provided through the anganwadi in an integrated manner to enhance their impact on childcare. Each anganwadi is run by an anganwadi worker supported by a helper in integrated service delivery, and improved linkages with the health system—thus increasing the capacity of community and women—especially mothers—for childcare, survival and development.

SERVICES AND BENEFICIARIES

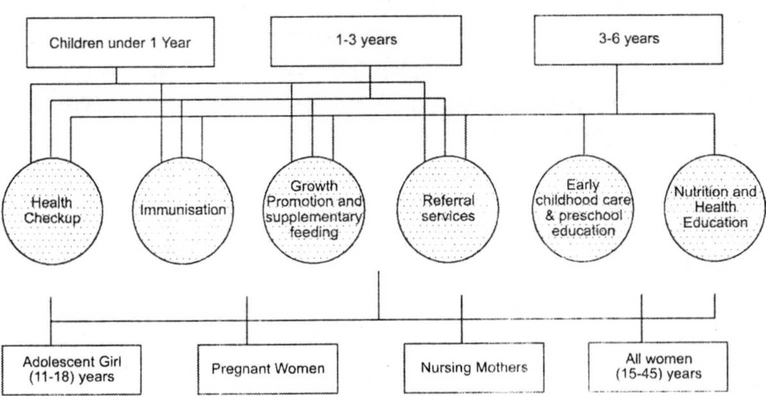

ICDS is unique because all basic sectoral services, related to early childhood care, preschool education, nutrition and health converge, through a community-based child care worker, that is, the anganwadi workers, on the same group of children, adolescent girls, pregnant and nursing mothers. Convergence of services is essential to address the inter-related needs of children and women, in a comprehensive and cost-effective manner. The child centred approach of ICDS is based on the rationale that care, psycho-social development and the child's health and nutritional well-being mutually reinforce each other.

In order to enhance the outreach of these services, particularly to the disadvantaged groups, and ensure their better utilisation, the anganwadi worker mobilises support from the community. All families in the community are surveyed by the anganwadi worker to identify pregnant and nursing mothers, adolescent girls and children below six years of age from the low income families and deprived sections of society.

Evaluation: Since its inception, the programme has generated interest among academicians, planners, administrators and those responsible for its implementation. Consequently, a large number of research studies have been conducted to evaluate and assess the impact of the programme. The Programme Evaluation Organisation (PEO) of the planning commission conducted a baseline survey of ICDS in 1976 and a repeat survey during 1977-78. Subsequent expansion of the ICDS was based on the positive results of these evaluations. A major chunk of the available ICDS research is focussed on health and nutrition components of the scheme. Most of these studies have been carried out by the Central Technical Committee (CTC). More recently, a joint multicentric study by the National Institute of Nutrition (NIN) and CTC (1995) highlights the impact of ICDS on psycho-social development. In addition to the above large scale studies, several micro-level researches, surveys as well as post graduate and doctoral dissertations have attempted to study the implementation of the programme and evaluate its impact on the beneficiaries. A review of these research studies indicates that ICDS has had a positive impact on beneficiaries and has potential of enhancing child survival and development. Definite improvement has been reported in major indicators of health and nutrition such as IMR, nutritional status, morbidity pattern, immunisation coverage and utilisation of health services.

ICDS—GOVERNMENT INITIATIVE FOR VOLUNTARY ORGANISATION

The scheme of ICDS is in existence since 1975-76. The ICDS represents a coordinated strategy aimed at improving the condition of children. The programme entails a package of services like supplementary nutrition, immunisation, health check-ups, referral services, nutrition and health education. Children in the age group of 6 months to 6 years as well as expectant and nursing mothers are the beneficiaries of this programme. The programme is administered by the State Governments. The expenditure of an ICDS project on salaries and honorarium of the staff, establishment and other recurring items is borne by the Government of India. Food for providing supplementary nutrition to the beneficiaries is made available by the State Governments, international agencies notably the CARE or the Government of India under its wheat based nutrition programme. UNICEF assists the ICDS in spheres of consultancy services, training, communications, certain initial supplies and equipment, monitoring, research and evaluation. The focal point for the delivery of services under the ICDS is the anganwadi. Generally, there is one anganwadi for a population of about 1000. The anganwadi is managed by an anganwadi worker, who is an honorary worker selected from the local community. The programme is supervised by ICDS supervisors and the CDPO who is overall incharge of a project.

The ICDS places great reliance on the coordinated efforts of different organisations and involvement of the local community. The government, in pursuance of its policy of offering greater role to the voluntary initiative in the socio-economic and other development programmes, thought of involving the voluntary organisations in the implementation of ICDS. It was expected that voluntary organisations would make it a peoples programme by increasing community participation. Moreover, it is generally believed that the services provided by these agencies cost less than that given by government agencies as they are unfettered by the rigid rules, that regulate the functioning of government. Besides, voluntary agencies also save considerably on use of manpower by adopting a multi-disciplinary approach in the use of their personnel. They are also expected to deliver the services more efficiently because of the flexibility in their method of work which is also conducive to innovativeness. Needless to say, the main strength of the voluntary agencies lies in their motivated manpower committed to their work. As a result of the efforts of the Department of Women and Child Development, Government of India, six organisations have been selected by the Central Government and the various State Governments to implement a number of ICDS projects. Voluntary action in this field has been negligible. Since voluntary action in implementation of the ICDS has been a recent phenomenon, the Department of Administrative Reforms and Public grievances was constituted.

1. To evaluate their performance and compare it with that of the government run projects so as to ascertain whether any advantages accrue to a programme implemented by voluntary agencies;
2. To find out solution to the problems, if any, faced by these organisations in implementing the programme, especially with regard to the release of grants-in-aid by government; and
3. In the process make some observations and recommendations for the efficient delivery of various services provided under the programme.

Out of the six projects implemented by voluntary agencies in the country, the team of the Department of Administrative

Reforms and Public Grievances studied the project at Sareni in District Raebareli run by the 'Literacy House' and a North Calcutta Project run by the Rama Krishna Mission Ashram. For comparison, two government projects run in the proximity of these two projects, namely the Lalganj Project in Raebareli and the Entally Project Calcutta were also studied.

Comparative Performance of Projects

Supplementary Nutrition

For both the projects, one being run by a voluntary organisation and the other by the Government in Raebareli, the Government of Uttar Pradesh provides the food materials for supplementary nutrition. A ready-to-eat food in powder form having 60 per cent wheat, 20 per cent soyabean, 10 per cent groundnut and 10 per cent sugar is supplied to the voluntary organisation run projects whereas the food supplied to the government run project consists of roosted gram, rice, dhal, etc. In West Bengal, the food for the government-run project is provided by CARE. It is corn soya blended with jaggery. For the RK Mission run project, nutrition is provided under the wheat based nutrition programme. The beneficiaries like better the food supplied under the wheat based nutrition programme as it offers them variety in taste. The beneficiaries of the Sareni Project were not happy with the food because of its insipid taste. Another noticeable feature was that whereas in Uttar Pradesh, food is served to all the beneficiaries in the age group of six months to six years, in West Bengal, it is served to children in the age group of three years to six years only. In the latter case, only malnourished children in the age group of six months to three years receive supplementary nutrition. The practice differs in the two states because of different instructions on the point contained in two sets of guidelines issued by the authorities.

Preschool Education

The pre-school education component was being emphasised considerably in all the four projects. The activities undertaken are games, songs, recitation of poems, teaching of the alphabet and counting of numbers etc. The activity is perceived to be an important component of the ICDS by the beneficiaries in all the four projects.

Health Services

In the voluntary organisation as well as the government run projects in Uttar Pradesh, lack of coordination between the Health Department and the project authorities results in non-fulfillment of immunisation targets assigned to them. The health check-ups and referral services provided to the beneficiaries leave much to be desired. Maintenance of records of immunisation and growth charts is also poor. On the other hand, in both the government and voluntary organisation run projects in Calcutta, 80 per cent of the children, have received proper immunisation and regular health check-ups are also provided to them. Records of immunisation and growth charts are maintained so well that one glance at the records would reveal the full status of a child's health.

Nutrition and Health Education

Education on nutrition and health in the government project in Raebareli as well as both the projects in Calcutta is given through the forum of fortnightly /monthly meetings of the Mahila Mandals. Many a time, such meetings are amended by ICDS supervisors, ANMs and LHVs. However, in the Literacy House (Voluntary agency) run project in Raebareli, the Programmes of adult literacy and ICDS have been amalgamated. The major feature of the amalgamation of the two programmes are that the adult education centres and anganwadis are located at the same place, one functions in the morning and the other in the afternoon. The anganwadi workers also function as adult education instructors only women attend adult literacy classes and education on nutrition and health constitute an important element of the curriculum of non-formal adult education.

Community Participation

In both the government and the voluntary agency run projects in Raebareli, community participation has been found to be insufficient. Barring a few exceptions, people in general do not help the project authorities in finding a place for running the anganwadi. Providing any monetary help or rendering any free service for the benefit of the projects is unheard of in the area. On the other hand, in both the projects in Calcutta, the community seems to be participating in a big way to make the programme a success. Local youth clubs help in providing accommodation for running the anganwadis. They also arrange picnics and other festivities for the children. In many cases mothers of the children attending the anganwadis have come forward to cook and distribute food in case the helper or the anganwadi's worker is absent.

Grants-in-aid

The team of the Department of Administrative Reforms and Public Grievances also studied the system of giving grants -in-aid by the government and the difficulties experienced by the organisation in receiving such grants. According to the guidelines issued by the Department of Women and Child Development, the implementation of the entire ICDS project or running of some anganwadis of such a project can be entrusted to a voluntary organisation by the State Government or by the Central Government. It will be open to a State Government, subject to its being satisfied about the bonafides and the capacity of an organisation, to entrust to it the whole or part of an ICDS project. In such a case, central grants available for that project or an amount proportionate to that part of the project, as the case may be, would be made available to the organisation along with the amount representing the supplementary nutrition component to be given from the State funds. In suitable cases, the Central Government may also entrust an ICDS project directly to an organisation of national repute. In the two organisations studied by this department, it was observed that to one, the Literacy House, the State Government (Government of Uttar Pradesh) has entrusted the implementation of ICDS, whereas to the others the Rama Krishna Mission, the implementation of the programme has been directly entrusted by the Central Government. Although the grants are given by different agencies, yet the problems faced by the organisation in both the cases are similar. Only after receiving the audited statement of expenditure pertaining to the previous year. It usually takes about three months for an organisation to get the statement audited by the Chartered Accountant and the government in turn takes two to three months in processing the statements. So, about six months delay usually occurs in giving the first installment to voluntary organisations. To run the programme uninterruptedly, the organisations have to make alternative arrangements for financing the programme during this period.

Salient Observations and Recommendations

The distinguishing features of voluntary organisations are supposedly a high degree of motivation of the persons, cost effectiveness, ability to mobilise community participation and innovativeness. An attempt was made by the study team to analyse these factors in the working of the voluntary organisations.

Selection of Voluntary agencies for running the ICDS

1. The agencies which have the necessary infrastructure and experience of organising health services should be tapped for implementing the ICDS. This would help in removing the organisation's dependence on the primary health centres for provision of health services. Thus, the poor performance in the sphere of health attributed to the lack of coordination with the health authorities could be avoided.

2. To enlist the much needed support of the community for the programme, the voluntary agencies which are in a position to provide some additional inputs in the form

of income/employment generating schemes etc should be encouraged to take up the ICDS.

3. Voluntary organisations should be encouraged to take up the ICDS projects in those areas in which they have established their credentials. Taking up programme for implementation at a new place doesn't place the organisation in an advantageous position vis-a-vis the government.

4. The agencies which are engaged in running the training courses to anganwadi workers should be requested to take up the implementation of the ICDS also. It would help in imparting practical knowledge to the trainees besides providing a forum of experimenting with new ideas for implementation of the programme.

GOVERNMENT ICDS PROJECTS

Guidelines have been issued by the Department of Women and Child Development vide MSW No. 19-9/85/CD (II) dated 13.8.1985 for considering the eligibility of anganwadi worker for direct recruitment to the posts of ICDS supervisor and providing certain benefits like age relaxation, etc. to them. It was pointed out by the staff working for the Rama Krishna Mission that while making such appointments, the Government of West Bengal does not give any such benefit to them whereas the staff working in the projects being implemented by the government enjoy these benefits. To make a discrimination of this sort appears to be unjustified as the nature of work performed by them is identical. This has resulted in a lot of heart-burn in the staff working for the voluntary agency. In order to remove this discrimination, it is recommended that the Department of Women and Child Development, Government of India should persuade State Governments to extend the benefits given for the services rendered anganwadi workers for appointment as ICDS supervisor to the anganwadi workers employed by the voluntary agencies also, subject, of course, to the fulfillment of the minimum eligibility conditions by such candidates.

Miscellaneous Operational Points

(i) ***Personnel:*** The performance of the better qualified anganwadi workers i.e., the graduates and the class XII pass candidates was distinctly superior to that of the matriculates. Frequent visits of the anganwadis by the supervisors and CDPO play a very important role in improving performance. The enterprising nature of the functionaries is more important than their working experience for achievement of better results.

(ii) ***Preschool education:*** Contrary to expectations, pre-school education is perceived to be an important component of the ICDS. Therefore, all care should be taken to organise this activity well, to evoke better response from the people towards this programme.

(iii) ***Nutrition:*** The food material supplied under the wheat based nutrition programme i.e., wheat and small amount of money to the beneficiary per day, given for purchasing other food stuff locally, gives maximum satisfaction to the beneficiaries as compared to the other items of food like corn soyabean, etc.

A lot of confusion persists with regard to the admissibility of supplementary nutrition to children of the age group of 6 months to 3 years, because of the contradictory instructions given in different publications on the subject. The hand book for anganwadi workers says that the supplementary nutrition to this group of beneficiaries should be restricted to the malnourished children only, whereas the booklet of the Department of Women and Child Development on ICDS does not mention this fact, thereby implying that supplementary nutrition should be provided to all the beneficiaries of the age group of 6 months to 3 years. It was observed that different project authorities were following different instructions on this subjects. For the achievement of the objectives of the ICDS, it would be better it supplementary nutrition is given to all children belonging to the age group of 6 months to 3 years. However, the Department of Women and Child Development, Government of India, should clarify the matter and send uniform instructions to the State Governments accordingly.

(iv) ***Health and Nutrition Education:*** For generating greater interest in women attending the meetings for receiving health and nutrition education topics like income generating opportunities and related matters should also be discussed.

(v) ***Maintenance of Records:*** In addition to recording merely the weights of the children on the growth charts, immunisation received by a child and any disease etc., contracted by him should also be indicated. This would give a comprehensive picture of the child's health at a glance which would help in supervisions the activities effectively.

(vi) ***Co-ordination with Health Authorities:*** The main reason for the lack of coordination of activities with the Health Department is the failure on part of the health authorities to treat the ICDS as their own programme, Anything done for the ICDS is considered a favour done to the ICDS project authorities. So, if the health authorities are some how made accountable for the implementation of the health components of the programme, then the staff would feel involved in its implementation. Perhaps if a system is evolved in which the ANM would send the report to pertaining immunisation etc in respect of the anganwadis under her jurisdiction to the Medical Officer who would then pass it on the CDPO, that would help the health authorities realise their responsibility towards this programme.

Innovations

It is recommended that the ICDS programme should provide flexibility to organisations to innovate to enable them to cater to the needs of the people of the area and to evoke an enthusiastic response from the beneficiaries and the community towards the programme.

THEORETICAL AND EMPIRICAL ISSUES ON ICDS AND CHILD RIGHTS

Children's rights are not, of course a new idea. The idea is conveyed in the Constitution, notably Article 39(f), which directs the state to ensure that "children are given opportunities and facilities to develop in a healthy manner and in conditions of freedom and dignity". This Article belongs to the Directive Principles, and should be read along with Article 37, which states that these principles are "fundamental to the governance of the country" and that "it shall be the duty of the state to apply these principles in making laws" As Article 39(f) illustrates, the Directive Principles (largely due to Ambedkar) include a visionary emphasis on "positive freedoms". The government's formal commitment to child rights and positive freedoms was further affirmed in the international Convention on the Rights of the child. In practice, however, little has been done to protect and promote the positive freedoms of children as a matter of right (Dreze, 2006).

We have a countrywide ICDS, whose main objective is the improvement of nutrition of pregnant and lactating women and young children. It operates at the village level and in urban slums through an anganwadi centre manned by a anganwadi worker who usually belongs to the village and dispenses services, including nutrition supplements to children, and pregnant and lactating women. The programme began in 1975 in 33 blocks and a few urban areas, and now after 30 years it covers most of the country. It is considered the biggest child welfare programme in Asia and probably in the world. The priority groups are low socio-economic group families, scheduled castes and scheduled tribes. The package of services consists of supplementary nutrition to children and to pregnant women during the last trimester of pregnancy and during lactation, as well as health and nutrition education and some activities for child development.

However, the functioning of the programme leaves much to be desired and much of the anganwadi workers' time is taken up by routine recording and reporting, and mindless weighing of children (growth monitoring) after which no action is taken or advice given to the caretaker. Her main responsibility should be health and nutrition education, encouraging women to breastfeed exclusively for six months and add semi-solid family food three to four times a day in appropriate quantities after that, which alone can improve nutrition. Teamwork with the auxiliary nurse midwife would result in better care of pregnant women, immunisation and management of any illness. However, the way the programme functions is that, even after 30 years, it has not been able to make a dent in the poor nutritional status of young children (Ghosh, S., 1997). However, in-depth nutrition education regarding feeding with foods within the family resources can help to improve nutrition (Ghosh, S., 2002). The Tenth Five Year Plan has not been very ambitious in this regard. It postulates a reduction of malnutrition from 47 per cent to 40 per cent. It is time, therefore, to change the direction of the programme and make it a true nutrition and child development programme (Ghosh, S. and Shah, D., 2004).

Shanti Ghosh makes two related points that have a crucial bearing on the revival to ICDS. First, she stresses the need to pay much greater attention to children under the age of three years. This is the critical period in the development of the child, when his or her "capabilities" (health, nutrition, learning abilities, etc.) are largely determined. For instance, this is the time when 90 per cent of the brain develops. Further, as the author points out, it is between the age of six months and two years that the nutritional status of Indian children deteriorates in an irreversible way. "If we are serious about preventing malnutrition", she says, "we have to focus on the age group of 6 months to 2 years".

The second point is that, during this period, much can be done through better feeding practices at home. For instance, it is well known that faulty weaning plays a major role in the onset of child malnutrition. Better knowledge and practice of appropriate feeding at home can go a long way in addressing this problem, even without additional economic resources. This requires interventions such as home visits and nutrition counselling. As Shanti Ghosh reiterates, these interventions were part of the original vision of ICDS, but have not been taken seriously.

Arun Gupta's paper on "infant and young child feeding" (IYCF) echoes many of these arguments, with special focus on breastfeeding and related matters. The author presents specific prescriptions on IYCF: "exclusive breastfeeding for the first six months (starting within one hour of birth) and continued breastfeeding for two years or beyond, along with adequate and appropriate complementary feeding beginning after six months". This prescription, described as "optimal IYCF", reflects "a unique global consensus on issues related to optimal infant and young child feeding". Arun Gupta summarises the scientific evidence on the benefits of optimal IYCF, and makes a strong case for nutrition counselling as a critical means of promoting better feeding practices at home. The effectiveness of this approach has already been established in various contexts, including a recent experiment conducted by the Breastfeeding Promotion Network of India (BPNI) in Gujarat (Garg and Ghosh, 2006).

As things stand, health services under ICDS are quite patchy. The main activity is child immunisation, and in this respect, the programme does seem to play a useful role (Dreze and Sen, 2004).

As immunisation services illustrate, one of the key issues in the provision of health services through ICDS is smooth cooperation between the anganwadi worker and health workers such as the ANMs. As Sundararaman argues in his contribution to this collection, there is a strong case for integrating ICDS with "community health volunteer" programmes. The proposed appointment of an Accredited Social Health Activist (ASHA) in every village, under the

National Rural Health Mission, is a crucial opportunity in this respect (Government of India, 2006).

Aside from this, direct provision of basic health services at the anganwadi needs to be revived. For instance, many anganwadi workers interviewed in the FOCUS (Sinha, 2004) survey said that the supply of medical kits had been discontinued. This was a disappointment for them, as the provision of basic medicines at the anganwadi used to be quite popular, and enhanced their social status. Health check-ups at the anganwadi are also far from regular: while 59 per cent of the anganwadi workers stated that health check-ups had taken place during the preceding 30 days, only 38 per cent of the mothers were aware of such services. There are major gaps here that are waiting to be filled.

Pre-school education (PSE) is another neglected aspect of ICDS. In the FOCUS survey, Tamil Nadu was the only state with a really effective PSE programme. In Tamil Nadu, 89 per cent of the mothers said that PSE activities were taking place at the anganwadi, and among those, 91 per cent felt that these activities were "useful". In the sample as a whole, however, the corresponding proportions were only 47 per cent 64 per cent, respectively.

This gap is all the more unfortunate as PSE has much potential, as a "selling point" for ICDS. Mothers interviewed in the FOCUS survey frequently expressed a strong desire to see their child learn something at the anganwadi, so that he or she would be better prepared to enter primary school. Among those whose children were not enrolled at the local anganwadi, more than 70 per cent said that they would like their children to be enrolled. When they were asked why they thought this would be useful, PSE emerged as their prime aspiration (Deepa Sinha, 2004).

Action for ICDS

One of the sobering findings of the FOCUS survey is that community involvement in ICDS is low, almost everywhere. Village communities, or for that matter gram panchayats, are rarely involved in the management or supervision of the local anganwadi. There are, however, positive experiences of public action and community involvement in ICDS. The papers by Dipa Sinha and Samir Garg discuss two recent initiatives of this kind, located in Andhra Pradesh and Chhattisgarh respectively.

In Andhra Pradesh, child rights issues were taken up in a setting where reasonably functional community institutions (mainly, the gram panchayats) were in place. The first task of the MV Foundation was to create "a new social environment" for child rights, as Dipa Sinha puts it. The central feature of this new social environment is that the survival, well-being and rights of children become social issues, of interest to the whole community and not just to the mothers or families of the children concerned. For instance, MV Foundation tried to ensure that the birth or death of a child is seen as a community event. When a child is born, the panchayat issues a birth certificate and the community celebrates. When a child dies, there is an enquiry and a public discussion of how the death could have been prevented. As Dipa Sinha, 2004 puts it: "To change norms, the entire community has to be mobilised to protect the rights of women and children".

In this new social environment, a range of practical interventions are possible. For instance, monthly meetings are convened by the gram panchayat with the anganwadi worker, the ANM, the school headmaster and others to review the situation of children: births and deaths, the progress of immunisation, the functioning of the local anganwadi, and so on. A new rapport also develops between the anganwadi worker and the community, whereby the latter helps to address the concerns of the anganwadi worker but also holds her accountable.

Twenty five years after the introduction of the ICDS programme the Supreme Court (order dated 28 November 2001) ordered that every settlement must have a disbursement centre and that every child aged 0-6, every pregnant and nursing mother and every adolescent girl be covered under the ICDS. Four years after the Government of India (GOI) and the state governments are yet to implement this order on 29 April 2004 the Supreme Court issued another order directing the government to file (with in three months) a time–bound plan for compliance once again the deadline passed with no concrete action or plan. Based on the report filed by the commission, another order was passed on 7 October 2004 nothing that the Government of India has not filed its plan and that state governments are far from ensuring universal access to supplementary nutrition.

The time has come to turn the ICDS programme upside down doing away with the model and thinking afresh on how best we can reach out to the most vulnerable. We need to plan separately for different sub groups of children looking at the specific needs of home based care and out reach services upto 3 years and a centre based approach for the 3+ group. It may be worth while discussing the possibility of splitting the ICDS programme into two—

(a) Dedicated home based programme to promote health and nutrition of children in the 0-3 group; health and nutrition of adolescent girls and pregnant and lactacting mothers.

(b) A centre-based nutrition and preschool education programme for 3-6 years. These are essential services about reaching out to this very important segment of out-population. Poor health, malnutrition and frequent bouts of illness at this stage have an irreversible impact on the overall health and well-being of children. Given the enormous diversity in the country and different administrative environments, political leadership and awareness levels among the people, the government needs to initiate a state-wise revisioning exercise to revisit the objectives of the ICDS programme with in the agreed ICDS conceptual

framework. This is essential to secure the commitment of the state leadership to the core objectives of the programme. This needs to be followed by stakeholders meetings at the state and district levels, with political leaders and other important opinion makers in the State.

3

Methodology

The study entitled "Reflection of Child Rights in the Integrated Child Development Services" was conducted in Chittoor District of Andhra Pradesh. As the largest child development programme it caters to the:

1. Health and nutritional needs of pregnant and lactating women;
2. Health, nutrition and education needs of children under six;
3. Life skill educational needs of adolescent girls.

ICDS programme launched well before the declaration of child rights is intended to address the important rights of India's children between 0-6 years. The programme since its inception in the year 1975 grew both in its coverage and services. ICDS unlike other programmes strengthened its structure, components, package of services, training and administration by retaining the original framework and adding on improvements. The programme is able to address the current issues with regard to children and mothers. ICDS is one programme which covers the child rights; Article-5; Article-6, Article-24, Article-28, Article-31. Further the programme encompasses five out of ten of the actions emphasised in the child rights document. Though the ICDS programme is not framed on the basis of child rights, it is necessary to revisit the programme in the light of child rights. There is every need to adopt rights approach to all child development programmes. The child's needs have become their rights, fulfillment of which are the responsibility of parents, family and the State.

The study is a evaluative one has two phases; in the first phase, the services of ICDS at the field level as perceived by anganwadi workers and mothers of anganwadi children was assessed. In the second phase, the child rights knowledge, attitudes and practises of anganwadi workers and mothers of anganwadi children was assessed.

The study attempts to examine the perceptions of anganwadi workers and mothers on ICDS, services at the field level in the context of child rights.

RESEARCH DESIGN

To facilitate the implementation of research study, a research design was developed after the review of relevant literature and visits to the ICDS projects which is given in flow chart 3.1. (*See on next page*)

The research design indicates the various steps in the research project envisaged by the researcher. It serves as a blue print for execution of research work planned.

LOCALE OF THE STUDY

The Chittoor district in Andhra Pradesh was selected purposively for the following reasons: It is one of the backward districts in the state interms of distribution of rural and urban population, degree of female literacy and other socio- economic parameters.

The physiography of the Chittoor District is as follows: The district is bounded by the states of Karnataka and Tamil Nadu on all sides except on the northern and part of the eastern sides. It is one of the four drought prone districts of the Rayalaseema region of Andhra Pradesh. The district has an area of 15,152 square kilometers and forms 5.5 per cent of the state area. Of this 14968.7 sq.km (98.79 per cent) is the rural area and 183.3 Sq.km (1.21 per cent) is the urban

3.1. Flow Chart

Research Design

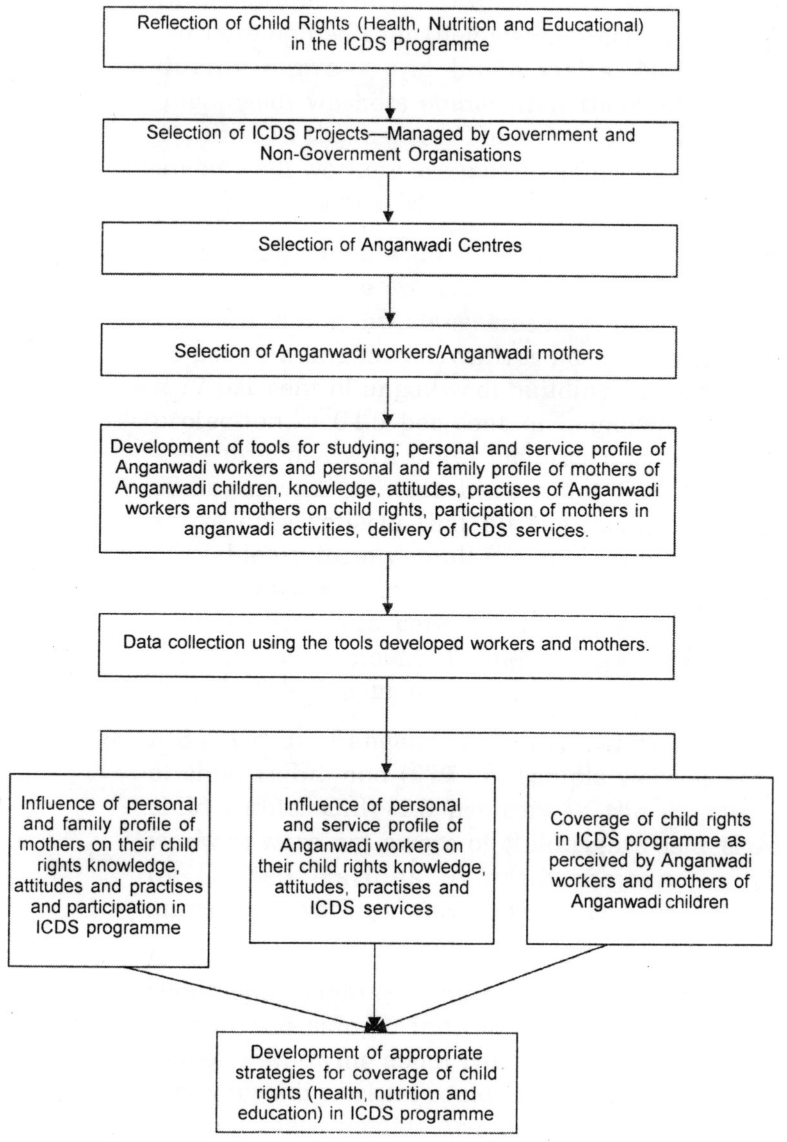

Map of Chittor District Revenue Mandals

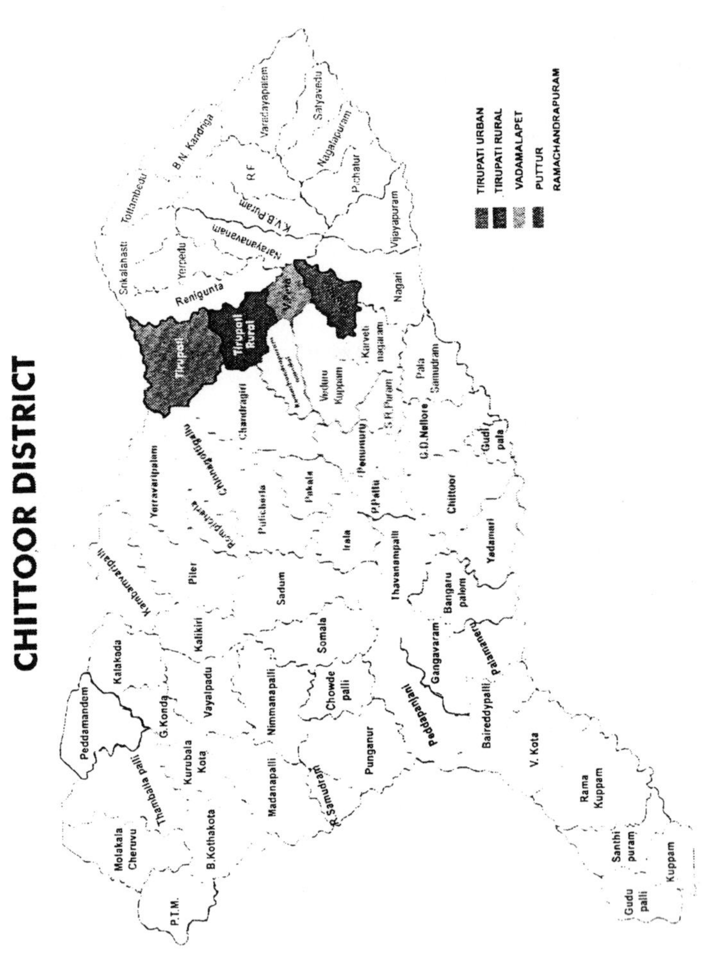

area. The district is divided into 66 mandals covering 1485 villages. The population of the district is 37,45,875, of whom 78.35 per cent (29,34,845) lived in rural areas and 21.65 per cent (8,11,030) lived in urban areas. The child population is 12.95 per cent of total population i.e., 4,85,584, of whom 80.05 per cent (3,88,755 children) lived in rural areas and 19.95 per cent (96,829 children) lived in urban areas as per 2001 census data.

SELECTION OF THE SAMPLE

Integrated Child Development Services (ICDS) projects are implemented by the government and non-governmental organisations and they are located in urban, rural and tribal areas. In order to study the influence of management, the location of anganwadi and place residence of sample which are also included as independent variables in the study. The ICDS projects functioning under the management of government and non-government organisations, which are located in neighbouring mandals were selected for the study. A multistage random sampling procedure was used for the selection of sample as shown in flow chart 3.2. (*See on next page*)

Comprised of two hundred mothers of anganwadi children and two hundred anganwadi workers, out of which hundred anganwadi workers and mothers were drawn from government run ICDS project and the remaining hundred mothers and hundred anganwadi workers were drawn from ICDS project functioning under non-governmental organisation management.

In order to examine the health, nutrition and early childhood education/preschool education services rendered to the children of anganwadi centres, ten anganwadi centres from each ICDS project were selected and from each anganwadi centre ten children were selected. Thus the sample comprised of 100 anganwadi children from each ICDS project that is 200 anganwadi children from the two ICDS projects were selected. All the two hundred children selected are the children of mothers who are respondents of the study.

3.2. Flow Chart

Selection of the Sample

ICDS Projects in Chittoor District (21)

Selection of ICDS Project

- ICDS Projects Managed by Government Organisation in Puttur, Ramachandrapuram, Vadamalapeta Mandals
- ICDS Projects Managed by Non-Government Organisation (RASS) in Tirupati Urban and Rural Mandals

Selection of Anganwadi Centers

- 142 Anganwadi Centers
- 111 Anganwadi Centers

Selection of Anganwadi Workers and Mother of Anganwadi Children

Government (142 Anganwadi Centers):

- 100 Anganwadi Workers
- Mothers of Anganwadi Children from 10 Anganwadi Centres → From each Centre 10 Mothers of Anganwadi Children i.e., 100 Mothers from Government Organisaiton ICDS Project
- Children from 10 Anganwadi Centres → From each Anganwadi Center 10 Children i.e., 100 Children from ICDS Project Managed by Government → Assessment of Health, Nutrition, Educational Services and Nutritional Status

Non-Government (111 Anganwadi Centers):

- 100 Anganwadi Workers
- Mothers of Anganwadi Children from 10 Anganwadi Centers → From each Centre 10 Mothers of Anganwadi Children i.e., 100 Mothers from Non-Government Organisaiton ICDS Project
- Children from 10 Anganwadi Centres → From each Anganwadi Center 10 Children i.e., 100 Children from ICDS Project Managed by NGO → Assessment of Health, Nutrition, Educational Services and Nutritonal Status

SELECTION OF VARIABLES

In this study the child rights knowledge, attitudes, practises, ICDS services, participation of mothers are the dependent variables and the major independent variables are age. educational status, marital status, place of residence, type of family, family income, size of family, access to public facilities, location of the anganwadi, length of service, training received, sources of knowing child rights information. The working definitions for each of the above variables are as follows:

(i) Child Rights

The rights of the child to survival, development, protection and participation is embodied in the UN convention on the rights of the child and ratified by the Government of India. All the forty six rights stated in the child rights declaration were considered as the child rights.

(ii) Child Rights Knowledge

The child rights education information known to the respondent is considered as child rights knowledge of the respondent. This is a resultant of various independent variables.

(iii) Child Rights Attitudes

Attitude is a complex opinion of the respondent about an issue. The attitudes are formed based on one's positive and negative experiences which influences the acceptance or rejection of an education programme. The attitudes formulated based on the child rights declared by United Nations were considered as the attitudes of the sample under study.

(iv) Child Rights Practise

The child rights implemented in the day to day activities is considered as the practise. The word "Practise" is used instead of the noun "Practice" in the thesis as it is more relevant.

(v) ICDS Services

ICDS a nation-wide child development programme covering children below 6 years of age, expectant and nursing mothers and women, delivers a package of services to meet its objectives.

The quality of services, delivered to the beneficiaries at anganwadi level as perceived by the mothers of anganwadi children and anganwadi workers were considered.

(vi) Age

The chronological age of the subjects in completed years was taken as age.

(vii) Education Status

The process by which one's mind develops through learning at school, college or university. Educational status is measured interms of the academic programme completed/ studied.

(viii) Marital Status

The anganwadi workers' and mothers' of anganwadi children, marital status *viz.*, married, unmarried, divorced/ separated was considered as marital status.

(ix) Place of Residence

The location or place of residence of anganwadi workers *viz.*, urban, urban slum, rural, remote area were considered as place of residence.

(x) Type of Family

The structure of the family of the respondents *viz.*, nuclear two parent, nuclear single parent, extended and joint family were included as a variable.

(xi) Annual Income

The total income earned by the family in a year was considered as the annual family income. The annual income determines the purchasing power of the family, which inturn influences the material possession of the family and the family's ability to provide for the various needs of the child.

(xii) Size of the Family

The number of members residing in a family is considered as the size of the family.

(xiii) Access to Public Services

The public services provided by the state and local Government bodies for healthy civic life *viz.*, health, sanitation, education, water, power, law and order were included as a variable.

(xiv) Location of Anganwadi

The place where the anganwadi is situated is taken as location of anganwadi such as urban, urban slum, rural.

(xv) Length of Service

The number of years of experience as anganwadi worker that is total number of years of service from the date of entry was considered as length of service.

(xvi) Training Received

Training given to anganwadi workers under the ICDS is taken as a variable.

xvii. Sources of Knowing Child Rights

The source from which the anganwadi could know about the child rights information was taken as a variable.

(xviii) ICDS Health Services

The immunisation, deworming tablets for worm infestation, the nutritional supplements *viz.*, iron, folic acid, vitamin A, riboflavin, health check-up and treatment received were considered as the health services of anganwadi children.

(xix) ICDS Nutritional Services

Recording of the anthropometric measurements of the child *viz.*, weight, height, mid upper arm circumference and supplementary nutrition provided as per the grades of malnutrition and regularity of supplementary nutrition.

(xx) ICDS Preschool Education Services

The quality of preschool education programme on the basis of ICDS objectives and use of play and educational material.

(xxi) Anthropometric Measurements

Measurements of physical dimensions of children is termed as anthropometric measurements of children.

(xxii) Weight

The beam balances in anganwadi centres were used to measure the weight of children in grams, weight reflects current nutritional status.

(xxiii) Height

The length or vertical height reflects the total increase in size of a child. Standing height of children in centimeters was measured using a vertical measuring wooden scale.

(xxiv) Mid Upper Arm Circumference

Circumferences of mid-upper arm (MUAC) and calf are recognised to indicate the status of muscle development in the body. The MUAC may be useful not only in identifying malnutrition but also in determining the mortality risk in children. The measurements of MUAC correlate well with weight, weight for height and clinical signs of protein energy malnutrition (PEM).

RELATIONSHIP AMONG INDEPENDENT AND DEPENDENT VARIABLES

The independent variables influence the dependent variables, very often it is difficult to determine the direction of influence of each variable especially with regard to socio-economic data. An attempt was made to present the direct and indirect routes through which the independent variables influence the dependent variables (Flow chart—3.3).

3.3. Flow Chart
Relationship Among Independent and Dependent Variables

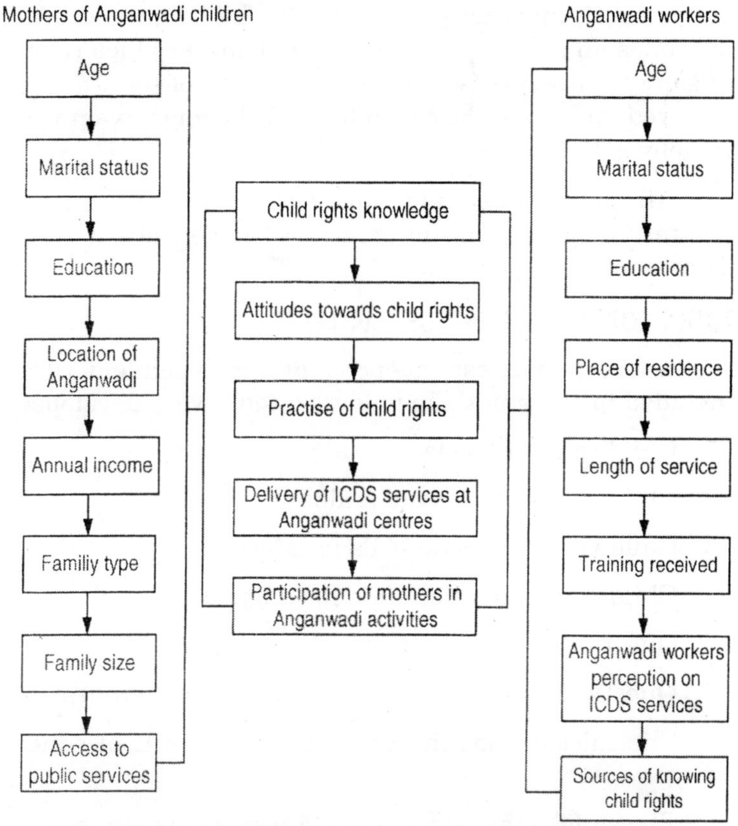

Flow chart 3.3 shows that knowledge, attitudes and practise influence the delivery of ICDS services which inturn influence the participation of mothers. Age, education, location of anganwadi may influence child rights knowledge and attitudes. marital status, family income, family type, family size and access to public facilities may determine the decision making power and freedom of mothers to practise child rights. They also determine the amount of time available to participate in ICDS activities. All the independent variables related to mothers of anganwadi children may influence the dependent variables as shown in the flow chart. 3.3.

The anganwadi workers' age, educational status, place of residence may have influence on child rights knowledge, attitudes and practise. The independent variables related to anganwadi workers' service such as length of service, training received, influence the capabilities of the anganwadi workers to deliver ICDS services.

All the independent variables related to anganwadi workers may have an influence on the dependent variables as presented in flow chart 3.3.

TOOLS FOR ASSESSMENT OF VARIABLES

In order to assess Independent and dependent variables included in the study the following tools were developed:

1. Child rights knowledge scale
2. Child rights attitudinal scale
3. Child rights practise scale for Mothers
4. Child rights practise scale for anganwadi workers
5. Questionnaire for anganwadi workers
6. Questionnaire for mothers of anganwadi children
7. Checklist on health, nutrition and preschool education services.

The child rights approach and perspective are new areas in research. Hence there were no tools or scales available on child rights assessment. A need is therefore felt for the development of appropriate tools to assess child rights knowledge, attitudes and practise and also their reflection in the existing ICDS programme.

Child Rights Knowledge Scale

The child rights stated in the child rights convention document were examined and forty seven questions were framed based on forty six child rights and the final scale consisted of thirty eight statements these questions were arranged in the form of a scale with a simple response pattern of 'Yes', 'No', 'Do not-know'. For the response 'Yes' a score of '1' was assigned, for the response 'No' a score of '0' is assigned. For the response 'Do not know' a score of '-1' is assigned. Thus, the child rights knowledge scale consisted of thirty eight (38) as maximum score and '-1' as minimum score. The scale was prepared both in English and Telugu (Vernacular language).

(a) Standardisation

The different process undertaken during standardisation are basically aimed at establishing the reliability and validity of the tool. Reliability concerns the extent to which measurements are repeatable, stable and dependable. Validity concerns the extent to which a test measure what it purports to measure.

(b) Validity

The content validity is concerned with whether the content of the test covers the child rights knowledge in correct proportion or not. This was established during the development of items and by seeking experts opinion. The child rights knowledge scale was submitted to (18) eighteen experts who were conversant with the subject. They were asked to give their opinion and suggestions on coverage and relevance of content given in the scale. Based on experts opinion and suggestions necessary modifications were done in the child rights knowledge scale.

(c) Reliability

Repetition of a test is a simplest method used to establish the reliability of a scale. The test retest method was used to calculate reliability co-efficient of child rights knowledge scale. The scale was administered on a sample of sixty anganwadi workers and sixty mothers of anganwadi children and repeated on the same group after a month. The correlation computed between the first and the second set of scores and the reliability co-efficient of 0.92 was obtained, which shows that there is high correlation between the first and second tests.

Child Rights Attitudinal Scale

Sustainability of any education programme will depend on the attitudes of the learners. Similarly for child rights education also it is important to assess the attitudes of anganwadi workers and mothers. A child rights attitudinal scale was developed. The scale consisted of thirty statements which were rated on a three point scale as 'strongly agree', 'agree' and 'disagree'. For the response 'strongly agree' a score of '2' was assigned, for the response 'Agree' a score of '1' was assigned, for the response 'disagree' a score of '0' was assigned. Thus the child rights attitudinal scale consisted of thirty statements with a maximum score of sixty and a minimum score of zero. The scale was prepared both in English and Telugu (Local language). Prior to standardisation the child rights attitudinal scale was submitted to eighteen experts who are conversant with the subject. They were asked to give their opinion and suggestions on coverage and relevance of content of the items included in the scale. Their suggestions were considered and modifications in the language and presentation style were made. Then the scale was subjected to item analysis.

(a) Item Analysis

The child rights attitudinal scale was administered to sixty anganwadi workers and sixty mothers of anganwadi children. The discriminating power of each item was calculated by applying the formula $ULI = \frac{R_U - R_I}{f}$, ULI stands for "Upper Lower Index" in the discriminating power, R_u stands for respondent giving right answers in 27 per cent lot and R, for respondent giving right answers in lower 27 per cent lot. In this context right answer means the answer which tallies with the value of '2' in the scoring sheet and 'f' stands for the number of respondents. The items having discriminating power of less than '2' were eliminated.

(b) Reliability

Repetition of a test is a simplest method used to establish the reliability of a scale. The test-retest method was used to calculate reliability co-efficient of child rights attitudinal scale. The scale was administered on a sample of sixty anganwadi workers and sixty mothers of anganwadi children and repeated on the same group after a month. The correlation computed between the first and the second set of scores and the reliability coefficient of 0.90 was obtained, which shows that there is highest correlation between the first and second tests.

Child Rights Practise Scale

The word "practise" denotes use or implementation. For the study the word practise is preferred over the word practice. The mothers and anganwadi workers practise of child rights at anganwadi centre and at home was assessed using child rights practise scales, developed separately for anganwadi workers and mothers as the role and activities of anganwadi workers towards anganwadi children is different from those of mothers role and her activities towards her children at home.

Child Rights Practise Scale for Mothers

In order to assess the levels of practise of child rights by the mothers of anganwadi children, a scale was developed. The scale consisted of thirty six questions grouped under five major areas; health and nutritional rights, educational rights, psycho-social and recreational rights, familial rights and rights of challenged/differently abled children.

A mixed pattern of responses are used in the scale in order to collect more accurate practises. The 'Yes' or 'No' type, multiple choice type of responses were included. The 'Yes' or 'No' type of responses were rated as '1' and '0' respectively. The multiple choice responses were rated as '3', '2', '1', '0' respectively. Thus the child rights practise scale of mothers consisted '67' as maximum score and '0' as minimum score. The scale was prepared both in English and Telugu.

Child Rights Practise Scale for Anganwadi Workers

The scale consisted of twenty two questions grouped under 3 major areas such as; health and nutritional rights, educational rights and psycho-social rights. The questions in this scale consisted of responses in the form 'Yes' or 'No' type and "multiple choice" type. The 'Yes' or 'No' type responses were rated as '1' and '0' respectively. The multiple choice responses were rated as '3'. '2', '1', '0' respectively.

The child rights practise scale for mothers and anganwadi workers was also submitted to expert panel consisting of eighteen experts who are conversant with the subject. Their recommendations and suggestions were incorporated in the scale, care was taken to avoid statements with ambiguity and complex concepts.

Reliability

Both the child rights practise scales (Mothers and anganwadi workers) were administered on a sample of sixty anganwadi workers and sixty mothers of anganwadi children and repeated on the same group after a month. The correlation computed between the first and the second set of scores and the reliability co-efficient of 0.8 was obtained, which shows that there is high correlation between the first and second tests.

Questionnaire for Anganwadi Workers

A general questionnaire was developed to collect data on the variables related to personal profile, service profile and ICDS services. The questions framed had "Yes" (or) "No" type and multiple choice response patterns. The final questionnaire consisted of thirty questions. The questionnaire was standardised by administering with a sample of sixty anganwadi workers and making modifications based on the results of pilot test.

Questionnaire for Mothers of Anganwadi Children

A general questionnaire to gather data regarding the personal, family profile of mothers their participation in anganwadi programme, was framed in English and Telugu. The questionnaire consisted of age, place of residence, educational status, occupation, income, family size, type of family, number of children, public services accessible to the family, participation in ICDS programme. The questionnaire was standardised by administering with a sample of sixty anganwadi mothers and making modifications based on the results of pilot test:

Checklist on Health, Nutrition and Preschool Education Services of ICDS

A checklist was formulated based on the health, nutrition and pre-school education services that a anganwadi centre is expected to render as per the ICDS programme. The investigator visited all the twenty anganwadi centres belonging to two ICDS projects spread in five Mandals of Chittoor district. After observing the programmes at each anganwadi centre, the investigator filled in the checklist. Thus the health, nutrition and pre-school education services at all the twenty anganwadi centres were rated on a checklist. The results were pooled and interpreted.

Assessment of Nutritional Status of Children

In order to examine the nutritional status of anganwadi children a sample of two hundred children were selected whose mothers were also the respondents of the study. Their age, heights, weights and mid upper cum circumference were measured using height standard, weight scale and MUAC tape and compared with the National Centre for Health Statistics (NCHS) standards (Banji, Rao and Reddy, 1996). The ICDS uses the Indian Academy of Paediatric (IAP) classification for growth monitoring. The IAP method was used to classify the sample as per their nutritional status. Similarly the children were classified as per their mid upper arm circumference measurements as normal (above 13.5 cms) mildly malnourished (12.5 to 13.5 cms) and severely malnourished (less than 12.5 cms). The heights of children were compared with the NCHS standards and were classified as above normal, and below normal.

DATA COLLECTION

The data for the study was collected from two sources that is anganwadi workers and the mothers of anganwadi children. The respondents were administered with the relevant tools *viz.*, child rights knowledge scale, child rights attitudinal scale, child rights practise scale (Mothers) child rights practice scale (Anganwadi workers), questionnaire for anganwadi workers, questionnaire for mothers of anganwadi children, by following the procedure for administration explained under the tools for assessment of variables.

With a prior written permission from the child development project officers (CDPOs) of non-governmental organisation and government organisation projects, the researcher made use of anganwadi workers monthly meeting at ICDS project office as venue for administering the research tools for data collection. The anganwadi workers were requested to assemble in the meeting hall, where the investigator introduced herself and the research topic. A brief and clear instructions were given about the tools and how to fill up each of the scales. Then tools were distributed one after the other that is after completion of questionnaire, the child rights knowledge scale was administered, after completion of which child rights attitudinal scale was administered later the child right practise scale was administered. Thus all the four tools were administered, within four hours and in two sessions. Thus using all the four tools, data was collected from two hundred anganwadi workers working in two ICDS projects.

With regard to mothers the investigator personally visited the homes of selected children. The visits were made generally during afternoons and evenings by prior intimation

THE INVESTIGATOR COLLECTING DATA FROM MOTHERS

NTR COLNY

అంగన్ వాడి
సెంటర్

THE INVESTIGATOR COLLECTING DATA FROM ANGANWADI WORKERS OF GO AND NGO ICDS PROJECTS

The mothers were interviewed for obtaining data on questionnaire. The child rights knowledge, attitudes and practise scales were administered and filled in by the mothers. In case of illiterates the scales were filled in by the investigator using interview method. Thus the data was collected from two hundred mothers.

Scoring

For scoring the tools the procedure followed in the pilot study for standardisation of tools was used in the final study too.

Rescaling

The scales developed for collection of data on various parameters had questions. Since each parameter had unequal number of questions, they have been rescaled to fifty.

For example: The child rights knowledge scale had 38 questions and the maximum score was 38. If 38 questions have a maximum score of 38, their 50 questions will have

$\frac{50}{38} \times 38 = 50$ score.

STATISTICAL TECHNIQUES

The scores for each tool administered with sample selected were calculated. The total scores obtained by each of two hundred anganwadi workers and two hundred mothers of anganwadi children on all the variables included in the study were computed. The data was carefully analysed by employing appropriate statistical techniques.

The following statistical techniques were employed to study the difference among the sample with regard to child rights knowledge, attitudes and practises to study the association and correlation between independent and dependent variables. Besides the above techniques simple analysis *viz.*, percentage, mean, standard deviations were also done.

Percentage

$$\frac{\text{Obtained number}}{\text{Sample number}} \times 100$$

Mean

Add up all the numbers and divide it by the number of them $\bar{X} = \frac{\sum x}{N}$

Standard Deviation

The standard deviation is based on squared deviations or distance from the mean

$$S.D. = \frac{\sum x^2}{n} - (\bar{x})^2$$

χ^2 – test to find the association between the variables

The chi-square test represents a useful method of comparing experimentally obtained results with those to be expected theoretically on some hypothesis. x^2 is one of the Non-parametric test, which is a quick, easy and quite popular among researchers. The equation for chi-square (x^2) is stated as follows:

$$\chi^2 = \left[\frac{(f_0 - f_e)^2}{f_e}\right]$$

(Chi-square formula for testing agreement between observed and expected results) in which fO = frequency of occurrence of observed of experimentally determined facts:

f_e = expected frequency of occurrence on some hypothesis

The differences between observed expected frequencies are squared and divided by the expected number in each case, and the sum of these quotients is χ^2. The more closely the observed results approximate to the expected, the smaller the chi-square and the closer the agreement between observed data and the hypothesis being tested. Contrariwise, the larger the chi-square the greater the probability of a real divergence of experimentally observed from expected results.

Examine the formula and the calculation they reveal several points of interest about χ^2

1. χ^2 cannot be negative because all discrepancies are squared; both positive and negative discrepancies make a positive contribution to the value of χ^2 .
2. χ^2 will be zero only in the unusual event that each observed frequency exactly equals the corresponding expected frequency.
3. Other things being equal, the larger the discrepancy between the f_e *S* and their corresponding f_o '*S*, the larger χ^2.
4. It is not the size of the discrepancy alone that accounts for a contribution to the value of χ^2; rather, it is the size of the discrepancy relative to the magnitude of the expected frequency.
5. The value of χ^2 depends on the number of discrepancies.

ANOVA

The value of analysis of variance in testing experimental hypothesis is most strikingly demonstrated in those problems in which the significance of upon which the differences among several means are desired. While the variability within a set of scores is ordinarily given by the standard deviation or σ, variability may also be expressed by the "variance" or σ^2. A very considerable advantage of variances over *SD's* is the fact that variances are often additive and sum of the squares, variances are based, always are. If the *f-test* refutes the null hypothesis we may use the *t-test* to evaluate mean differences. If the *f-test* does not refute the null hypothesis there is no justification for further testing, as differences between pairs of means will not differ significantly unless there are a number of them in which case one or two might by chance equal or approach significance.

Post Hoc Test

The tests we use to make these specific comparisons are called post hoc comparisons or a posterior (Latin, meaning "what comes later" comparisons.

Post hoc tests generally employ sampling distributions that compare the means of many samples. In short, post hoc tests projects us from making too many type I errors by requiring a bigger difference (between sample means) before we can declare that difference to be statistically significant.

There are several commonly used post hoc tests. The only real difference among them is that some are more conservative than others. In ascending level of conservativeness with regard to type I errors (but descending power), we could choose from among such tests as Duncan's multiple-range test. To use any one of these tests, our F ratio must first be significant.

't' Test

The significance of the difference between the means of two populations.

Limitations

1. If the variance of the populations is known, a more powerful test is available.
2. The test is accurate if the populations are normally distributed. If the populations are not normal, the test will give an approximate guide.

Method

Consider two populations with means μ_1 and μ_2. Independent random samples of size n_1 and n_2 are taken from which sample means $\bar{x}_1$ and x_2, together with sums of squares

$$SS_1 = \sum_{i=1}^{n_1} (x_i - \bar{x}_1)^2$$

and

$$SS_2 = \sum_{i=1}^{n_2} (x_i - \bar{x}_1)^2$$

are calculated. The best estimate of the population variance is found as $s = (SS_i + SS_2)/(n_1 + n_2 - 2)$. The test statistic is

$$t = \frac{(\bar{x}_1 - \bar{x}_2) - (\mu_1 - \mu_2)}{s\left(\frac{1}{n_1} + \frac{1}{n_2}\right)}$$

which may be compared with Student's *t*-distribution with $(n, + n_2 - 2)$ degrees of freedom. The test may be either one-tailed or two-tailed.

Pearson's Correlation

Pearson's correlation coefficient is best suited to measuring the association between two variables that are each continuous and quantitative. A correlation shows the relationship between pairs of scores. In its simplest form, the Pearson correlation coefficient is defined as follows *z* score formula for the correlation coefficient.

$$r = \frac{\sum(Zx\, Zy)}{n}$$

where n is the number of pairs of scores. To find *r*, we must convert each raw score to a *z* score. Then for each pair of *z* scores we multiply the scores, sum the results, called the cross products, and divide by the number of pairs of scores. Thus, *r* is the mean of the cross-products of the paired *z* scores. Deviation-score formula for the correlation coefficient.

$$r = \frac{\sum(X - \bar{X})(Y - \bar{Y})}{n\, Sx\, Sy}$$

Where *n* is again the number of pairs of scores and *sx* and *sy* are the standard deviation of the two samples. Pearson's *r* using this formula because doing so will help us see what factors make the coefficient positive or negative and what factors result in a high or low value.

Coefficient of correlation are indices ranging over a scale which extends from –1.00 through .00 to 1.00. A positive correlation indicates that large amounts of the one variable tend to accompany large amounts of the other; a negative correlation indicates that small amounts of the one variable tend to accompany large amounts of the other. A zero correlation indicates no consistent relationship.

4

Results and Discussion

The data collected was subjected to quantitative and qualitative statistical analysis and the results were interpreted and discussed in this chapter.

Efforts were made to present and discuss the results systematically:

1. Tabulation of data and descriptive analysis of personal, family and service profile of anganwadi workers and also personal, family profile of mothers of anganwadi children.
2. Analysis of the data on child rights knowledge, attitudes and practise by the anganwadi workers and mothers of anganwadi children.
3. Descriptive analysis of the relationship among the personal, family, service variables of the sample with the child rights, knowledge, attitudes and practise of anganwadi workers.
4. Descriptive analysis of the relationship among the variables related to personal, family, ICDS participation and child rights knowledge, attitudes and practise of mothers of anganwadi children.
5. Difference, association and correlation among the variables related to personal, family, service profile of the sample and their child rights knowledge, attitudes and practise of the anganwadi workers.

6. Difference, association and correlation among the variables related to personal, family, ICDS participation and child rights, knowledge, attitudes and practise of mothers of anganwadi children.
7. Descriptive analysis of coverage of child rights of children infected with AIDS and children affected with AIDS.

PERSONAL PROFILE OF ANGANWANDI WORKERS

ICDS is sponsored 100 per cent by the status and uniquely relies on the honorary anganwadi worker (AWW), who is a woman, recruited and chosen by the community, aged 21-45 years and middle-school educated. The anganwadi worker was responsibility for 2000 households or 1000 persons in rural areas and 700 persons in tribal areas. The anganwadi worker is crucial to the functioning of the programme and receives an honorarium of Rs. 225-275 per month for implementing the ICDS programme; anganwadi workers have helpers who are paid Rs. 110 per month. Training over a 3 months period is conducted at the Bal Sevika Training Institute by the Indian Council of Child Welfare (ICCW). Additional health personnel and their role and the number of persons/per area anganwadi workers are responsible for, equipment, and functions are also described. The anganwadi worker is responsible for non-formal preschool education, organisation of supplementary nutrition feeding, health and nutrition education of women and families, immunisation of women and children, treatment and referral of common illnesses, growing monitoring, and community participation (Lal and Sachar, 1993).

Age

On the basis of age the sample of anganwadi workers were divided into three groups, *viz.*, those falling between 20-25 years, 25-30 years and 30-35 years. Studies have shown that age seems to influences the perception of child rights by women. Hence, age was included as one of the parameters in the present study.

Table 4.1: Distribution of the Anganwadi Workers According to their Age

S.No.	Age (yrs)	Number	Percentage
1.	20 – 25	33	16.5
2.	25 – 30	69	34.5
3.	30 – 35	98	49.0
	Total	**200**	**100.0**

From Table 4.1, it is evident that majority of anganwadi workers' that is (49%) of anganwadi workers were aged between 30-35 years, followed by 34.5 per cent aged between 25-30 years and only 16.5 per cent belonged to the age group of 20-25 years.

Fig. 4.1: Distribution of the Anganwadi Workers According to their Age

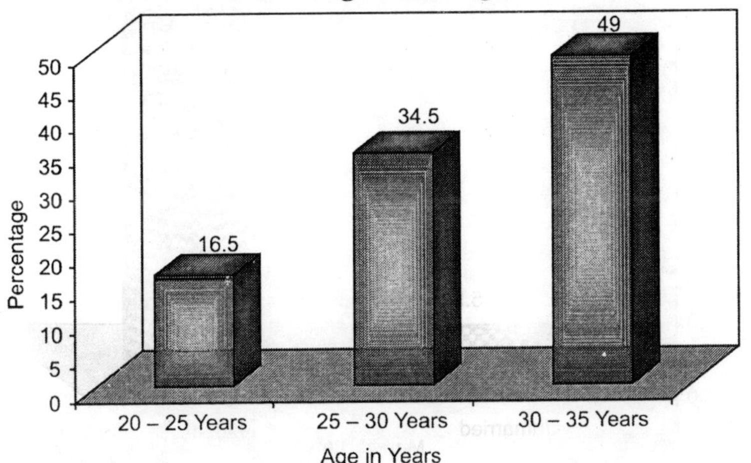

Marital Status

The marital status of anganwadi workers may have an influence on their perception of child rights. The experiences of married women, especially those having children may have awareness on the needs of children. Hence, marital status of the sample was included as a variable in the study. The anganwadi workers were divide into two groups *viz.*, married and unmarried as shown in Table 4.2.

Table 4.2: Distribution of the Anganwadi Workers According to their Marital Status

S.No.	Marital Status	Number	Percentage
1.	Unmarried	11	5.5
2.	Married	189	94.5
	Total	**200**	**100.0**

The table 4.2 shows that majority of anganwadi workers (94.5%) were married and only 5.5 per cent were unmarried.

Fig. 4.2: Distribution of the Anganwadi Workers According to their Marital Status

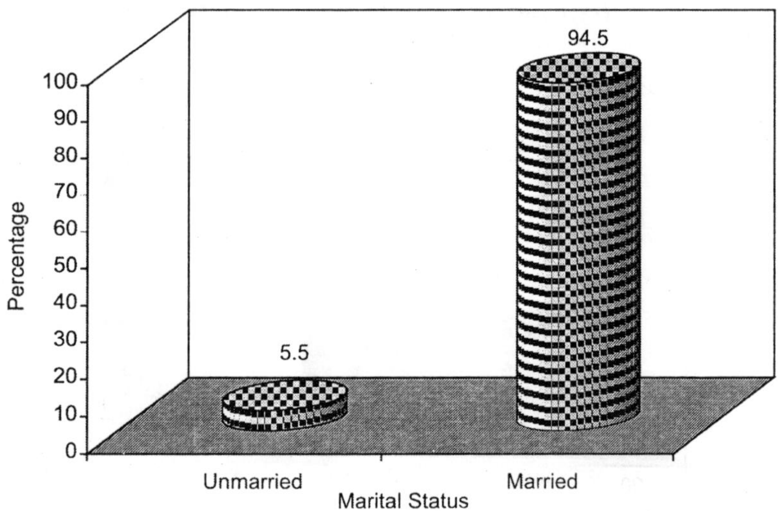

Place of Residence

The place one resides has an influence on their exposure to mass media and other sources of information. The place of residence is usually determined by one's occupation and economic status. The anganwadi workers were classified into four groups that is rural, urban, urban slum, remote area (*See Table* 4.3).

Table 4.3: Distribution of the Anganwadi workers according to their Place of Residence

S.No.	**Place of Residence**	***Number***	***Percentage***
1.	Rural	69	34.5
2.	Urban	45	22.5
3.	Urban slum	51	25.5
4.	Remote area	35	17.5
	Total	**200**	**100.0**

Around (34.5%) of anganwadi workers were residing in rural areas, a 22.5 per cent were residents of urban area, a 25.5 per cent were urban slum dwellers and 17.5 per cent were living in remote areas on the outskirts of towns. This shows that only a small percentage lived in urban areas. Mostly anganwadis are established in rural and urban slum areas for the benefit of women and children residing in those area anganwadi workers also might be residing near to anganwadis.

Fig. 4.3: Distribution of the Anganwadi Workers According to their Place of Residence

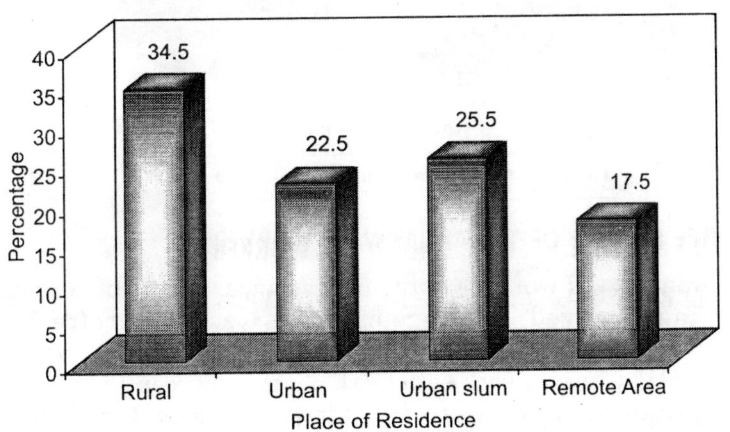

Educational Status of Anganwadi Workers

The formal education received by the sample was recorded. The educational status of the sample ranged from 10th class to degree level.

Table 4.4: Distribution of Anganwadi Workers According to their Educational Status

S.No.	Educational Status	Number	Percentage
1.	10th class	123	61.5
2.	Intermediate	58	29.0
3.	Degree	19	9.5
	Total	**200**	**100.0**

According to Table 4.4 most of the anganwadi workers (61.5%) were educated upto 10th class. Around 29 per cent had intermediate education and only 9.5 per cent of the sample were educated upto degree level.

Fig. 4.4: Distribution of the Anganwadi Workers According to their Educational Status

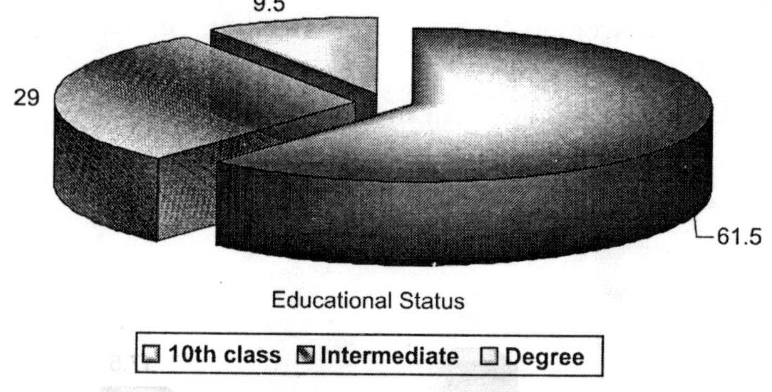

SERVICE PROFILE OF THE ANGANWADI WORKERS

The anganwadi workers entry into service, length of service, training received, reading materials received, refresher training attended, sources of knowing child rights information, there work satisfaction, there perceptions about anganwadi services were included as parameters under service profile of anganwadi workers.

Length of Service

The number of years of experience as anganwadi workers was considered as length of service. Job experience may contribute to work efficiency and improvement of skills. Working with children may provide insight into their needs and perception of their rights. Based on the length of service the anganwadi workers were divided into four groups *viz.*, less than 5 years, 6-10 years, 11-15 years and above 15 years as shown in Table 4.5.

Table 4.5: Distribution of the Anganwadi Workers According to their Length of Service

S.No.	*Length of Service*	*Number*	*Percentage*
1.	Below 5 years	137	68.5
2.	6 – 10 years	18	9.0
3.	11 – 15 years	28	14.0
4.	Above 15 years	17	8.5
	Total	**200**	**100.0**

Majority of the sample (68.5%) had service below 5 years, a 9 per cent of anganwadi workers had 6-10 years of service, a 14 per cent had a service between 11-15 years and only 8.5 per cent had service above 15 years. The wages for anganwadi workers are meagre, which may be reason for very few had service more than six years.

Training Received

Training for the job as anganwadi worker generally includes equipping the trainees with necessary skills to perform their work effectively. The performance of trained anganwadi workers may vary from those who are not trained. Hence "training" was included as one of the parameters in the present study. The sample were divide into two groups *viz.*, trained and not trained.

Table 4.6: Distribution of the Anganwadi Workers According to Training Received

S.No.	*Training Status*	*Number*	*Percentage*
1.	Not training received	161	80.5
2.	Training received	39	19.5
	Total	**200**	**100.0**

From the Table 4.6, it is clear that majority (80.5%) of anganwadi workers were not trained. Only a 19.5 per cent were trained. This may be due to the anganwadi workers changing their jobs as unmarried anganwadi workers leaving the place and their jobs after their marriage.

Number of Anganwadi Workers who Received ICDS material

National Institute of Public Co-operation and Child Development (NIPPCD) is designated as the apex body for the training of ICDS functionaries. The functions of the institute include planning, coordination and monitoring. The training of ICDS functionaries, formulation of training strategies, development and updation of training methodologies, aids, curriculum and materials such as manuals, guide books, hand books etc., are also given by NIPPCD.

Table 4.7: Distribution of the Anganwadi Workers According to the ICDS Materials Received by them

S.No.	*Received materials from*	*Number*	*Percentage*
1.	Yes	196	98.0
2.	No	4	2.0
	Total	**200**	**100.0**

Majority (98%) of the sample received materials from ICDS, only 2 per cent have not received materials as shown in Table 4.7. ICDS usually supplies materials such as manuals, guide books and handbooks to anganwadi workers.

Information about ICDS Activities

The welfare and development programmes tend to under go some changes depending on the needs of beneficiaries and social changes. The ICDS has also made changes in their activities monitoring and evaluation in order to deliver the services more effectively and also increase the accountability of its functionaries and involve people. The changes introduced are usually published in their news bulletins and other publications published by ICDS apex body NIPCCD. Communication of relevant information to the field functionaries is the responsibility of trainers and supervisors. The awareness and knowledge about the organisations for which one works creates confidence and may influence their quality of work.

The responses of the anganwadi workers to the questions; do you get any briefing about current information in ICDS from the supervisors and do you get current information on ICDS in the form of newsletter is given in Table 4.8.

Table 4.8: Current Information about ICDS to the Anganwadi Workers

S.No.	*Current information about ICDS*	*Number*	*Percentage*
1.	Do you receive current information about ICDS from supervisors		
	Yes	198	99.0
	No	2	1.0
	Total	**200**	**100.0**
2.	Do you receive current information about ICDS in the form of newsletter		
	Yes	193	96.5
	No	7	3.5
	Total	**200**	**100.0**

From the Table 4.8 it is clear that majority (99%) and (96.5%) of anganwadi workers received current information about ICDS from the supervisors and also in the form of newsletters at the time of data collection. Currently a monthly magazine "*Indiara Darshini*" is published and distributed to anganwadi centres.

Refresher Training received by Anganwadi Workers

Anganwadi workers received 3 months basic job training after their indections into the job, followed by monthly visits from a medical team and subsequent refresher courses.

Refresher training is important after one and half years, in order to update their knowledge and skills. Hence, an attempt was made to collect details on the refresher trainings and their frequency.

Table 4.9: Distribution of the Anganwadi Workers According to their Refresher Training

S.No.	*Anganwadi workers Refresher Training*	*Number*	*Percentage*
1.	Anganwadi workers who did not received refresher training	58	29.0
2.	Anganwadi workers who received refresher training	142	71.0
	Total	**200**	**100.0**
3.	Anganwadi workers who received refresher training 5 years before	110	77.46
4.	Anganwadi workers who received refresher training before 10 years	18	12.65
5.	Anganwadi workers who received refresher training before 15 years	10	7.04
6.	Anganwadi workers who received refresher training above 15 years	4	2.82
	Total	**142**	**100.0**

From the table 4.9, it is evident that 29 per cent of anganwadi workers did not receive refresher training. A good majority (71%) of the sample received refresher training once in their service. Data regarding the year of refresher training revealed that among those who received training (77.46%) of anganwadi workers received training 5 years before that is from the date of data collection (during the year 2004) for the present study. Around 12.6 per cent of the sample received refresher training 10 years before, a 7.04 per cent of the sample and 2.82 per cent of the sample received refresher training before 15 years and above 15 years respectively. This shows that the refresher training is not received by the anganwadi workers periodically, which is essential for updating their knowledge.

ANGANWADI WORKER'S PERCEPTIONS ON ICDS SERVICES AT THEIR ANGANWADI

Anganwadi worker (AWW) is a good resource who if properly trained and supervised, can achieve a great deal in collaboration with the health system. Instead of ensuring that the job she is assigned is done as stipulated, she is being pulled in different directions for domiciliary care of the newborn, for integrated management of childhood illness and so on. She has become a handy frontline worker for every programme that the government starts rather than being left alone to carry out her own responsibilities. She needs to be trained well for the jobs she is supposed to do in the ICDS programme, retain what is essential in the programme for improving growth, nutrition and development of children, and get rid of the rest. Shanti Ghosh (2004) opined that we need to convert the ICDS into a true health, nutrition and development programme and not limit it to a food dole programme.

The ICDS field level units – anganwadi centres are mostly housed in private accommodations. Most of these anganwadi centres are not ideally suitable for organising anganwadi programmes, as they are not pucca buildings. Even if there are pucca buildings their size is very small and not sufficient to accommodate all the children and equipment. In some areas there is no out door space. Toilet, water facilities are also not accessible to anganwadi children.

Child rights though light on basic amenities of children such as water, sanitation, hygiene, privacy, recreation etc. Hence, data on these parameters was also collected to assess the quality of services rendered at anganwadi centres. Inadequacy of civic facilities in such services may deprive children of their opportunities to be trained in certain self help skills *viz.*, toilet, washing, cleaning.

Mothers Meetings

The anganwadi worker organises mothers' meetings on second Saturday of every month at the anganwadi centre. In mothers' meetings the anganwadi workers explain and discuss about childcare, supplementary nutrition, immunisation, early childhood education and other issues related to ICDS services. These meetings improve the rapport between the anganwadi workers and mothers and there by improve the utilisation of ICDS services. They are highly useful in preparing and educating mothers on aspects related to child and maternal care and health. Almost all the anganwadi workers under study conducted mothers' meetings once a month. The anganwadi worker's perceptions on "How the mothers' meetings are useful to mothers" was gathered and is presented in Table 4.10.

Table 4.10: Uses of Mothers' Meetings as Perceived by Anganwadi Workers

S.No.	*Uses of Mothers Meetings*	*Number*	*Percentage*
1.	Awareness on child care	153	76.5
2.	Knowledge on child nutrition	146	73.0
3.	Knowledge about maternal and child health	98	49.0
4.	All the above	188	94.0

From Table 4.10, it is clear that (76.5%) of anganwadi workers felt that mothers' meetings create awareness on childcare. 73 per cent stated that they impart knowledge on child nutrition, a 49 per cent of anganwadi workers felt that mothers meetings were helpful in gaining knowledge on maternal and child health. Around 94 per cent of anganwadi workers perceived that all the above three were learned by the mothers during mothers' meetings. (*See also Fig. 4.5 on next page*)

Job Satisfaction of Anganwadi Workers

The anganwadi worker's perception on her job satisfaction at anganwadi centre is included as a variable, as the job satisfaction influences performance. Satisfaction about work comes when the anganwadi workers possess the required knowledge and skills related to her work, when the infrastructure facilities, equipment and other resources needed to conduct the programme are accessible and available.

Fig. 4.5: Uses of Mothers Meetings as Perceived by Anganwadi Workers

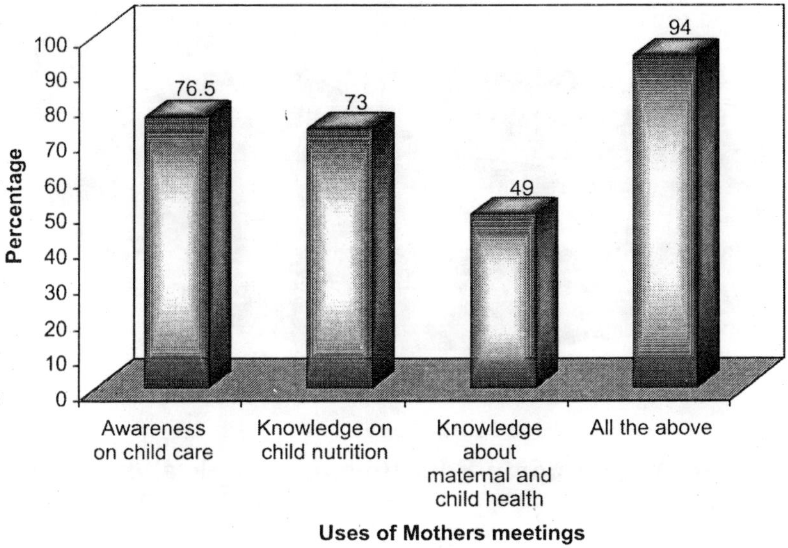

Table 4.11: Job Satisfaction of Anganwadi Workers

S.No.	*Levels of Job Satisfaction*	*Anganwadi Workers*	
		Number	*Percentage*
1.	Adequately	5	2.5
2.	Able to do some work	8	4.0
3.	Able to do all works	63	31.5
4.	Need to develop	59	29.5
5.	Working with limitations	65	32.5
	Total	**200**	**100.0**

The Table 4.11 shows that only 2.5 per cent of the anganwadi workers had adequate job satisfaction, a 4 per cent of the anganwadi workers were able to do some works, 31.5 per cent were able to do all works, a 29.5 per cent stated that they need to develop and 32.5 per cent of anganwadi workers expressed that they are working with limitations. Thus, the data indicates only a small percentage of anganwadi workers had adequate satisfaction.

Fig. 4.6: Distribution of the Anganwadi Workers According to the Job Satisfaction

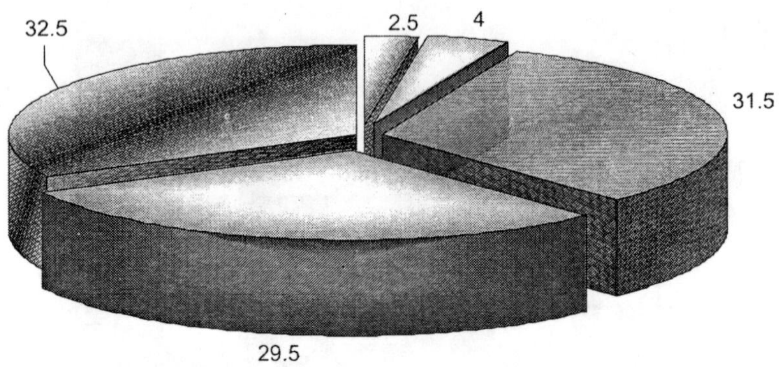

Role of Anganwadi in Educating the People about ICDS Services

To improve the utilisation of ICDS services, the anganwadi workers are given with the information and are asked to publicise to the ICDS services within their jurisdiction, so as to enable the young children and women in that local area to avail the ICDS services.

Table 4.12: Opinion of Anganwadi Workers on their Role in Educating the People on ICDS Services

S.No.	*Role of Anganwadi*	*Anganwadi Workers*	
		Number	*Percentage*
1.	Nominal	0	0.0
2.	Spreading message during surveys and home visits	15	7.5
3.	Using local events and public meetings for spreading ICDS information	125	62.5
4.	Pasting posters and distribution of handouts on ICDS services	60	30.0
	Total	**200**	**100.0**

The responses of the sample to the question; "Role of anganwadi in educating the people about the services extended by the anganwadi, in your opinion" was collected and presented in Table 4.12. It shows that majority of anganwadi workers (62.5%) were educating people about ICDS services by utilizing local events and public meetings. Around 30 per cent of the anganwadi workers indicated that pasting posters and distribution of handouts on ICDS services is the mode of spreading ICDS information. Only a 7.5 per cent of anganwadi workers opined that they were spreading messages during surveys and home visits. None of the anganwadi workers opined that their efforts were nominal in this aspect. Thus the data reflects that anganwadi workers are making efforts in educating the people about ICDS services in their areas.

Facilities available at Anganwadi Centres

According to Sarada (2006) the anganwadi centres due to paucity of funds could not be located in good buildings with safety and sanitary conditions. This is very much so in urban slums. The physical facilities at the anganwadi centre are inadequate to the conduct of the programme efficiently. Information on the accessibility, building, sanitation, safety, water facilities and toilet facilities available at anganwadi centres were gathered and is given in Table 4.13.

Table 4.13: Facilities Available at Anganwadi Centres

S.No.	*Facilities available*	*Anganwadi workers*		
		Percentage Yes	*Percentage No*	*Total*
1.	Accessible	99.0	1.0	100
2.	Pucca building	54.5	45.5	100
3.	Sanitation	96.0	4.0	100
4.	Protection/safety	77.0	23.0	100
5.	Water facilities	64.5	35.5	100
6.	Toilet facilities	34.0	66.0	100

From the above Table 4.13 which shows that all most all anganwadi workers (99%) stated that their centres are accessible to all the people, 54.5 per cent of anganwadi centres have pucca building, 96 per cent anganwadi centres have good sanitation, a 77 per cent of anganwadi buildings are providing protection, a 64.5 per cent of anganwadi centres were provided with water facilities and 34 per cent of anganwadi centres have toilet facilities. The above data reflects that all the facilities are not available uniformly in all the anganwadis. Some of the anganwadis have inadequate facilities. This need to be taken care because it will affect the all round development of children who are in crucial period of development.

SOURCES OF KNOWING CHILD RIGHTS INFORMATION

The anganwadi workers awareness on child rights, their efforts to know about child rights and their opinion about inclusion of certain services in the ICDS programme was gathered using the questionnaire developed for the study.

Awareness on Child Rights

The responses of the anganwadi workers to the questions "are you aware of child rights" and "are you aware of the child rights as declared by United Nations", are recorded. Which showed that 3 per cent of anganwadi workers were not aware of child rights and 97 per cent of the anganwadi workers were aware of child rights. Only 1.5 per cent of the anganwadi workers were not aware of child rights as declared by United Nations. A great majority of the anganwadi workers were aware of child rights.

Table 4.14: Distribution of the Anganwadi Workers According to their Awareness on Child Rights

S.No.	*Awareness on child rights*	*Number*	*Percentage*
1.	Anganwadi workers aware of child rights	194	97.0
2.	Anganwadi workers not aware of child rights	6	3.0
	Total	**200**	**100.0**
1.	Anganwadi workers aware of child rights as declared by United Nations	197	98.5
2.	Anganwadi workers not aware of child rights as declared by United Nations	3	1.5
	Total	**200**	**100.0**

Sources of Knowing Child Rights

Anganwadi worker's who were aware of child rights were asked about the sources of knowing about ICDS and the results are given in Table 4.15.

Table 4.15: Anganwadi Workers Sources of Knowing about Child Rights

S.No.	***Sources of knowing about child rights***	***Number***	***Percentage***
1.	Through ICDS	169	85.8
2.	Family	1	0.5
3.	Media	7	3.6
4.	ICDS and family	17	8.6
5.	ICDS, family and media	3	1.5
	Total	**197**	**100.0**

From the above table, it shows that (85.8%) of anganwadi workers came to know about child rights through ICDS. Around 0.5 per cent of the sample indicated their family as the source of knowing about child rights. A 3.6 per cent of anganwadi workers could know about child rights through mass media. Around 8.6 per cent of the sample came to know about child rights through ICDS and their families. Only 1.5 per cent indicated ICDS, family and mass media as their sources of knowing about child rights. It is evident that ICDS is the major sources of knowing about child rights.

Hence the hypothesis 8 "The child rights component is not covered in the anganwadi workers training programme of ICDS" is rejected as the anganwadi workers indicated the sources of knowing about child rights as ICDS.

Changes in ICDS services on the basis of Child Rights

The anganwadi workers response to a question; "Do you want changes in the ICDS" services based on the child rights, was recorded and it was found that 40 per cent of anganwadi workers felt that there is no need for any change in the

ICDS programme. Around 60 per cent of the anganwadi workers felt that changes can be made in the ICDS programme on the basis of child rights.

PERSONAL AND FAMILY PROFILE OF MOTHERS OF ANGANWADI CHILDREN

In the present study the data on the mothers personal profile, family profile, accessibility to public services was collected in order to examine the living conditions of children attending to anganwadi and their families.

Child Rights Knowledge, Attitude, Practise of Mothers and the Independent variables

Most of the psychological and physical development of human being occurs in the first few years of life. Those are the years during while maximum development of brain occurs and the individual grows to his or her full genetic potential. If the milestones of development are not reached at the appropriate time, then lasting damage may be done to the complex processes of child's growth. UNICEF (1992), felt that there is no second choice, the children who are the victims of preventable malnutrition, disease and illiteracy are being most shamefully failed by the present world order. Today, the means are at hand to significantly enhance that protective ability. By mobilising all means of communication and support, parents everywhere can be empowered with knowledge about the importance of breastfeeding and immunisation; the special nutritional needs of the young child; the need to monitor child growth; the methods of preventing and coping with diarrhoeal disease, respiratory infections and malaria; the facts about domestic hygiene and protection against common disease (UNICEF, 1989).

The ICDS programme caters to the health, nutrition and educational needs of the children below 6 years, pregnant women, nursing mothers and adolescent girls in India. The ICDS programme attempts to fulfill the health, nutrition and educational rights of children through a package of services delivered to the beneficiaries through the field level units called anganwadi centres. The ICDS emphasises participation of mothers in the activities of anganwadi both as beneficiaries and also as stakeholders.

Age

The chronological age of mothers in completed years was collected. The mothers acquire knowledge through life experiences, which enhance their capabilities by improving their knowledge and skills. Hence age was included as a variable, the mothers were divided into three groups as per their age (See Table 4.16)

Table 4.16: Distribution of the Mothers according to their Age

S.No.	Age	Number	Percentage
1.	20 - 25 years	111	55.5
2.	25 - 30 years	65	32.5
3.	30 - 35 years	24	12.0
	Total	**200**	**100.0**

From the Table 4.16, it is clear that majority of mothers (55.5%) belonged to 20-25 years age group. A 32.5 per cent of the mothers were aged between 25-30 years and 12 per cent of mothers belonged to the age group of 30-35 years. (*also See Fig. 4.7 on next page*)

Location of Anganwadi

According to Vimala Ramachandran (2004) who accesses an anganwadi centre (AWC) is influenced by its physical location as well as the caste/community profile of its workers. The fifth report of the Commissioners (2004) notes that one of the primary reasons for poor coverage of needy groups under the scheme is the location of the anganwadi centre. Access to services by deprived communities like the SC and ST is restricted if the centre is located in upper caste predominant hamlets. Field visits also show what appears to

Fig. 4.7: Distribution of the Mothers According to their Age

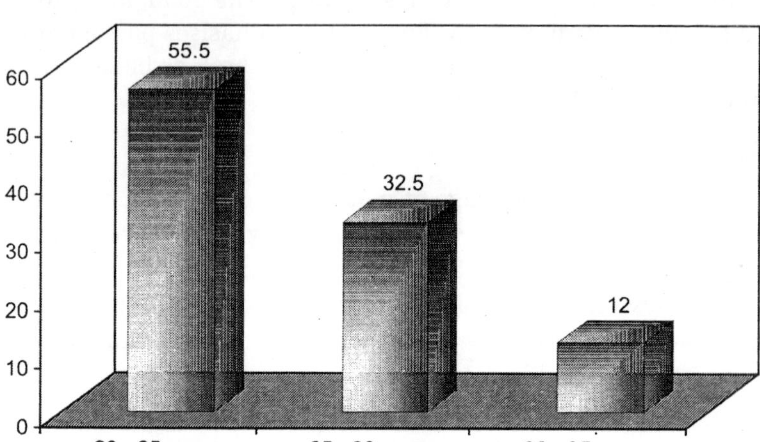

be a glaring lack of any proper method to assess the need and requirement as a result of which many of the SC/ST hamlets have been excluded. This not only reinforces the need for implementation of the order calling for a functional anganwadi in every habitation, but also suggests that priority must be given to initially cover the SC/ST populated habitations followed by others (Saxena and Sankaran, 2004).

Location influences the accessibility to public facilities, space available and exposure to mass media and other sources of information. Based on the location of anganwadi the samples were divided into three groups urban area, urban slum and rural area.

Table 4.17: Distribution of the Mothers According to their Location of Anganwadi

S.No.	*Place of Anganwadi*	*Number*	*Percentage*
1.	Urban slum	139	69.5
2.	Urban	24	12.0
3.	Rural	37	18.5
	Total	**200**	**100.0**

From the Table 4.17, it is evident that (69.5%) of the sample were children attending anganwadis located in urban slum 12 per cent of the children were attending anganwadis located in urban and 18.5 per cent of children of the sample were attending anganwadi centres located in rural areas. This shows that majority of anganwadis attended by children of the sample were located in urbanslum areas.

Fig. 4.8: Distribution of the Mothers According to their Location of Anganwadi

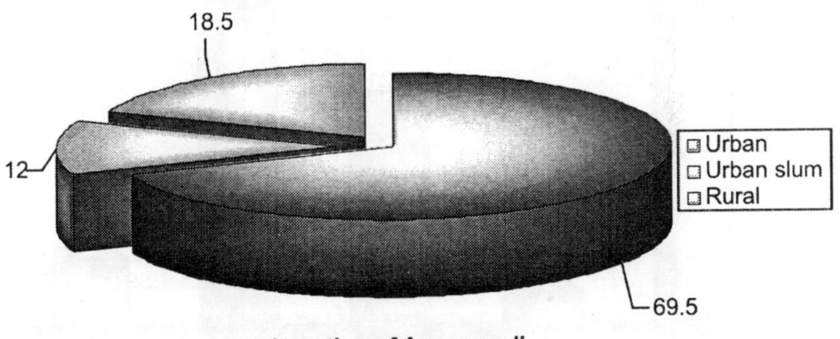

Educational Status

Education exposes people to select knowledge and gives necessary skills in acquisition of knowledge. The number of years of formal education received by the mothers was considered as their educational status. Based on the educational status the sample was classified as illiterates, literates, primary education, high school education and college education as shown in Table 4.18.

Table 4.18: Distribution of the Mothers According to their Educational Status

S.No.	*Educational Status*	*Number*	*Percentage*
1.	Illiterate	66	33.0
2.	Literates	10	5.0
3.	Primary Education	42	21.0
4.	High School Education	66	33.0
5.	College Education	16	8.0
	Total	**200**	**100.0**

The educational status of the mothers shows that 33 per cent were illiterates, 5 per cent were literates, 21 per cent had primary education, 33 per cent had high school education and 8 per cent had college education.

Fig. 4.9: Distribution of the Mothers According to their Educational Status

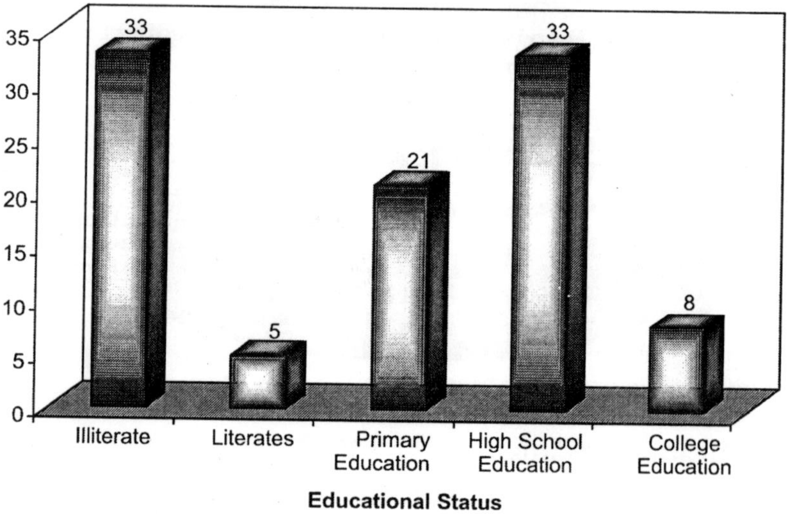

35
30
25
20
15
10
5
0
33
5
21
33
8
Illiterate
Literates
Primary Education
High School Education
College Education
Educational Status

Occupational Status of Mothers

Women of today continue to be a major section of workforce, especially in the un-organised sector. The occupation of mother affects the time available for care of children and also to herself. It further exposes the mother to various experiences, which may influence her knowledge, attitudes and practise of child rights. The sample were divided into five groups on their occupation *viz.*, daily wage labour, business, employed in private sector, employed in government sector, housewives.

The Table 4.19 shows that majority of mothers (60.5%) were housewives, 34.5 per cent were daily wage earners, followed by 3.5 per cent of women engaged in petty business, 0.5 per cent employed in private sector and 1 per cent

Table 4.19: Distribution of the Mothers According to their Occupation

S.No.	Occupational Status	Number	Percentage
1.	Daily wage earners	69	34.5
2.	Business	7	3.5
3.	Employed in private sector	1	0.5
4.	Employed in government sector	2	1.0
5.	Housewives	121	60.5
	Total	**200**	**100.0**

employed in government sector. This shows that majority of women were housewives who will be available to their children throughout the day unlike working mothers.

Annual Income

The money earned by the mothers in a year was considered as annual income of mothers. It is proved that money earned by women was better utilised for the family, especially for the fulfillment of family needs. As per the annual income, the mothers were divided into four groups as shown in Table 4.20.

Table 4.20: Distribution of the Mothers According to their Annual Income

S.No.	Annual Income (Rs.)	Number	Percentage
1.	Below 12,000	172	86.0
2.	12001 – 18000	21	10.5
3.	18001 – 24000	4	2.0
4.	Above 24001	3	1.5
	Total	**200**	**100.0**

From the above table it is evident that (86%) of mothers had an annual income of below Rs.12,000, around 10.5 per cent of the mothers had annual income between Rs.12,001 to 18,000, a 2 per cent had annual income between Rs.18,001 to 24,000 and 1.5 per cent had annual income above Rs.24,001. This shows that majority of mothers had income below poverty line.

Fig. 4.10: Distribution of the Mothers According to their Annual Income

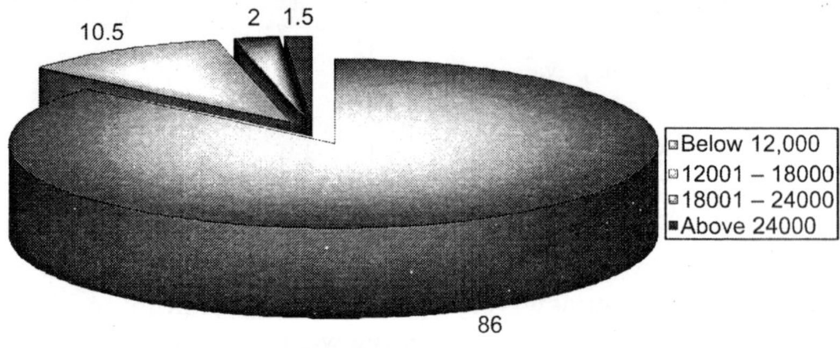

Ration Card

According to Sarada (2006) the Government of Andhra Pradesh like other state governments provides basic food materials such as rice, dhal, oil, sugar etc., at subsidised rates to the poor. The poor are identified and given a ration card which makes them entitled to receive the provisions at subsidised rates in the local outlets (shops). This is meant to ensure the availability of minimum nutrition to the poor who otherwise cannot purchase. Provision of food, health and nutrition are the responsibilities of state as per human rights declared by the United Nations.

The ration cards are issued to avail rice, wheat, sugar, oil, kerosene at subsidised rates from ration shops. This is a service provided to poor, middle income and other families to ensure minimum nutrition the ration cards are issued by Revenue Department and food materials are supplied by Civil Supplies/ Public distribution (PDS). In Andhra Pradesh white colour card issued to those living below poverty line and pink colour card to others. For white ration card, all the five provisions *viz.*, rice, wheat, sugar, oil, kerosene are given, for pink ration card holder only sugar is given. A white ration card helps poor families to acquire staple food and other provisions and supports the family nutritionally to some extent.

Table 4.21: Distribution of the Mothers According to their Ration Card

S.No.	*Ration Card*	*Mothers of Anganwadi Children*	
		Number	*Percentage*
1.	Mothers having ration card	111	55.5
2.	Mothers not having ration card	89	44.5
	Total	**200**	**100.0**
1.	Mothers having white ration card	97	87.37
2.	Mothers having pink ration card	14	12.63
	Total	**111**	**100.0**

The Table 4.21 shows ration card status of the mothers. Among the mothers studied (55.5%) were having ration card and remaining 44.5 per cent do not possess a ration card. Among the ration card holders (87.37%) had white ration card and 12.63 per cent had pink ration card. Although many of the mothers belonged to lower income group, they do not have a ration card.

Size of Family

The number of members in a family was considered as size of a family. As the family size increases the available family resources have to be distributed among more number of people. In a low income family, the large family size increases the pressure on its resources and deprives some of the members of their needs. Non-fulfillment of needs later leads to non-fulfillment of rights. Hence family size was included as a variable.

Table 4.22: Distribution of the Mothers According to their Family Size

S.No.	*Family Size*	*Number*	*Percentage*
1.	Below 4 members	18	9.0
2.	5 – 8 members	170	85.0
3.	Above 9 members	12	6.0
	Total	**200**	**100.0**

The family size of the sample is shown in Table 4.22, it indicates that majority (85%) of the mothers of anganwadi children had family size of 5–8 members. Around 9 per cent of the sample had small families of less than 4 members. Only 6 per cent had family size above 9 members.

Family Type

The family type influences the decision-making power and interpersonal relationships within the family. In a nuclear family the mother may have more freedom to implement her knowledge and practises in the case of a joint family there may be members elder to her, whose attitudes may have an influence on mothers decisions. Hence, family type was included as a variable.

In the present study the mothers' of anganwadi children were divide into four groups *viz.*, two parent family, single parent family, extended family and joint family. A (55.5%) of the mothers belonged to nuclear – two parent family, 3.5 per cent belonged to nuclear single parent family, 2.5 per cent were from extended families and 38.5 per cent were of joint families.

Number of Children

Children in the family demand more time from mothers for their care and management. The more the children in a family the amount of attention given to each child is reduced and the quality of care given to children may be affected. Further number of children in a family places demand on mothers time and also health.

In the present study (83%) of the mothers had 2 to 4 children. Whereas 17 per cent had less than 2 children.

MOTHERS ACCESS TO PUBLIC SERVICES

The public services are meant for the welfare and development of the families living in a particular area. These are provided by the state through its local governments. The services in the area of health, nutrition, sanitation, education,

Table 4.23: Distribution of the Mothers According to the Availability of Public Services to their Families

S.No.	*Availability of Public Services*	*Availability in percentage*					
		No	*Nominal*	*Average to some extent*	*Good*	*Very good*	*Total*
1.	Primary Health Centres	1.0	3.5	17.0	39.0	39.5	100
2.	Anganwadi Services	–	5.5	22.0	39.0	33.5	100
3.	Municipal/Panchayat water facilities	1.0	37.0	23.5	19.0	19.5	100
4.	Municipal/Panchayat services	55.5	3.0	17.5	24.0	–	100
5.	Civil supplies	23.0	4.0	29:0	26.5	17.5	100
6.	Primary School Education	1.0	4.0	36.5	47.5	11.0	100
7.	Non-formal Education	32.5	–	0.5	24.5	42.5	100
8.	Electricity facility	–	8.0	19.5	44.5	28.0	100
9.	Law and order services (Utilising constitutional legal provision)	33.0	1.5	16.5	33.0	16.0	100

utilities law and order were included in the human rights. The human rights are also child rights, hence availability and accessibility of these services were studied.

From the table 4.23, it is evident that (99%) of the sample have access to primary health centre, only 1 per cent did not have access to PHC services. Majority of the sample rated the PHC services as good and very good.

The ICDS anganwadi services are accessible to all the sample. This may be because the sample children are attending anganwadi centre. Majority of the sample rated the anganwadi services as good and very good (39%) and 33.5 per cent respectively. Only 5.5 per cent and 22 per cent rated anganwadi services availability as 'nominal' and 'to some extent' respectively.

The water facilities in Municipal and Panchayat areas are accessible to (99%) of the sample and for only 1 per cent it is not accessible. Majority of the sample rated water facilities as nominal and average. Only a 19 per cent rated water facilities as good and around 19.5 per cent rated it as very good.

With regard to Municipal/Panchayat services the (55.5%) of the respondents stated that they are not available. A 44.5 per cent stated that Panchayat and Municipal services are available and their ratings for these services ranged from nominal to good.

Around 23 per cent of the sample had no access to civil supplies and (77%) had access to civil supplies. The ratings for civil supplies indicate that nominal 4 per cent, average 29 per cent, good 26.5 per cent and very good 17.5 per cent.

Primary school education programme is available to (99%) of the sample. A 47.5 per cent rated the primary school education services as good and a 11 per cent rated it as very good. A 4 per cent and 36.5 per cent of the sample rated this services as a nominal and average respectively.

The non-formal education services are accessible to (67.5%) of the sample and not accessible to 32.5 per cent of the sample. A 24.5 per cent and 42.5 per cent of the sample rated non-formal education services as good and very good respectively.

Electricity facility is accessible to all the respondents. A good majority of the sample rated electricity facility as good (44.5%) and very good 28 per cent). Only 8 per cent and 19.5 per cent of the sample rated electricity facility as nominal and average respectively.

The law and order services were not accessible to 33 per cent of the sample. Only (67%) of the sample had access to these services. Around 1.5 per cent and 16.5 per cent of the sample rated law and order services as nominal and average respectively. A 33 per cent and 16 per cent of the sample rated these services as good and very good respectively.

CHILD RIGHTS, KNOWLEDGE, ATTITUDE AND PRACTISES OF ANGANWADI WORKERS

The child rights knowledge, attitudes and practises of anganwadi workers under study was assessed using child rights knowledge, attitudes and practises scales developed for the purpose. The child rights; knowledge scores, attitudes scores and practise scores of the sample was analysed statistically, the mean scores, standard deviation of the sample is given in Table 4.24.

Table 4.24: Child Rights, Knowledge, Attitudes and Practises of Anganwadi Workers

S. No	*Anganwadi workers*	*Knowledge*			*Attitude*			*Practise*		
		Max.	*Mean*	*SD*	*Max.*	*Mean*	*SD*	*Max.*	*Mean*	*SD*
1.	GO ICDS	38	37.57	0.70	·60	49.25	5.69	39	29.71	4.46
2.	NGO ICDS	38	37.25	0.72	60	49.35	4.96	39	31.05	3.64

From the Table 4.24, it is evident that the mean child rights knowledge scores of anganwadi workers belonging to government organised and non-government organised ICDS projects indicated that there is not much difference between mean knowledge scores of the anganwadi workers of two ICDS projects. They did not vary much in their scores as the standard deviation value for government organisation and non-government organisation anganwadi workers is 0.7 and 0.72 respectively. With regard to attitudes also there is not much difference between the anganwadi workers of two ICDS projects in their child rights attitudinal mean scores. The anganwadi workers varied in their attitudinal scores as the standard deviation values were 5.69 for government organisation anganwadi workers and 4.96 for non-government organisation anganwadi workers. The mean child rights practises scores of government organisation anganwadi workers was 29.71 and non-government organisation anganwadi workers was 31.05. The standard deviation values 4.46 and 3.64 indicate that the sample varied in their child rights practises.

The results in table 4.24, indicate that the mean knowledge, attitudes and practise scores of anganwadi workers of government and NGO ICDS projects were not low but were well above the average. Hence the following hypothesis were rejected.

Hypothesis 2: The child rights knowledge of anganwadi workers is low.

Hypothesis 4: The attitudes of anganwadi workers towards child rights is low.

Hypothesis 6: The practise of child rights by anganwadi workers is not adequate.

CORRELATION BETWEEN CHILD RIGHTS KNOWLEDGE, ATTITUDES AND PRACTISES SCORES OF ANGANWADI WORKERS

Knowledge on child rights enhances the awareness and understanding of children's needs. The knowledge may contributes to positive attitudes and help individual act favourably towards child rights, which inturn motivates people to practise child rights. Thus knowledge, attitudes and practise on child rights may lead to positive behaviour of anganwadi workers towards children and their rights. The correlation between the child rights knowledge, attitudes and practises was studied using Pearson's correlation as shown in Table 4.25.

Table 4.25: Correlation between Child Rights Knowledge, Attitudes and Practises Scores of Anganwadi Workers

S.No.	*Dependant Variables*	*Knowledge*	*Attitude*	*Practise*
1.	Knowledge	1.000	0.131	0.043
		–	0.065	0.546
		200.000	200.000	200.000
2.	Attitude	0.131	1.000	0.101
		0.065	–	0.153
		200.000	200.000	200.000
3.	Practise	0.043	0.101	1.000
		0.546	0.153	–
		200.000	200.000	200.000

Table 4.25 indicates that the anganwadi workers knowledge, attitudes and practises had no correlation with each other indicates that there is no consistent relationship. The anganwadi workers knowledge, attitudes and practises may not have an influence on each other.

CHILD RIGHTS KNOWLEDGE, ATTITUDE, PRACTISE AND THE INDEPENDENT VARIABLES OF THE ANGANWADI WORKERS

Age

The difference between the mean scores of child rights knowledge, attitude and practise and the age of the sample was examined using F-test. The anganwadi workers were classified into three groups on the basis of their age *viz.*, 20-25 years, 25-30 years, 30-35 years the difference between groups and with in groups with regard to their knowledge, attitude and practise on child rights was examined as shown in Table 4.26.

Table 4.26: Child Rights Knowledge, Attitude, Practise and the Age of the Anganwadi Workers

S. No.	*Dependant variables*	*Anganwadi workers*	*Sum of Squares*	*df*	*Mean Square*	*F-value*	*p-value*	*Remarks*
1.	Knowledge of Anganwadi workers	Between Groups	0.26	2	0.13	0.087	0.917	Not Significant
		Within Groups	300.97	197	1.52			
2.	Attitude of Anganwadi workers	Between Groups	795.97	2	397.98	1.841	0.161	Not Significant
		Within Groups	42596.78	197	216.227			
3.	Practise of Anganwadi workers	Between Groups	547.98	2	273.99	0.210	0.810	Not Significant
		Within Groups	256553.25	197	1302.30			

From the above table it is evident that the anganwadi workers did not differ with in the groups and between groups with regard to their knowledge, attitude, practise on child rights. Age did not seem to have an influence on the child rights knowledge, attitude, practise of the sample.

Child Rights Knowledge, Attitude, Practise and the Educational Status of the Anganwadi Workers

The difference between the mean scores of child rights knowledge, attitude, practise and the educational status of the anganwadi workers was examined using F-test. The sample was classified into three groups on the basis of their age *viz.,* 10th Class, Intermediate and Graduation. The difference between groups and with in groups with regard to their knowledge, attitude and practise on child rights was examined. (*See Table 4.27 on next page*)

From the Table 4.29, it is evident that the anganwadi workers did not differ within the groups and between groups with regard to their knowledge, attitude and practise on child rights. Educational status seems to had no influence on the child rights knowledge, attitude and practise of the anganwadi workers.

Child Rights Knowledge, Attitude and Practise and the Place of Residence of the Anganwadi Workers

The difference between the mean scores of child rights knowledge, attitude and practise and the place of residence of the anganwadi workers was examined using F-test. The anganwadi workers were classified into four groups on the basis of their place of residence *viz.*, Rural, Urban, Urban slum, remote area the difference between groups and with in groups with regard to their knowledge, attitude and practise on child rights.

From the table 4.28 (*See on page 179*), it is evident that the anganwadi workers did not differ with in the groups and between groups with regard to their knowledge, attitude and practise on child rights. Place of residence also seems to

Table 4.27: Child Rights Knowledge, Attitude, Practise and the Educational Status of Anganwadi Workers

S. No.	*Dependant variables*	*Anganwadi workers*	*Sum of Squares*	*df*	*Mean Square*	*F-value*	*p-value*	*Remarks*
1.	Knowledge of Anganwadi workers	Between Groups	3.40	2	1.70	1.126	0.326	Not Significant
		Within Groups	297.83	197	1.51			
2.	Attitude of Anganwadi workers	Between Groups	494.15	2	247.07	1.135	0.324	Not Significant
		Within Groups	42898.61	197	217.75			
3.	Practise of Anganwadi workers	Between Groups	3674.13	2	1837.06	1.428	0.242	Not Significant
		Within Groups	253427.10	197	1286.43			

Table 4.28 : Child Rights Knowledge, Attitude and Practise and the Place of Residence of Anganwadi Workers

S. No.	*Dependant variables*	*Anganwadi workers*	*Sum of Squares*	*df*	*Mean Square*	*f-value*	*p-value*	*Remarks*
1.	Knowledge of Anganwadi workers	Between Groups	5.16	3	1.72	1.139	0.335	Not Significant
		Within Groups	296.07	196	1.51			
2.	Attitude of Anganwadi workers	Between Groups	686.97	3	228.99	1.051	0.371	Not Significant
		Within Groups	42705.78	196	217.88			
3.	Practise of Anganwadi workers	Between Groups	9113.09	3	3037.69	2.401	0.069	Not Significant
		Within Groups	247988.13	196	1265.24			

have no influence on the child rights, knowledge, attitude and practise of the anganwadi workers.

Child Rights Knowledge, Attitude and Practise and Marital Status of Anganwadi Workers

The marital status of anganwadi workers was included as a variable in the present study with an assumption that marriage and motherhood may have an influence on anganwadi workers perception of children's needs and their skills on childcare. In order to examine difference between the married and unmarried anganwadi workers with regard to their child rights knowledge, attitude and practise, a *t-test* was employed for their mean scores on knowledge, attitude and practise as shown in Table 4.29. (*See on next page*)

The Table 4.29 shows that the anganwadi workers did not differ significantly on their child rights knowledge, attitude and practise on the basis of their marital status. The results may not be generalised as the number of unmarried anganwadi workers (11 members) were not proportionate to the number of married anganwadi workers (189 members), in the sample.

Child Rights Knowledge, Attitude and Practise and Length of Service of Anganwadi Workers

The number of years of job experience as anganwadi worker, from the date of are entry into ICDS was taken and was calculated as the length of service. The anganwadi workers were classified into four groups on the basis of their length of service *viz.*, below 5 years, 6-10 years, 11-15 years and above 15 years. The difference between groups and within groups with regard to child rights knowledge, attitude and practise was examined using F-test (ANOVA) as shown in Table 4.30. (*See on page 182*)

From the table 4.30, it is evident that the anganwadi workers did not differ significantly with regard to their knowledge and attitudes, either between groups or within groups. The anganwadi workers showed significant difference

Table 4.29: The Difference between the Married and Unmarried Anganwadi Workers with Regard to Child Rights Knowledge, Attitude and Practise

S. No.	*Dependant variables*	*Marital status of the Anganwadi workers*	*N*	*Mean*	*SD values*	*t-value*	*p-value*	*Remarks*
1.	Knowledge of Anganwadi workers	unmarried	11	49.8804	0.39673	1.516	0.131	Not Significant
		married	189	49.3038	1.25522			
2.	Attitude of Anganwadi workers	unmarried	11	91.8182	10.65767	1.506	0.157	Not Significant
		married	189	86.7108	14.94418			
3.	Practise of Anganwadi workers	unmarried	11	85.1010	10.18901	–0.464	0.646	Not Significant
		married	189	86.9929	36.90311			

Note: p-value >0.05 level of significance.

Table 4.30: Child Rights Knowledge, Attitude and Practise and Length of Service of Anganwadi Workers

S. No.	*Dependant variables*	*Anganwadi workers*	*Sum of Squares*	*df*	*Mean Square*	*f-value*	*p-value*	*Remarks*
1.	Knowledge of Anganwadi workers	Between Groups	5.99	3	1.99	1.327	0.267	Not Significant
		Within Groups	295.24	196	1.50			
2.	Attitude of Anganwadi workers	Between Groups	136.95	3	45.65	0.207	0.892	Not Significant
		Within Groups	43255.81	196	220.69			
3.	Practise of Anganwadi workers	Between Groups	11308.97	3	3769.65	3.006	0.032	Significant @ 5% Level
		Within Groups	245792.26	196	1254.04			

with regard to child rights practise. The job experience in general equips the anganwadi workers with skills needed to perform their work effectively. As the anganwadi workers differed significantly on their child rights practise scores a DUNCAN test was employed to examine difference between groups as shown in Table 4.30.

Child Rights Practise and Length of Service of Anganwadi Workers

Table 4.31: Post Hoc Tests Homogeneous Subsets

1. Duncan Multiple Range Test

S. No.	*Length of service of the Anganwadi Workers*	*N*	*Significant at 0.05% level*	
			1	*2*
1.	below 5 yrs	137	84.2052	
2.	6 to 10 yrs	18	82.0988	
3.	11 to 15 yrs	28		105.4563
4.	above 15 yrs	17	83.0065	
5.	Sig.		0.844	1.000

The Table 4.31 shows that there is no significant difference between the anganwadi workers having a length of service, below 5 years, 6-10 years and above 15 years with regard to their child right practise. There is significant difference between the anganwadi workers having 11-15 years of service and other groups with regard to child rights practises.

Hence part of the hypothesis 10 "There is no relationship between personal and service profile of anganwadi workers and their knowledge, attitude and practise on child rights is rejected". As there was significance difference between the anganwadi workers having 11-15 years of service and other groups with regard to child rights practises.

Child Rights Knowledge, Attitude and Practise and Training of Anganwadi Workers

Trainings build the capacities of the anganwadi workers to perform their work effectively. Further trainings provide

Table 4.32: Child Rights Knowledge, Attitude and Practise and Training of Anganwadi Workers

S. No.	*Dependant variables*	*Anganwadi workers*	*Sum of Squares*	*df*	*Mean Square*	*f-value*	*p-value*	*Remarks*
1.	Knowledge of Anganwadi workers	Between Groups	8.92	4	2.23	1.489	0.207	Not Significant
		Within Groups	292.31	195	1.49			
2.	Attitude of Anganwadi workers	Between Groups	3301.29	4	825.32	4.014	0.004	Not Significant
		Within Groups	40091.47	195	205.59			
3.	Practise of Anganwadi workers	Between Groups	564.34	4	141.08	0.107	0.980	Not Significant
		Within Groups	256536.88	195	1315.57			

opportunities to interact with their co-trainees and the trainers which help in understanding their role and responsibilities as anganwadi workers, the sample were divided into two groups *viz.*, trained, not trained. Further, from the data of study how many years ago the training was received was also calculated in order to know its influence on child rights knowledge, attitude and practise. In order to examine the difference between the groups and within the groups with regard to their child rights knowledge, attitude and practise a F-test (ANOVA) was employed as shown in Table 4.32. (*See on next page*)

From the Table 4.32, it is clear that the anganwadi workers did not differ significantly either between groups or within groups with regard to their child rights knowledge and practise with training received. The anganwadi workers showed significant difference for the child rights attitudes and the training received. In order to examine the difference between groups with regard to child rights attitudes a Duncan Multiple Range Test was employed. If ANOVA is significant for any of the parameters it is followed by a post-Hoc test; Duncan test, as shown in Table 4.32.

Training Status and Child Rights Attitudes of Anganwadi Workers

Table 4.33: Training Status and Child Rights Attitudes of Anganwadi Workers

S. No.	*Training Status*	*N*	*Significant at 0.05% level*	
			1	*2*
1.	Not received training	161		86.9772
2.	below 5 yrs*	8		88.7500
3.	6 to 10 yrs*	2	50.8333	
4.	11 to 15 yrs*	13		93.8462
5.	above 15 yrs*	16		85.2083
6.	Sig.		1.000	0.0330

*The number of years before the date of data collection, the training received.

From the Table 4.33, it is evident that the anganwadi workers, who have received training 6-10 years ago differed significantly with other groups *viz.*, not trained, below 5 years, 11-15 years and above 15 years with regard to their child rights attitudes.

Child Rights Knowledge, Attitude and Practise of Anganwadi Workers and ICDS Management

The ICDS functioning under the management of governmental organisation and non-governmental organisation were selected for the study in order to examine the efforts of management in providing child rights information to the field level functionaries of ICDS. The supervision, monitoring and evaluation of activities of anganwadi centres and the performance appraisal of anganwadi worker may be done regularly or sporadically depending on the management. Hence, management was also included in the study as a parameter.

In order to examine the difference between the anganwadi workers belonging to governmental organisation and non-governmental organisation management with regard to their child rights knowledge, attitude and practise, a *t-test* was employed as shown in Table 4.34. (*See on next page*)

The Table 4.34 indicates that the anganwadi workers belonging to government organisation and non-governmental organisation management did not differ significantly on their child rights attitudes and practises, but significant difference was found between two groups of the anganwadi workers with regard to their child rights knowledge.

ASSOCIATION OF CHILD RIGHTS KNOWLEDGE, ATTITUDE AND PRACTISE WITH THE INDEPENDENT VARIABLES

The relationship between dependent variables *viz.*, child rights knowledge, attitudes and practises of anganwadi workers with the independent variables *viz.*, age, place of residence, educational status and type of management was studied using chi-square test.

Table 4.34: Child Rights Knowledge, Attitude and Practise of Anganwadi Workers and ICDS Management

S. No.	*Dependant variables*	*I CDS Management of Anganwadi workers*	*N*	*Mean*	*SD values*	*t-value*	*p-value*	*Remarks*
1.	Knowledge of Anganwadi workers	Government organisaion management, Puttur	100	49.15	1.47	–2.058	0.041	*Significant at 5% Level
		Non-Government organisation management, Tirupati	100	49.51	0.89			
2.	Attitude of Anganwadi workers	Government organisaion management, Puttur	100	85.43	16.39	–1.497	0.136	Not Significant
		Non-Government organisation management, Tirupati	100	88.55	12.83			
3.	Practise of Anganwadi workers	Government organisaion management, Puttur	100	82.52	12.39	–1.724	0.087	Not Significant
		Non-Government organisation management, Tirupati	100	91.25	49.03			

* p-value <0.05 level of significant.

Table 4.35: Association between Age and Child Rights Knowledge Attitude and Practise of Anganwadi Workers

S. No.	*Dependent Variables*	*χ^2 calculated value*	*df*	*χ^2 table value*	*Remarks*
1.	Knowledge of Anganwadi workers	0.35	2	3.84	Not Significant
2.	Attitudes of Anganwadi workers	16.99	4	13.28	**Significant at 1% level
3.	Practises of Anganwadi workers	0.98	4	9.49	Not significant

** Significant at the 0.01 level.

The Table 4.35 indicates that there is no association between child rights knowledge and the age of anganwadi workers. Similarly no association was found between child rights practises and the age of anganwadi workers, but there was an association between the child rights attitude and the age of anganwadi workers. Although the results of ANOVA for the above variables indicated no significant difference among the anganwadi workers with regard to child rights knowledge, attitude and practise, the chi-square test indicated an association between child rights attitudes and the age of anganwadi workers.

Association of Educational Status with Child Right Knowledge, Attitude and Practise of Anganwadi Workers

The formal education received by the anganwadi workers was considered as their educational status. Based on the educational status, the anganwadi workers were divided into three groups *viz.*, 10th Class, Intermediate and Graduation.

The association between child rights knowledge, attitude, practise and the educational status of the sample was studied using chi-square test. From the Table 4.36, it is clear that

Table 4.36: Association between Educational Status and Child Rights Knowledge, Attitude and Practise of Anganwadi Workers

S. No.	*Dependent Variables*	*χ^2 calculated value*	*df*	*χ^2 table value*	*Remarks*
1.	Knowledge of Anganwadi workers	1.07	2	3.84	Not Significant
2.	Attitudes of Anganwadi workers	4.40	4	9.49	Not Significant
3.	Practises of Anganwadi workers	1.68	4	9.49	Not Significant

** Significant at the 0.01 level.

there is no association between anganwadi workers child rights knowledge, attitude, practise and educational status. This shows that there is no significant relationship between the child rights knowledge, attitude, practice and the educational status of anganwadi workers. The ANOVA test employed to examine the difference between the educational status and child rights knowledge attitude, practise of anganwadi workers also showed no significant difference.

Association of Child Rights Knowledge, Attitude and Practise with the Place of Residence of Anganwadi Workers

Place of residence may have an influence on the perception of child rights of anganwadi workers. Place of residence plays a role in accessibility to information, media, services and exposure which inturn have an influence on awareness knowledge, attitudes and skills of a person. Hence place of residence of anganwadi workers was included as a variable in this study. The relationship between place of residence and child rights knowledge, attitude and practise of anganwadi workers was studied with the help of chi-square test as shown in Table 4.37.

Table 4.37: Association of Knowledge, Attitude and Practise with the Place of Residence of Anganwadi Workers

S. No.	*Dependent Variables*	*χ^2 calculated value*	*df*	*χ^2 table value*	*Remarks*
1.	Knowledge of Anganwadi workers	3.99	3	7.82	Not Significant
2.	Attitudes of Anganwadi workers	7.32	6	12.59	Not Significant
3.	Practises of Anganwadi workers	12.17	6	12.59	Not Significant

From the Table 4.37, it is evident that there is no association between child rights knowledge, attitudes, practise and the place of residence, of anganwadi workers. This indicates that there is no significant relationship between child rights knowledge, attitude, practise and the place of residence of anganwadi workers. The results of ANOVA test conducted for the same variables showed that the anganwadi workers did not differ significantly with regard to their child rights knowledge, attitude and practise. This further affirms that place of residence may not have an influence on child rights knowledge, attitude and practise of anganwadi workers.

Association of Child Rights Knowledge, Attitude and Practise of Anganwadi Workers with ICDS Project Management

The ICDS projects are functioning under government and non-government organisation management. In the present study ICDS projects from each management was selected purposefully to know the relationship between the type of management and child rights, knowledge, attitude and practise of anganwadi workers. The Puttur ICDS project is functioning under government management whereas the Tirupati ICDS project is functioning under Rastriya Seva Sanstha (RASS) a non-governmental organisation.

Table 4.38: Association of Child Rights Knowledge, Attitude and Practise of Anganwadi Workers with ICDS Project Management

S. No.	*Dependent Variables*	*χ^2 calculated value*	*df*	*χ^2 table value*	*Remarks*
1.	Knowledge of Anganwadi workers	0.61	1	3.84	Not Significant
2.	Attitudes of Anganwadi workers	14.42	2	13.82	***Significant
3.	Practises of Anganwadi workers	2.89	2	3.84	Not Significant

*** Significant at 0.001 level

From the table 4.38, it is evident that the dependent variables *viz.,* child rights knowledge, child rights practises had no association with the independent variable, ICDS project management. The relation between child rights attitudes and ICDS project management was found. Through the above results indicates that there is significant relationship between anganwadi workers child rights attitudes and ICDS project management. The *t-test* computed for the same variables indicate that the anganwadi workers showed, significant difference with regard to their child rights knowledge. This may not be attributed to management efforts, as during the study period none of the managements provided child rights information to their anganwadi workers.

CHILD RIGHTS KNOWLEDGE, ATTITUDE AND PRACTISE OF MOTHERS OF ANGANWADI CHILDREN

The mother through their participation in ICDS programme, through mass media *viz.,* Radio, Television, Newspapers, Magazines, Books, Meetings of self help groups and others may have been exposed to child rights information. The mothers by virtue of their motherhood and experiences within the family and community may develop insight into children's needs and rights. The mothers perceptions of child rights may motivate her to make efforts to improve her capabilities in child care and management. Hence, an attempt was made in this study to assess the child rights knowledge, attitudes and practises of mothers of anganwadi children and also to study the relationship between mothers child rights knowledge, attitude and practise and their participation in anganwadi centres activities and also their personal and family variables.

Child Rights Knowledge, Attitude and Practise of Mothers of Anganwadi Children

The mothers child rights knowledge were assessed using child rights knowledge and attitude scale developed and administered for anganwadi workers. A separate tool for assessing the child rights practise scales of mothers was developed and administered to the mothers. The scores of child rights knowledge, attitude and practise scale for mothers are presented in Table 4.39. (*See on next page*)

From the table 4.39, it is evident that the mean child rights knowledge scores of mothers of Government (GO) and Non-government (NGO) ICDS projects were 37.6 and 37.3 respectively, and the standard deviation values were 0.7 and 0.72 respectively. This shows that there is not much variation among mothers with regard to their child rights knowledge scores. The mean child rights attitudes scores of mothers, whose children attending ICDS projects of government and non-government mothers were 49.3 and 49.4. The standard deviation values were 5.7 and 5.0 respectively, that is the mothers varied in their child rights attitudes scores. The mean child rights practise scores of government and non-government mothers were 39.19 and 40.63 respectively. The standard deviation values were 3.79 and 3.27 respectively. This shows that though the mothers did not vary in their child rights knowledge scores, variation was observed among the mothers with regard to attitudes and practises. The results in the Table 4.39 indicate that the mean knowledge, attitudes and practise scores of mothers of anganwadi children

Table 4.39: Child Rights Knowledge, Attitude and Practise of Mothers

S. No	*Mothers with Anganwadi Children*	*Participation in ICDS Programme*			*Knowledge*			*Attitude*			*Practise*		
		Max	*Mean*	*S.D*	*Max*	*Mean*	*S.D*	*Max*	*Mean*	*S.D*	**Maxi**	**Mean**	**S.D**
1.	GO ICDS	34	25.11	4.99	38	37.6	0.70	60	49.3	5.7	67	39.19	3.79
2.	NGO ICDS	34	20.61	5.00	38	37.3	0.72	60	49.4	5.0	67	40.63	3.27

attending government and NGO ICDS projects were not low but were well above the average. Hence the following Hypothesis were rejected:

Hypothesis 3: The child rights knowledge of mothers of Anganwadi children is low.

Hypothesis 5: The attitudes of mothers of anganwadi children towards child rights is low.

Hypothesis 7: The practise of child rights by mothers of anganwadi children is not adequate.

CORRELATION BETWEEN CHILD RIGHTS KNOWLEDGE, ATTITUDE AND PRACTISES AND PARTICIPATION OF MOTHERS OF ANGANWADI CHILDREN

Several behaviour modification experiments and studies conducted in India, in the area of health and nutrition education and interventions revealed that the knowledge, attitudes and practises of people are interrelated. For sustainable practises it is necessary to bring out changes in the knowledge and attitude of the people or beneficiaries. In order to examine the relationship between the child rights knowledge, attitude, practise and participation of mothers in anganwadi activities 'Pearson correlation' test was employed and the results are given in Table 4.40.

Table 4.40: Correlation between Child Rights Knowledge, Attitude and Practises and Participation of Mothers of Anganwadi Children

S. No.	*Dependant Variables*	*Participation of Mothers*	*Knowledge*	*Attitude*	*Practise*
1.	Participation of Mothers	1.000	-0.168*	–0.115	0.272**
2.	Knowledge of Mothers	–0.168*	1.000	–0.016	–0.084
3.	Attitudes of Mothers	–0.115	–0.016	1.000	–0.065
4.	Practise of Mothers	0.272**	–0.084	–0.065	1.000

* Correlation is significant at 0.05 level

** Correlation is significant at 0.01 level

From the Table 4.40, it is evident that the participation of mothers in anganwadi activities had significant negative correlation at 0.05 level with the child rights knowledge of mothers. The negative correlation between participation of mothers child rights knowledge indicates that participation showed inverse relation to the child rights knowledge. But the participation of mothers had no significant correlation with their child rights attitudinal scores. The participation of mothers showed significant positive correlation at 0.01 level with the child rights practise of mothers. That is the samples' participation in anganwadi activities showed significant correlation with child rights knowledge and practises but not with child rights attitudes.

The child rights knowledge of mothers of anganwadi children showed significant (negative) correlation at 0.05 level with their participation in anganwadi activities. But the child rights knowledge scores of mothers had no significant correlation with child rights attitudes and practises. The child rights attitudes of the sample had no correlation with their participation in anganwadi activities, child rights knowledge and child rights practises. The child rights practises of mothers of anganwadi children showed significant positive correlation with the participation and had no correlation with their child rights knowledge and attitudes. Thus the correlation values indicate that the mothers participation in anganwadi activities showed significant positive correlation with their child rights practises and a significant negative correlation with child rights knowledge, though no significant correlation was found between mothers child rights knowledge, attitudes and practise.

THE CHILD RIGHTS KNOWLEDGE, ATTITUDE, PRACTISE, PARTICIPATION AND THE INDEPENDENT VARIABLES OF MOTHERS

The participation of mothers in the ICDS programme is found to be passive Majority of mothers of children attending government managed ICDS programme (63 per cent) was low, around 31 per cent of mothers participation was moderate and only 6 per cent should high participation.

Among the mothers of children attending NGO managed ICDS projects 59 per cent. 59 per cent showed low participation, 37 per cent moderate participation only 4 per cent showed high participation. This allows to accept the hypothesis 9. "The participation of mothers in the ICDS programme is not adequate". Efforts should be made to improve the participation of mothers in the ICDS programme.

Age

The approximate chronological age of the mothers was taken as age in years. The mothers were classified as three groups on the basis of their age *viz.*, 20-25 years, 25-30 years and 30-35 years. In order to study the difference between mothers with regard to their child rights, knowledge, attitude, practise and their age, *F-test* was employed and the results are given in Table 4.41. (*See on next page*)

The table 4.41 shows that the mothers did not differ significantly on their child rights knowledge, attitude and practise either between groups or within groups. This indicates that age had no influence on child rights knowledge, attitude and practise of mothers of anganwadi children.

Child Rights Knowledge, Attitude, Practises, Participation and Location of Anganwadi Centre

The location of anganwadi centre determines the amount of space available for conducting anganwadi activities and also the type of accommodation available to house the anganwadi centre. In the study area most of the anganwadi centres were accommodated in rented houses. Around sixty per cent of anganwadi centres of government ICDS project were accommodated in small thatched houses, and forty per cent of anganwadi centres in non-government ICDS projects were accommodated in small thatched houses.

The anganwadi centres located in rural areas have access to outdoor space or ground whereas the anganwadi centers located in urban and urban slums have little or no outdoor space. The quality of anganwadi centers activities involving

Table 4.41: The Child Rights Knowledge, Attitude, Practise and the Age of Mothers

S. No.	*Dependant variables*	*Mothers*	*Sum of Squares*	*df*	*Mean Square*	*f-value*	*p-value*	*Remarks*
1.	Standard score of knowledge of mothers	Between Groups	0.08	2	0.04	0.061	0.941	Not Significant
		Within Groups	129.97	197	0.66			
2.	Standard score of attitude of mothers	Between Groups	189.85	2	94.92	0.599	0.550	Not Significant
		Within Groups	31216.13	197	158.45			
3.	Standard score of practise of mothers	Between Groups	491.85	2	245.92	2.218	0.112	Not Significant
		Within Groups	21847.07	197	110.89			
4.	Standard score of participation of mothers	Between Groups	43.07	2	21.53	0.006	0.994	Not Significant
		Within Groups	668388.87	197	3392.83			

mothers and adolescent girls also depends on the space available. Hence location of anganwadi centre was included in the present study.

The anganwadi centres under study were classified into three groups based on their location *viz.*, urban, urban slum and rural areas. The difference between child rights knowledge, attitudes, practise and participation of mothers and the location of anganwadi centre was examined with help of ANOVA test, as shown in table 4.42. (*See on next page*)

From the Table 4.42, it is evident that there was significant difference between mothers with regard to their child rights knowledge, attitudes and participation in anganwadi activities and the location of anganwadi centre. But the mothers did not differ significantly with regard to their child rights practises and the location of anganwadi centre. As the significant difference was found for child rights knowledge, attitudes and participation with regard to location of anganwadi centres a Duncan multiple range test was employed, to examine the difference within groups.

Location of Anganwadi and Child Rights Knowledge of Mothers

From the table 4.43 (*See table on page 200*) it is clear that there is no significant difference between the mothers whose children were attending anganwadi located in urban area and rural area with regard to child rights knowledge. There is no significant difference between mothers whose children are attending anganwadi located in rural area and urban slum with regard to their child rights knowledge. There is significant difference in knowledge between mothers whose children were attending anganwadi located in urban area and urban slum.

Location of Anganwadi and Child Rights Attitude of Mothers

From the Table 4.44, (*See table on page 200*) it is evident that the mothers of children attending anganwadi in rural area differed significantly with regard to their child rights

Table 4.42: Location of Anganwadi and Child Rights Knowledge, Attitude, Practise and Participation of Mothers

S. No.	*Dependant variables*	*Mothers*	*Sum of Squares*	*df*	*Mean Square*	*f-value*	*p-value*	*Remarks*
1.	Standard score of knowledge of mothers	Between Groups	4.38	2	2.19	3.433	0.034	Significant at 5% level
		Within Groups	125.67	197	0.63			
2.	Standard score of attitude of mothers	Between Groups	1091.93	2	545.96	3.548	0.031	Significant at 5% level
		Within Groups	30314.05	197	153.87			
3.	Standard score of practise of mothers	Between Groups	116.26	2	58.13	0.515	0.598	Not Significant
		Within Groups	22222.65	197	112.80			
4.	Standard score of participation of mothers	Between Groups	21650.54	2	10825.27	3.297	0.039	Significant at 5% level
		Within Groups	646781.39	197	3283.15			

Table 4.43 : Location of Anganwadi and Child Rights Knowledge of Mothers

S. No.	*Place of Anganwadi*	*N*	*Significant at 0.05% level*	
			1	*2*
1.	Urban Area	139	49.403	
2.	Rural	37	49.679	49.679
3.	Urban Slum	24		49.780
	Sig.		0.126	0.576

Table 4.44: Location of Anganwadi and Child Rights Attitude of Mothers

S. No.	*Location of Anganwadi*	*N*	*Significant at 0.05% level*	
			1	*2*
1.	Rural area	37	63.3333	
2.	Urban slum	24		68.8889
3.	Urban area	139		69.4125
	Sig.		1.000	0.851

attitudes with the mothers of children attending anganwadi in urban slum and urban area where as the mothers of children attending anganwadi in urban slum and urban area did not differ significantly in their child rights attitudes.

Location of Anganwadi and Participation of Mothers in Anganwadi Activities

Table 4.45: Location of Anganwadi and Participation of Mothers in Anganwadi Activities

S. No.	*Location of Anganwadi*	*N*	*Significant at 0.05% level*	
			1	*2*
1.	Urban slum	24	74.65	
2.	Rural	37	80.85	
3.	Urban	139	100.71	
4.	Sig.		0.056	

From the table 4.45, it is clear that the ANOVA shows that there is significant difference in participation of mothers of children attending anganwadi in urban, urban slum and rural areas. However Duncan multiple range test shows insignificant difference between pairs of urban slum and rural, rural and urban, urban slum and urban.

When there are more than two groups to be compared at a time ANOVA (F-test) is employed, if any attribute/ parameter is significant through ANOVA it followed by Duncan multiple range test. Duncan test was employed for location of anganwadi and; child rights knowledge of mothers, child rights attitudes of mothers and participation of mothers.

Child Rights Knowledge, Attitude, Practise, Participation and Educational Status of Mothers

The mothers' formal education in number of years was considered as their educational status. Based on the educational status the mothers were classified into five groups *viz.*, illiterates, literates, primary education, high school education and college education. In order to examine the difference between the educational status of mothers and their child rights knowledge, attitude and practise ANOVA was employed as shown in Table 4.46. (*See on next page*)

From table 4.46 it is evident that there was no significant difference between mother's educational status with regard to child rights knowledge, attitude and practise. But significant difference was found between the educational status of mothers and their participation in anganwadi activities. Though the mothers did not differ significantly in their child rights knowledge, attitude and practise on the basis of their educational status, significant difference was seen for participation in anganwadi activities. This shows that education of mothers had an influence on their participation in anganwadi activities.

Educational Status and Participation of Mothers in Anganwadi Activities

As the F-test revealed that the mothers differed significantly with regard to their participation in anganwadi

Table 4.46: Child Rights Knowledge, Attitude, Practise, Participation and Educational Status of Mothers

S. No.	*Dependant variables*	*Mothers*	*Sum of Squares*	*df*	*Mean Square*	*f-value*	*p-value*	*Remarks*
1.	Standard score of knowledge of mothers	Between Groups	2.73	4	0.68	1.048	0.384	Not Significant
		Within Groups	127.31	195	0.65			
2.	Standard score of attitude of mothers	Between Groups	974.41	4	243.60	1.561	0.186	Not Significant
		Within Groups	30431.56	195	156.05			
3.	Standard score of practise of mothers	Between Groups	195.20	4	48.80	0.430	0.787	Not Significant
		Within Groups	22143.72	195	113.55			
4.	Standard score of participation of mothers	Between Groups	43691.56	4	10922.89	3.409	0.010	Significant at 1% level
		Within Groups	624740.38	195	3203.79			

activities. Duncan test was employed to examine the difference between the groups which is as shown in Table 4.47.

Table 4.47 : Educational Status and Participation of Mothers in Anganwadi Activities

S. No.	*Educational Status*	*N*	*Significant @ 0.05% level*		
			1	*2*	*3*
1.	Illiterate	66	77.1465		
2.	Literate	10			134.1667
3.	Primary Education	42	100.7937	100.7937	100.7937
4.	High School Education	66	95.2020	95.2020	
5.	College Education	16		114.5833	114.5833
6.	Sig.		0.183	0.277	0.059

From the Table 4.47, it is clear that the mothers who were illiterate, high school educated and primary school educated did not differ significantly in their participation in anganwadi activities, similarly the mothers who were high school educated, primary school educated and college educated did not differ significantly in their participation. Like-wise the mothers who were primary school educated, college educated and literates did not differ in their participation in anganwadi activities.

But there is significant difference between mothers who were illiterates and college educated, high school educated and literates and also illiterate and literate mothers.

Child Rights Knowledge, Attitudes, Practise Participation and Occupation of Mothers

Occupation of mothers determines the amount of quality time available for childcare and participation in anganwadi activities. Occupation of mothers also determines the amount of physical stress the mother undergoes, which also influences the mothers ability to attend to her children, especially in absence of domestic assistance/help. In the present study the sample were classified into five groups on the basis occupation *viz.,* (1) Daily wage labour, (2) Business, (3) Employed in private sector, (4) Employed in government sector, (5) Housewives.

In order to examine the difference between mothers with regard to their occupation and their child rights knowledge, attitude, practise and participation in anganwadi activities, ANOVA was employed, the results are shown in Table 4.48. (*See on next page*)

From the Table 4.48 it is clear that mothers did not differ significantly with regard to their occupation and child rights knowledge and practises. The sample show significance difference on their occupation and child rights attitudes and participation in anganwadi activities. This shows that occupation of mothers had an influence on their child rights attitudes and their participation in anganwadi activities.

As significant difference was found between occupation and child rights attitudes of mothers and also between occupation and participation of mothers in anganwadi activities. Duncan multiple range test was employed to examine the difference between groups of mothers with regard to their child rights attitudes and participation.

Occupation and Child Rights Attitudes of Mothers

The Table 4.49 (*See table on page 206)* shows that there is no significant difference between housewives and others (employed in private sector, government sector and business) with regard to child rights attitudes. But these two groups of mothers differed significantly with the daily wage earners.

Occupation and Participation of Mothers in Anganwadi Activities

From the Table 4.50, (*See table on page 206)* it is clear that the ANOVA shows that there is effect of different groups of occupation on mothers' participation. However Duncan test shows insignificant difference between pairs daily wage earners and others, housewives and others, daily wage earners and housewives with respect to participation.

Table 4.48: Child Rights Knowledge, Attitudes, Practise, Participation and Occupation of Mothers

S. No.	*Dependant variables*	*Mothers*	*Sum of Squares*	*df*	*Mean Square*	*f-value*	*p-value*	*Remarks*
1.	Standard score of knowledge of mothers	Between Groups	0.18	2	0.09	0.143	0.867	Not Significant
		Within Groups	129.86	197	0.65			
2.	Standard score of attitude of mothers	Between Groups	3359.80	2	1679.90	11.800	0.000	Significant at 1% level
		Within Groups	28046.18	197	142.36			
3.	Standard score of practise of mothers	Between Groups	186.13	2	93.06	0.828	0.439	Not Significant
		Within Groups	22152.79	197	112.45			
4.	Standard score of participation of mothers	Between Groups	38918.69	2	19459.34	6.090	0.003	Significant at 1% level
		Within Groups	629513.24	197	3195.49			

Table 4.49: Occupation and Child Rights Attitudes of Mothers

S. No.	*Occupational Status of Respondents*	*N*	*Significant @ 0.05% level*	
			1	*2*
1.	Daily wage earners	69		73.8647
2.	Housewives	121	65.3306	
3.	Others	65	64.3333	
4.	Sig.		0.770	1.000

Table 4.50: Occupation and Participation of Mothers in Anganwadi Activities

S. No.	*Occupational Status of Mothers*	*N*	*Significant @ 0.05% level*
1.	Daily wage earners	69	74.7585
2.	Others	10	99.1667
3.	Housewives	121	104.4077
4.	Sig.		0.0084

Child Rights Knowledge, Attitude, Practise, Participation and Family Size

The number of members living in the respondents family was considered as their family size. Family size influences the work load of the mother, the demand on the available family resources *viz.*, income, food, space, utilities and other human and material resources. Family size may have an influence on the anganwadi childrens, mothers' time for childcare, participation in anganwadi activities and also on their child rights knowledge attitude and practise. On the basis of the family size the sample was classified into three groups *viz.*, below four member, five to eight members, above nine members. ANOVA test was employed to study the difference between the mothers with regard to their family size and their child rights knowledge, attitudes, practise and participation in anganwadi activities. The results are given in Table 4.51.

The Table 4.51 shows that the mothers of anganwadi children did not differ on their family size and their child rights knowledge, attitude, practise and participation in

Table 4.51: Child Rights Knowledge, Attitude, Practise, Participation and Family Size

S. No.	Dependant variables	Mothers	Sum of Squares	df	Mean Square	f-value	p-value	Remarks
1.	Standard score of knowledge of mothers	Between Groups	0.93	2	0.46	0.716	0.490	Not Significant
		Within Groups	129.11	197	0.65			
2.	Standard score of attitude of mothers	Between Groups	73.14	2	36.57	0.230	0.795	Not Significant
		Within Groups	31332.84	197	159.05			
3.	Standard score of practise of mothers	Between Groups	330.69	2	165.34	1.480	0.230	Not Significant
		Within Groups	22008.22	197	111.71			
4.	Standard score of participation of mothers	Between Groups	2484.50	2	1242.25	0.367	0.693	Not Significant
		Within Groups	665947.44	197	3380.44			

anganwadi centres activities. It indicates that the family size may not have an influence on the participation of mothers and their child rights knowledge, attitude and practise.

Annual Income of Mothers and Child Rights Knowledge, Attitude, Practise and Participation

The annual income of respondents family was considered as their family's income. The income influences the purchasing power of the family and also their living conditions. The family income indirectly influences the family's access to electronic and mass media, work load of the mother and also her participation in anganwadi activities. Hence an effort was made to examine the difference between the mothers with regard to their family income and child rights knowledge, attitude, practise and participation in anganwadi activities.

The mothers was classified into two groups on the basis of their family annual income *viz.,* less than Rs.12,000 and Rs.12,001 to 18,000. As the mothers size for the income groups, Rs.18,001 to 24,000 were less than five, they were included under Rs.12,000 to 18,000 group.

The difference between the mothers of anganwadi children with regard to their annual income and their child rights knowledge attitude practise and participation was examined with the help of *t-test* as shown in Table 4.52. (*See table on next page*)

The Table 4.52 shows that there was no significant difference between mothers belonging to less than Rs.12,000 and 12,001 to 18,000 with regard to child rights knowledge, attitudes, practise and participation in anganwadi activities. It indicates that the family income may not have an influence on mothers child rights knowledge, attitude, practise and participation in anganwadi activities.

Types of Family and Child Rights Knowledge, Attitude, Practise and Participation of Mothers in Anganwadi Activities

The family type determines the decision making power of the mother and also the amount of freedom available to

Table 4.52: ***t-Test*** **for Annual Income of Mothers**

S. No.	*Dependant variables*	*Annual Income*	*N*	*Mean*	*SD values*	*t-value*	*p-value*	*Remarks*
1.	Standard score of knowledge of mothers	below 12000	172	49.46	0.81	–1.544	0.124	Not Significant
		12001-18000	28	49.71	0.74			
2.	Standard score of attitude of mothers	below 12000	172	68.38	12.62	0.444	0.660	Not Significant
		12001-18000	28	67.26	12.34			
3.	Standard score of practise of mothers	below 12000	172	117.13	10.75	–0.892	0.378	Not Significant
		12001-18000	28	118.90	9.58			
4.	Standard score of participation of mothers	below 12000	172	92.73	58.10	–0.720	0.476	Not Significant
		12001-18000	28	101.19	57.54			

Note: p-value > 0.05 level of significant

participate in anganwadi activities. Hence an attempt was made to examine the difference between the mothers with regard to their family type and their child rights knowledge, attitude, practise and participation using *t-test*. The mothers were divided into four groups *viz.*, nuclear two parent family, nuclear single parent family, extended family and joint family.

As the sample size for nuclear single parent family and extended family were less than five. They were included under nuclear family for the purpose of computing *t-test*. The results of *t-test* are given in Table 4.53. (*See table on next page*)

From the Table 4.53, it is clear that the mother of anganwadi children did not differ significantly with regard to their family types and their child rights knowledge, attitude, practise and participation in anganwadi activities.

Hypothesis 11: "There is no relationship between personal and family profile of the mothers and their knowledge, attitude and practise on child rights and participation in anganwadi activities" is rejected as:

(a) ***Age:*** The mother's age had no influence on knowledge, attitude and practise of child rights and also on their participation in anganwadi centers' activities.

(b) ***Location of Anganwadi Centre:*** The mothers significantly differed in their rights knowledge, attitudes and participation with regard to location of anganwadi centre, but did not differ significantly with regard to their child rights practises and location of anganwadi centre.

(c) ***The Educational Status:*** There was no significant difference between mother's educational status with regard to child right knowledge, attitude and practise. But significant difference was found between the educational status of mothers and their participation in anganwadi activities.

(d) ***Occupation of Mothers:*** Occupation of mothers had an influence on their attitudes on participation

Table 4.53: Type of Family and Child Rights Knowledge, Attitude, Practise and Participation of Mothers

S. No.	*Dependant variables*	*Family types*	*N*	*Mean*	*SD values*	*t-value*	*p-value*	*Remarks*
1.	Standard score of knowledge of mothers	nuclear-both parents	118	49.4982	0.80542	–0.37	0.970	Not Significant
		joint family	82	49.5026	0.81767			
2.	Standard score of attitude of mothers	nuclear-both parents	118	69.1808	12.07516	1.273	0.205	Not Significant
		joint family	82	66.8496	13.18593			
3.	Standard score of practise of mothers	nuclear-both parents	118	117.5972	10.60096	0.343	0.732	Not Significant
		joint family	82	117.0732	10.64416			
4.	Standard score of participation of mothers	nuclear-both parents	118	91.5960	61.50317	–0.698	0.486	Not Significant
		joint family	82	97.2561	52.62412			

in anganwadi activities but had no influence on their child right knowledge and practises.

(e) ***Family Size and Family Type:*** Family size and Family Type of the mothers had no influence on their child rights knowledge, attitudes and practise and participation in anganwadi centre's activities.

Thus, among the variables related to personal and family profile of mothers' only age, family size and type did not have an influence on the child rights knowledge, attitudes and practise of the sample. Hence the hypothesis No.11 is rejected.

ICDS Project Management and Child Rights Knowledge, Attitude, Practise and Participation of Mothers

The ICDS projects functioning under government management and non-government organisation management were selected for the study, that is Puttur and Tirupati ICDS projects respectively. The management either government or NGO has their functioning style which influences the staff attendance, performance and utilisation of services by the beneficiaries. Further the management's efforts to provide child rights information to their personnel especially to those working at field level and distribution of such information to the beneficiaries may also depend on the type of management.

In the present study the sample was divided into two groups based on the type of ICDS project management in which their children are attending anganwadi programme that is government (Puttur) and NGO (Tirupati). The difference between the mothers whose children are attending anganwadis run by government and non-government organisation and their child rights knowledge, attitude, practise and participation in anganwadi activities were examined using *t-test* as shown in Table 4.54.

From the Table 4.54, it is clear that the mothers did not differ significantly on their child rights knowledge. But significant difference was found between the two groups of mothers for child rights attitudes, practises and participation.

Table 4.54: ICDS Project Management and Child Rights Knowledge, Attitude, Practise and Participation of Mothers

S. No.	*Dependant variables*	*Management of Anganwadi*	*N*	*Mean*	*SD values*	*t-value*	*p-value*	*Remarks*
1.	Standard score of knowledge of mothers	GO mothers	100	49.52	0.71	0.459	0.646	Not Significant
		NGO mothers	100	49.47	0.89			
2.	Standard score of attitude of mothers	GO mothers	100	78.16	8.61	18.338	0.000	**Significant at 1% Level
		NGO mothers	100	58.28	6.58			
3.	Standard score of practise of mothers	GO mothers	100	115.26	11.15	-2.878	0.004	**Significant at 1% Level
		NGO mothers	100	119.50	9.60			
4.	Standard score of participation of mothers	GO mothers	100	81.08	55.46	–3.204	0.002	**Significant at 1% Level
		NGO mothers	100	106.75	57.81			

Note: p-value > 0.01 level of significant

This shows that the type of management had an influence on the mothers child rights attitudes, practises and participation in anganwadi activities.

ASSOCIATION OF CHILD RIGHTS KNOWLEDGE, ATTITUDE AND PRACTISE, PARTICIPATION WITH THE INDEPENDENT VARIABLES OF THE MOTHERS OF THE ANGANWADI CHILDREN

The relationship between dependent variables *viz.,* child rights knowledge, attitudes, practise and participation of mothers with the independent variables *viz.,* age, location of anganwadi, annual income, family type, number of children was studied using chi-square-test.

Association of Child Rights Knowledge, Attitude and Practise, Participation with the Age of the Mothers of Anganwadi Children

The association between age and child rights knowledge, attitudes practises and participation of mothers was studied using chi-square test as shown in Table 4.55.

Table 4.55: Association of Child Rights Knowledge, Attitudes Practises with the Age of Mothers of Attending Anganwadi Children

S. No.	*Dependent Variables*	*χ^2 calculated value*	*df*	*χ^2 table value*	*Remarks*
1.	Child rights knowledge of mothers	0.57	2	5.99	Not Significant
2.	Child rights attitudes of mothers	4.76	4	9.49	Not Significant
3.	Child rights practise of mothers	8.64	4	9.49	Not Significant
4.	Participation of mothers	0.40	4	9.49	Not Significant

From the Table 4.55, it is evident that there was no association between the age of the mothers and their child rights knowledge, attitudes practises and participation in anganwadi activities. Similar results were also found in ANOVA test that is, the mothers did not differ either between groups or within the groups with regard to their age and child rights knowledge, attitudes, practises and participation in anganwadi activities. It indicates that the age had no influence on child rights knowledge, attitudes, practises and participation of mothers in this study.

Association of Child Rights Knowledge, Attitudes, Practises and Participation with the Location of Anganwadi of the Mothers of attending Anganwadi Children

The association between the location of anganwadi and the child rights knowledge, attitudes, practises and participation was studied with the help of chi-square-test as shown in Table 4.56.

Table 4.56: Association of Child Rights Knowledge, Attitudes, Practises with the Location of Anganwadi of the Mothers of attending Anganwadi Children

S. No.	*Dependent Variables*	*χ^2 calculated value*	*df*	*χ^2 table value*	*Remarks*
1.	Child rights knowledge of Mothers	6.29	2	5.99	*Significant at 0.05 level
2.	Child rights attitudes of Mothers	20.22	4	18.47	***Significant at 0.001 level
3.	Child rights practise of Mothers	4.49	4	9.49	Not Significant
4.	Participation of Mothers	17.11	4	9.49	*Significant at 0.05 level

* Significant level at 0.05

*** Significant level at 0.001

From the above table, it is evident that the location of anganwadi is significantly associated with child rights knowledge, attitudes and participation in anganwadi activities. The location of anganwadi was not significantly associated with the child rights practises. It shows that location of anganwadi may have an influence on child rights knowledge, attitudes and participation of mothers.

Association of Child Rights Knowledge, Attitudes, Practises and Participation with the Annual Income of Mothers

The association between the annual income and the child rights knowledge, attitudes, practises and participation of mothers is given in Table 4.57.

Table 4.57: Association of Child Rights Knowledge, Attitudes, Practises and Participation with the Annual Income of Mothers

S. No.	*Dependent Variables*	*χ^2 calculated value*	*df*	*χ^2 table value*	*Remarks*
1.	Child rights knowledge of mothers	4.69	1	3.84	*Significant
2.	Child rights attitudes of mothers	0.18	2	5.99	Not Significant
3.	Child rights practise of mothers	3.45	2	5.99	Not Significant
4.	Participation of mothers	1.99	2	5.99	Not Significant

* Significant value at 0.05 level

From the above table, it is clear that there is an association between the annual income of mothers and their child rights knowledge. But no association found between the annual income of mothers and their child rights attitudes, practises and participation in anganwadi activities.

Association of Child Rights Knowledge, Attitude, Practise and participation with the Family Type of Mothers

The relationship between the family type and child rights knowledge, attitudes, practises and participation of mothers in anganwadi centre activities is presented in Table No.4.58.

Table 4.58: Association of Child Rights Knowledge, Attitudes, Practises and Participation with the Family Type of Mothers

S. No.	*Dependent Variables*	*χ^2 calculated value*	*df*	*χ^2 table value*	*Remarks*
1.	Child rights knowledge of mothers	0.05	1	3.84	Not Significant
2.	Child rights attitudes of mothers	2.65	2	5.99	Not Significant
3.	Child rights practise of mothers	0.09	2	5.99	Not Significant
4.	Participation of mothers	2.50	2	5.99	Not Significant

From the Table 4.58, it is clear that there is no association found between the family type and child rights knowledge, attitudes, practises and participation of mothers in anganwadi activities.

Association between type of management and Child Rights Knowledge, Attitude, Practises and Participation of Mothers in Anganwadi Activities

The relationship between the type of management that is the ICDS projects functioning under government and non-government organisation managements and child rights knowledge, attitudes, practises and participation of mothers in the anganwadi activities was examined using chi-square test is given in Table 4.59.

From the Table 4.59, it is clear that the type of management showed significant association with the child rights attitudes, practises and participation of mothers. There was no association between the type of management and child rights knowledge of mothers. This shows that the type of management had an influence on child rights attitudes,

Table 4.59: Association between Type of Management and Child Rights Knowledge, Attitudes, Practises and Participation of Mothers in Anganwadi Activities

S. No.	*Dependent Variables*	*χ^2 calculated value*	*df*	*χ^2 table value*	*Remarks*
1.	Child rights knowledge of mothers	0.92	1	3.84	Not Significant
2.	Child rights attitudes of mothers	85.81	2	13.82	***Significant at 0.001 level
3.	Child rights practise of mothers	6.86	2	5.99	*Significant at 0.05 level
4.	Participation of mothers	22.95	2	13.82	***Significant at 0.001 level

*** Significant value at 0.001 level
* Significant value at 0.05 level

practises of mothers and also on their participation in anganwadi activities.

NUTRITIONAL STATUS OF ANGANWADI CHILDREN

The ICDS programme was expected to prevent the incidence of severe malnutrition of the kind that has been reported in some parts of the country. However, after 30 years of operation, the ICDS is yet to have an impact on the poor nutritional status of children. The ICDS has to be converted into a true health, nutrition and development programme, and not limited to a food dole programme (Ghosh, S. 2004).

According to Vimala Ramachandran (2005) in Rajasthan and Uttar Pradesh there was not even a single instance where the anganwadi worker (AWW) had monitored a grade 3 or 4 malnourished child and used the opportunity to demonstrate the effectiveness of supplementary feeding. anganwadi workers find it easier to manage older children and are not motivated to provide home-based care or services. Monitoring systems currently used do not capture the range and quality of services provided to under 3 years.

In order to examine the implications of nutrition services rendered at the anganwadi centres, an attempt was made to assess the nutritional status of children selected for the study from 20 anganwadi centres of two ICDS projects. For assessment of nutritional status, the anthropometric measurements *viz.*, height, weight and mid upper arm circumference (MUAC) was selected as they are commonly used in anganwadis.

The age of children was taken from the attendance registers. Using the equipment available at the anganwadi centre *viz.*, beam balance, height stand and MUAC tape, the weights heights and MUAC of the sample were collected at each anganwadi. Thus weights, heights and MUAC of all the two hundred children from 20 anganwadi centres were collected and pooled.

Hypothesis 12: There is no difference between mothers of children attending anganwadi centers run by government organisations and non governmental organisations management with regard to their child rights knowledge, attitude and practise.

The type of management had an association with the child rights attitudes, practise and participation of mothers, but had no significant association with the child right knowledge of mothers, hence hypothesis 12 is rejected.

Hypothesis 13: There is no relationship between child rights knowledge, attitude and practise of anganwadi workers and mothers. The hypothesis 13 is accepted as there is no relationship between mothers and anganwadi workers with regard to their child rights knowledge, attitudes and practises.

Weight for Age

The age, weights and heights of each child was compared with the national centre for health statistics (NCHS) standards in order to calculate percentage of NCHS values. The weights of children for their age were classified using Indian Academy of Paediatrics (IAP) classification in order to grade their nutritional status; as normal, grade-I, grade-II, grade-III and grade-IV, as shown in Table 4.60.

Table 4.60: Distribution of Children according to their Weight for Age

S. No.	Age in years	Percentage of Children					Total
		Normal	Grade-I	Grade-II	Grade-III	Grade-IV	
1.	2 – 3	83	14	3	-	-	100
2.	4 – 5	77	15	8	-	-	100

From the above table, it is clear that majority of children in the age group 2 to 3 years and 4 to 5 years were normal. Around 14 per cent and 3 per cent of children in the age group of 2 to 3 years had mild and moderate malnutrition respectively. Similarly 15 per cent and 8 per cent of children in the age group of 4 to 5 years had mild and moderate malnutrition respectively.

None of the children found to have grade-III and grade-IV malnutrition. This may be attributed to the nutrition services of anganwadi centres.

Height for Age

Height for age is a measure of stunting. It is well known that height for age is less only when children are exposed to malnutrition over a long period. Using height for age of NCHS standards, children were classified into different grades of stunting as shown in table No.4.61.

Table 4.61: Classification of Children according to their Height for Age

S. No.	Age of Children	Percentage of Children			Total
		Normal	Stunting	Severe stunting	
1.	2 – 3	79	21	-	100
2.	4 – 5	61	39	-	100

From the Table 4.61, it is evident that (79%) of children in the age group of 2-3 years and (61%) of children in the age group of 4-5 years were found to be normal. Around 21 per cent of children in the age group of 2-3 years and 39 per cent of children in the age group of 4 to 5 years found to be stunted, that is their percentage heights for age of NCHS median values were less than two standard deviation (<2 SD). This shows that though majority of children had normal heights for their age, considerable percentage of children showed stunted growth.

Mid Upper Arm Circumference of Children

The arm circumference increases rapidly from birth to one year from 11 cms to 16 cms between the first and fifth years, it remains fairly constant at about 16 to 17 cms among well nourished children. During this time, the fat of early infancy is replaced by muscle. A value of 16.5 cm is the reference cut off point used as standard. The children are classified based on their MUAC into grades of malnutrition *viz.,* normal (above 13.5 cms), mild malnutrition (12.5 to 13.5 cms) and severely malnourished (less than 12.5 cms).

Table 4.62: Distribution of Children according to their Grades of Malnutrition for MUAC

S. No.	*Age of Children*	*Percentage of Children*			*Total*
		Normal > 13.5 cms	*Grade-I 12.5-13.5 cms*	*Grade-II <12.5 cms*	
1.	2 – 3	81	19	-	100
2.	4 – 5	75	25	-	100

From the above table, it is clear that majority of the children fell in the category of normal. Whereas 19 per cent of children aged between 2-3 years and 25 per cent of children aged between 4-5 years had grade-I malnutrition as their MUAC values were between 12.5 to 13.5 cms.

Thus the nutritional status of children under study indicates majority of children found to be normal. When children were graded for their nutritional status on the basis of their height for age and MUAC considerable percentage of children were found to have mild malnutrition. When weight for age was used for classification of children into different grades of malnutrition, a small percentage of children fell in the category of moderate malnutrition. This shows that considerable percentage of children were malnourished, requiring nutritional intervention.

The anganwadi workers should share the information related to nutritional status of children with their mothers, in order to educate them and guide them in monitoring the nutritional status and growth of children. Growth is a irrecoverable process, the timely intervention is the only solution to prevent the losses of malnutrition.

QUALITY OF HEALTH, NUTRITION AND EDUCATION SERVICES DELIVERED AT THE ANGANWADI CENTRES

The goal of the anganwadi programme was to provide a set of services that consisted of supplementary nutrition for pregnant women and young children, and education, immunisations, and preventive medicine for poor and lower-caste children. The immunisation programme was operated by the health department, which ran the primary health centers (PHCs). It thus took advantage of the presence of a large number of children and "atrisk" women in the anganwadi to inoculate children, pregnant women, and nursing mothers against the most common diseases. After experimenting with supplementary nutrition programmes that produced generally poor results (Tandon, Ramachandran, and Bhatnagar 1981: 382), the ICDS programme was initiated to provide a package of well-integrated services that would combine nutrition, health, education, and day care for children under six years of age, and nutrition and health for pregnant women (Heaver 1989; Sharma 1986; Tandon, Ramachandran, and Bhatnagar 1981).

The health, nutrition and education services included in the package of services expected to be delivered to the beneficiaries of ICDS programme at the anganwadi centre were included in a 'check list' developed to assess the quality of services. The investigator observed whole days programme at twenty anganwadi centres belonging to two ICDS projects and interacted with the anganwadi workers, helpers, children and mothers. The checklists were filled in by the investigator based on her observations and interactions with the stakeholders at the anganwadi level.

Another area of concern was the quantity given to each child. Given the village milieu, the anganwadi workers distributed the supplements to any child who came to the centre. In two anganwadi centres of Rajasthan, we also observed old women (who had little or no family support) and men coming to the centre for food. We did not come across any child who was officially getting double rations even though nearly all the registers recorded two to four children as being given double rations. The anganwadi workers were at a loss trying to name the children who were identified as the recipients of double rations (Vimala Ramachandran, 2005).

The anganwadi workers is expected to distribute iron folic acid tablets, vitamin A and riboflavine to children and expectant mothers. In majority of anganwadi workers iron folic acid tablets are given to children and mothers but riboflavine is not distributed in all the anganwadi centres. The ratings for nutritional supplements indicate that (35%) of anganwadi centres were rated as very good, 55 per cent of anganwadi centres were rated as good and only 10 per cent of anganwadi centres were rated as average.

Worm infestation is common health problem among anganwadi children. The treatment includes one tablet of Mebendazole with water twice a day for 3 consecutive days. The anganwadi worker is expected to provide this service to anganwadi children with the help of Medical Officer of ANM.

The health, nutrition and education services rendered to the beneficiaries were rated on a five point scale given in the check list *viz.,* very good, good, average, poor and very poor which is shown in Table 4.63.

Table 4.63: Quality of Health, Nutrition and Preschool Education Services of ICDS Programme

S. No.	*Description of Services*	*Very Good*	*Good*	*Avg.*	*Poor*	*Very Poor*
1.	Health check-up once in 3 months Medical Officer/ Local Health Visitor/ Auxillary Nurse Mid wife	45	30	25	-	-
2.	Vital statistics in MMR (Birth rate, still birth rate, infant mortality rate, morality rate, maternal mortality rate) pregnant and lactating women	70	30	-	-	-
3.	Immunisation to children (BCG, DPT, Polio, TT, Hepatitis B), immunisation to pregnant women	100	-	-	-	-
4.	Nutritional supplements to pregnant and lactating women	35	55	10	-	-
	Nutritional supplements vitamin A, iron, folic acid, riboflavin					
5.	Deworming to children, deworming to mothers and child family	90	10	-	-	-
6.	Children and pregnant women, nutritional status assessment	100	-	-	-	-
7a.	Supplementary nutrition to children	100	-	-	-	-
b.	Supplementary nutrition to malnourished children	100	-	-	-	-
c.	Supplementary nutrition to pregnant and lactating women	100	-	-	-	-

(Contd...)

8.	Health nutrition, child care and population education to mothers.	20	35	15	20	10
9.	Promotion of breadfeeding	35	65	-	-	-
10.	Pre-school education use of play, educational material	15	30	30	15	10
11.	Screening of HIV/AIDS infected (Mothers and children)	80	20	-	-	-

From the Table 4.63, it is evident that health check-up was rated as very good in (45%) of centres, as good in 30 per cent of centres and as average in 25 per cent of centres. This indicates that the health check-up, which is to be done at least once in three days, is not done regularly in the anganwadi centres under study.

The monthly monitoring reports should include vital statistics *viz.,* Birth rate, still birth rate, infant mortality rate, under five mortality rate, maternal mortality rate, number of pregnant and lactating women in the anganwadi area. This responsibility of anganwadi workers was rated as very good (70%) and good (30%).

All the children and pregnant women in the anganwadi area are covered under immunisation programme. Hence this service of ICDS was rated as very good in all the centres.

Supply of nutritional supplements *viz.,* iron folic acid tablets and vitamin-A for pregnant women and nursing mothers along with nutritional counselling was included in the package of services of ICDS. Only iron folic acid (IFA) are distributed to women as and when the supply was received. This service of ICDS was rated as very good in 35 per cent centres and good in 55 per cent centres and average in 10 per cent of centres.

Deworming tablets are provided to children once a year in majority of anganwadi centres. But these tablets are not given to child's mothers and family members, from whom the child has the easy possibility of getting infested again. The Deworming of children was rated as very good in 90 per cent of centres and good in 10 per cent of centres.

One of the prime duties of the anganwadi workers is to monitor the growth of children through monthly assessment of nutritional status. While majority of anganwadi workers maintains the records for nutritional status accurately, the information was not shared with the mothers of children to improve the nutritional status. Mere provision of supplementary nutrition and assessment of nutritional. Status may not alleviate the problem of under-nutrition. This service of anganwadi was rated as very good in all the of anganwadi centres.

The supplementary nutrition to children in anganwadi centres was rated as very good in all the twenty-anganwadi centres. The regular supplementary nutrition given to normal children provides 300 K.Cals and 8-10 gms of protein. The supplementary nutrition given to severely malnourished (Grade III and Grade IV) children should provide 600 K.Cals and 18-20 gms of protein in three to four feeds out of which at least 2 feeds should be given at the anganwadi. This service is not observed in any of the anganwadis as there were no severely malnourished children in any of the anganwadis.

According to Dipa Sinha (2004) the ICDS provides one kind of food for all children in this age group, and another more nutritious powder for children who suffer from grade III and grade IV malnutrition. There is no explanation about whether this is enough, whether the child should be fed anything else, or how many times a day the feed should be given and in what form. There are instances where the parents did not feed the child anything else once they got powder from the anganwadi worker, which is actually not enough for the entire day. Further, when some children contract diarrhoea on eating this food, other mothers stop feeding the child anganwadi food. Clearly, there is no one who will tell them about the right practice when something like this happens.

The supplementary nutrition given to pregnant and lactating women provides 500 K.Cals of energy and 20-25 gms of protein per day. All the anganwadi centres understudy distributes the supplementary nutrition regularly to the pregnant and lactating women enrolled. Hence this service of anganwadi were rated as very good for all the anganwadi centres under study.

An Integrated Child Development Service (ICDS) survey of 52 anganwadi community workers and 156 mothers of ICDS beneficiary children in Nelamangala, Bangalore, India, in order to ascertain the practices of mothers in managing diarrhoea and respiratory infections and nutrition. The results would be applied to improving health education and developing appropriate and effective communication about nutrition and health between the anganwadi workers and the mothers (Vasundhara, Harish, 1993).

Health and nutrition education to adolescent girls, women, mothers is one of the enlisted activities of anganwadi centre. The anganwadi workers are unable to deliver this service effectively to adolescent girls and women owing to several factors. This service of anganwadi centres were rated as very good in 20 per cent of centres, good in 35 per cent centres, average in 15 per cent centres, poor in 20 per cent centres and very poor in 10 per cent of anganwadi centres under study.

All the anganwadi centres celebrates international week for promotion of breast-feeding from 1st to 7th August. The anganwadi workers role in promotion of breast-feeding in their anganwadi area was rated as very good in 35 per cent and good in 65 per cent of centres.

The early childhood care and preschool education (ECCE) component of the ICDS may well be considered as the backbone of the ICDS programme. This is also the most joyful play way daily activity, visibly sustained for three hours a day. It brings and keeps young children at the anganwadi centre – an activity that motivates parents and communities.

ECCE, as envisaged in the ICDS, focusses on the total development of the child, in the age range of up to six years, from the under privileged groups. The early childhood pre-school education programme, conducted through the medium of play, aims at providing a learning environment for the promotion of social, emotional, cognitive, physical and aesthetic development of the child. It also contributes to the universalisation of primary education.

The quality of preschool education offered in anganwadi centres depends on the interest and commitment of the anganwadi workers. It was observed that except for few anganwadi centres, in many of the anganwadi centres the early childhood education programme is confined to four walls of anganwadi centre and the activities were conducted as a routine. The ratings for the preschool education programme was very good in 15 per cent, good in 30 per cent, average in 30 per cent, poor in 15 and very poor in 10 per cent centres.

The ICDS programme under its health services does not specify any service to mothers infected with AIDS, children infected with AIDS and children affected with AIDS. It was observed that majority of anganwadi centres of both ICDS projects under study had HIV/AIDS positive cases enrolled in ICDS as beneficiaries. During the interaction with the anganwadi workers, helpers and mothers it was revealed that

1. The pregnant and nursing mothers infected with HIV/AIDS were sent to nearby voluntary counselling and testing centres (VCTCs).
2. The children infected with AIDS (CIAs) and children of HIV/AIDS (CAAs) patients were also allowed to participate in anganwadi activities.
3. Although there is no visible discrimination of CIAs and CAAs in the anganwadi centres with regard to supplementary nutrition and education.

The children were not mingling with the CIAs, the ICDS services for HIV/AIDs infected mothers and children were rated as very good in (80%) and good in 20 per cent centres.

The ICDS may include provision of additional nutrition supplementation to the pregnant, lactating women and children infected with HIV/AIDS as they are in need of such nutritional support.

The health, nutrition and education services provided under ICDS programme at the anganwadi centres were assessed for their quality in selected anganwadi centres, which showed that immunisation and supplementary nutrition to children and mothers were rated as very good for all twenty centres under study. Only the health and nutrition education services to women and adolescent girls and pre-school education programme to children found to be poor and very poor in 30 per cent and 35 per cent of centres respectively. The remaining 9 services were rated as very good to average. This indicates that the quality of preschool education to children and health and nutrition education services to mothers and adolescent girls education has to be improved in order to achieve long lasting results in the area of health, nutrition and education. The coverage of child rights in ICDS programme is inadequate.

Hypothesis 1: "The coverage of child rights in ICDS programme is inadequate" is accepted.

According to Sarada (2006) the ICDS programme is very much relevant to the needs of children and all of its services are not well utilised by the beneficiaries. The main reason being-lack of awareness regarding the services. The quality of physical facilities available in the anganwadi centres was also found to be poor and makes it difficult for the anganwadi worker to conduct a quality programme for the children. The ICDS being the largest national programme encompassing children and mother centered services such as health, nutrition, early childhood education, needs to be improved in terms of physical facilities and publicity. The participation of mothers was found to be inadequate. The mothers, knowledge and skills on child care needs to be improved.

The anganwadi workers need to show greater empathy and reachout to children who are in dire need of proper nutrition and health care services. They have to transform themselves into 'professional care-givers', working with and giving attention to fewer numbers of children. This is especially true for children in poverty situation. All this does not only mean more resources, but a lot more care and attention. Can we not involve mothers in the nutrition component of the ICDS programme. May be this is asking too much of a system that is so enormous and impersonal. But there are no shortcuts – children need care, love and, above all, individualised attention.

The time has come to turn the ICDS programme upside down – doing away with the existing model and thinking afresh on how best we can reach out to the most vulnerable. We need to plan separately for different sub-groups of children – looking at the specific needs of home-based care and outreach services upto 3 years and a centre based approach for the 3+ group. It may be worthwhile discussing the possibility of splitting the ICDS programme into two : (a) a dedicated home-based programme to promote health and nutrition of children in the 0-3 group; health and nutrition of adolescent girls and pregnant and lactating mothers; (b) a centre-based nutrition and pre-school education programme for 3-6 years. This is essential if we are serious about reaching out to this very important segment of our population. Poor health, malnutrition and frequent bouts of illness at this stage have an irreversible impact on the overall health and well being of children.

Given the enormous diversity in the country and different administrative environments, political leadership and awareness levels among the people, the government needs to initiate a state-wise revisioning exercise to revisit the objectives of the ICDS programme – within the agreed ICDS conceptual framework. This is essential to secure the commitment of the state leadership to the core objectives of the programme. This needs to be followed by stakeholders' meetings at the state and district levels, with political leaders and other important opinion makers in the State.

MAJOR FINDINGS

- Majority of anganwadi workers that is (49%) were aged between 30-35 years, followed by 34.5 per cent aged between 25-30 years, and only 16.5 per cent belonged to the age group of 20-25 years.
- Majority of anganwadi workers (94.5%) were married and only 5.5 per cent were unmarried.
- Around 34.5 per cent of anganwadi workers were residing in rural areas, a 22.5 per cent were residents of urban area, a 25.5 per cent were urban slum dwellers and 17.5 per cent were living in remote areas on the out skirts of towns. This shows that only a small percentage lived in urban areas.
- Most of the anganwadi workers (61.5%) were educated upto 10th class. Around 29 per cent had intermediate education and only 9.5 per cent of the sample were educated upto degree level.
- Majority of the sample (68.5%) had service below 5 years, a 9 per cent of anganwadi workers had 6-10 years of service, a 14 per cent had a service between 11-15 years and only 8.5 per cent had service above 15 years.
- Majority (80.5%) of anganwadi workers was not trained. Only a 19.5 per cent were trained. This may be due to the anganwadi workers changing their jobs as unmarried anganwadi workers leaving the place and their jobs after their marriage.
- Majority (98%) of the sample received materials from ICDS, only 2 per cent have not received materials.
- Majority of anganwadi workers received current information about ICDS from the supervisors and also in the form of newsletters at the time of data collection. Currently a monthly magazine "*Indira*

Darshini" is published and distributed to anganwadi centres.

- A 29 per cent of anganwadi workers did not receive refresher training. A good majority (71%) of the anganwadi workers received refresher training once in their service. Data regarding the year of refresher training revealed that among those who received training (77.46%) of anganwadi workers received 5 years before that is from the date of data collection (during the year 2004) for the present study. Around 12.6 per cent of the sample received refresher training 10 years before, a 7.04 per cent of the sample and 2.82 per cent of the anganwadi workers received refresher training before 15 years and above 15 years respectively. This shows that the refresher training is not received by the anganwadi workers periodically, which is essential for updating their knowledge.

- A 76.5 per cent of anganwadi workers felt that mothers' meetings create awareness on childcare. 73 per cent stated that they impart knowledge on child nutrition, a 49 per cent of anganwadi workers felt that mothers meetings were helpful in gaining knowledge on maternal and child health. Around 94 per cent of anganwadi workers perceived that all the above three were learned by the mothers during mothers' meetings.

- Only 2.5 per cent of the anganwadi workers had adequate job satisfaction, a 4 per cent of the anganwadi workers were able to do some works, 31.5 per cent were able to do all works, a 29.5 per cent stated that they need to develop and 32.5 per cent of anganwadi workers expressed that they are working with limitations. Thus, the data indicates only a small percentage of anganwadi workers had adequate satisfaction.

- Majority of anganwadi workers (62.5%) were educating people about ICDS services by utilising local events and public meetings. Around 30 per cent of the anganwadi workers indicated that pasting posters and distribution of handouts on ICDS services is the mode of spreading ICDS information. Only a 7.5 per cent of anganwadi workers opined that they were spreading messages during surveys and home visits. None of the anganwadi workers opined that their efforts were nominal in this aspect. Thus the data reflects that anganwadi workers are making efforts in educating the people about ICDS services in their areas.

❖ Almost all anganwadi workers (99%) stated that their centres are accessible to all the people, 54.5 per cent of anganwadi centres have pucca building, 96 per cent anganwadi centres has good sanitation, a 77 per cent of anganwadi buildings are providing protection, a 64.5 per cent of anganwadi centres were provided with water facilities and 34 per cent of anganwadi centres have toilet facilities. The above data reflects that all the facilities are not available uniformly in all the anganwadis. Some of the anganwadis have inadequate facilities. This need to be taken care because it will affect the allround development of children who are in crucial period of development.

❖ A 3 per cent of anganwadi workers were not aware of child rights and (97%) of sample were aware of child rights. Only 1.5 per cent of the anganwadi workers were not aware of child rights as declared by United Nations. A great majority of the anganwadi workers were aware of child rights.

❖ A (85.8%) of anganwadi workers came to know about child rights through ICDS. Around 0.5 per cent of the sample indicated their family as the source of knowing about child rights. A 3.6 per cent of anganwadi workers could know about child rights through mass media. Around 8.6 per cent of the sample came to know about child rights through ICDS and their families. Only 1.5 per cent indicated ICDS, family and mass media as their sources of knowing about child rights.

- A 40 per cent of anganwadi workers felt that there is no need for any change in the ICDS programme. Around 60 per cent of the anganwadi workers felt that changes can be made in the ICDS programme on the basis of child rights.
- Majority of mothers (55.5%) belonged to 20-25 years age group. A 32.5 per cent of the sample were aged between 25-30 years and 12 per cent of mothers belonged to the age group of 30-35 years.
- A (69.5%) of the anganwadi children were attending anganwadis located in urban slum, 12 per cent of the children are attending anganwadis located in urban areas and 18.5 per cent of children of the sample were attending anganwadi centres located in rural areas. This shows that majority of anganwadis attended by children of the sample were located in urban slum.
- The educational status of the mothers shows that 33 per cent were illiterates, 5 per cent were literates, 21 per cent had primary education, 33 per cent had high school education and 8 per cent had college education.
- Majority of mothers (60.5%) were housewives, 34.5 per cent were daily wage earners, followed by 3.5 per cent of women engaged in petty business, 0.5 per cent employed in private sector and 1 per cent employed in government sector. This shows that majority of women were housewives who will be available to their children throughout the day unlike working mothers.
- A (86%) of mothers had an annual income of below Rs.12,000, around 10.5 per cent of the sample had

annual income between Rs.12,001 to 18,000, a 2 per cent had annual income between Rs.18,001 to 24,000 and 1.5 per cent had annual income above 24,001. This shows that majority of mothers had income below poverty line.

- Among the mothers studied 55.5 per cent were having ration card and remaining 44.5 per cent do not possess a ration card, among the ration card holders 87.37 per cent had white ration card and 12.63 per cent had pink ration card. Although many of the mothers belonged to lower income group, they do not have a ration card.

- Majority (85 per cent) of the mothers of anganwadi children had family size of 5-8 members. Around 9 per cent of the sample had small families of less than 4 members. Only 6 per cent had family size above 9 members.

- A 55.5 per cent of the mothers belonged to nuclear–two parent family, 3.5 per cent belonged to nuclear single parent family, 2.5 per cent were from extended families and 38.5 per cent were from joint families.

- A 83 per cent of the mothers had 2-4 children. Whereas 17 per cent had less than 2 children.

- A 99 per cent of the sample have access to primary health centre, only 1 per cent did not have access to PHC services. Majority of the sample rated the PHC services as good and very good.

- Majority of the sample rated the anganwadi services as good and very good, (39% and 33.5%) respectively. Only 5.5 per cent and 22 per cent rated anganwadi services availability as 'nominal' and 'to some extent' respectively.

- The water facilities in Municipal and Panchayat areas were accessible to 99 per cent of the sample and for only 1 per cent it is not accessible. Majority of the sample rated water facilities as nominal and average. Only a 19 per cent rated water facilities as good and around 19.5 per cent rated it as very good.

- With regard to Municipal/Panchayat services the 55.5 per cent of the respondents stated that they are not available. A 44.5 per cent stated that Panchayat and Municipal services are available and their ratings for these services ranged from nominal to good.
- Around 23 per cent of the sample had no access to civil supplies and 77 per cent had access to civil supplies. The ratings for civil supplies indicate that nominal 4 per cent, average 29 per cent, good 26.5 per cent and very good 17.5 per cent.
- Primary school education programme is available to (99%) of the sample. A 47.5 per cent rated the primary school education services as good and 11 per cent rated it as very good. A 4 per cent and 36.5 per cent of the sample rated this services as a nominal and average respectively.
- The non-formal education services are accessible to (67.5%) of the sample and not accessible to 32.5 per cent of the sample. A 24.5 per cent and 42.5 per cent of the sample rated non-formal education services as good and very good respectively.
- Electricity facility is accessible to all the respondents. A good majority of the sample rated electricity facility as good (44.5%) and very good (28%). Only 8 per cent and 19.5 per cent of the sample rated electricity facility as nominal and average respectively.
- The law and order services were not accessible to 33 per cent of the sample. Only (67%) of the sample had access to these services. Around 1.5 per cent and 16.5 per cent of the sample rated law and order

services as nominal and average respectively. A 33 per cent and 16 per cent of the sample rated these services as good and very good respectively.

- Child rights knowledge scores of anganwadi workers belonging to government and non-government organisation ICDS projects indicated that there is not much difference between mean knowledge scores of the anganwadi workers of two ICDS projects. They did not vary much in their scores as the standard deviation value for government and non-government organisation anganwadi workers is 0.7 and 0.72 respectively. With regard to attitudes also there is not much difference between the anganwadi workers of two ICDS projects in their child rights attitudinal mean scores. The anganwadi workers varied in their attitudinal scores as the standard deviation values were 5.69 for government anganwadi workers and 4.96 for non-government organisation anganwadi workers. The mean child rights practises scores of government organisation anganwadi workers were 29.71 and non-government organisation anganwadi workers were 31.05. The standard deviation values 4.46 and 3.64 indicate that the anganwadi workers varied in their child rights practises.

- The anganwadi workers knowledge, attitudes and practises had no correlation with each other indicates that there is no consistent relationship. The anganwadi workers knowledge, attitudes and practises may not have an influence on each other.

- Age did not seem to have an influence on the child rights knowledge, attitude, practise of the anganwadi workers. The anganwadi workers did not differ with in the groups and between groups with regard to their knowledge, attitude, practise on child rights.

- Educational status seems to had no influence on the child rights knowledge, attitude and practise of the anganwadi workers. The anganwadi workers did not differ with in the groups and between groups with regard to their knowledge, attitude and practise on child rights.
- Place of residence also seems to had no influence on the child rights, knowledge, attitude and practise of the anganwadi workers. The anganwadi workers did not differ with in the groups and between groups with regard to their knowledge, attitude and practise on child rights.
- The anganwadi workers did not differ significantly on their child rights knowledge,. attitude and practise on the basis of their marital status. The results may not be generalised as the number of unmarried anganwadi workers (11 members) were not proportionate to the number of married anganwadi workers (189 members), in the sample.
- The job experience in general equips the anganwadi workers with skills needed to perform their work effectively. The anganwadi workers did not differ significantly with regard to their knowledge and attitudes, either between groups or within groups. The anganwadi workers showed significant difference with regard to child rights practise.
- No significant difference between the anganwadi workers having a length of service, below 5 years, 6-10 years and above 15 years with regard to their child right practise, there is significant difference between the anganwadi workers having 11-15 years of service and other groups with regard to child rights practises.
- Anganwadi workers did not differ significantly either between groups or with in groups with regard

to their child rights knowledge, practise and the training received. The anganwadi workers showed significant difference for the child rights attitudes and the training received. In order to examine the difference between groups with regard to child rights attitudes a Duncan Multiple Range Test was employed. The anganwadi workers, who have received training 6-10 years ago differed significantly with other groups *viz.*, not trained, below 5 years, 11-15 years and above 15 years with regard to their child rights attitudes.

- ❖ The anganwadi workers belonging to government organisation and non-governmental organisation management did not differ significantly on their child rights attitudes and practises, but significant difference was found between two groups of the anganwadi workers with regard to their child rights knowledge.
- ❖ There is no association between child rights knowledge and the age of anganwadi workers. Similarly no association was found between child rights practises and the age of anganwadi workers, but there was an association between the child rights attitude and the age of anganwadi workers. Although the results of ANOVA for the above variables indicated no significant difference among the anganwadi workers with regard to child rights knowledge, attitude and practise. However, the chi-square test indicated an association between child rights attitudes and the age of anganwadi workers.
- ❖ There is no association between anganwadi workers child rights knowledge, attitude and practise and educational status. This shows that there is no significant relationship between the child rights knowledge, attitude, practise and the educational status of anganwadi workers. The ANOVA test employed to examine the difference between the

educational status and child rights knowledge attitude, practise of anganwadi workers also showed no significant difference.

- ❖ There is no association between anganwadi workers child rights knowledge, attitude, practise and the place of residence of anganwadi workers. This indicates that there is no significant relationship between child rights knowledge, attitudes, practise and the place of residence of anganwadi workers. The results of ANOVA test conducted for the same variables showed that the anganwadi workers did not differ significantly with regard to their child rights knowledge, attitude and practise. This further affirms that place of residence may not have an influence on child rights knowledge, attitude and practise of anganwadi workers.
- ❖ The dependent variables *viz.*, child rights knowledge, child rights practises had no association with the independent variable, ICDS project management. The relation between the child rights attitudes and ICDS project management was found though the above results indicates that there is significant relationship between anganwadi workers child rights attitudes and ICDS project management. The *t-test* computed for the same variables indicate that the anganwadi workers showed, significant difference with regard to their child rights knowledge. This may not be attributed to management efforts, as during the study period none of the managements provided child rights information to their anganwadi workers.
- ❖ The mean child rights knowledge scores of mothers of government and non-government ICDS projects were 37.6 and 37.3 respectively, and the standard deviation values were 0.7 and 0.72 respectively. This shows that there is not much variation among mothers with regard to their child rights knowledge

scores. The mean child rights attitudes scores of mothers, whose children attending ICDS projects of government and non-government mothers were 49.3 and 49.4 respectively. The standard deviation values were 5.7 and 5.0 respectively, that is the mothers varied in their child rights attitudes scores. The mean child rights practise scores of government and non-government mothers were 39.19 and 40.63 respectively. The standard deviation values were 3.79 and 3.27 respectively. This shows that though the mothers did not vary in their child rights knowledge scores, variation was observed among the mothers with regard to attitudes and practises.

❖ The participation of mothers in anganwadi activities had significant negative correlation at 0.05 level with the child rights knowledge of mothers. The (negative) correlation between participation of mothers child rights knowledge indicates that participation showed inverse relation to the child rights knowledge. But the participation of mothers had no significant correlation with their child rights attitudinal scores. The participation of mothers showed significant positive correlation at 0.01 level with the child rights practise of mothers. That is the samples' participation in anganwadi activities showed significant correlation with child rights knowledge and practises but not with child rights attitudes.

❖ The child rights knowledge of mothers of anganwadi children showed significant (negative) correlation at 0.05 level with their participation in anganwadi activities. But the child rights knowledge scores of mothers had no significant correlation with child rights attitudes and practises. The child rights attitudes of the sample had no correlation with their participation in anganwadi activities, child rights knowledge and child rights practises. The child rights practises of mothers of anganwadi children showed significant positive correlation with the participation and had no correlation with their child rights knowledge and attitudes. Thus the correlation values indicate that the mothers participation in anganwadi activities showed significant positive correlation with their child rights practises and a significant negative correlation with child rights knowledge, though no significant correlation was found between mothers' child rights knowledge, attitudes and practises.

- The mothers did not differ significantly on their child rights knowledge, attitude and practise either between groups or within groups. This indicates that age had no influence on child rights knowledge, attitude and practise of mothers of anganwadi children.

- Significant difference between mothers with regard to their child rights knowledge, attitudes and participation in anganwadi activities and the location of anganwadi centre. But the mothers did not differ significantly with regard to their child rights practises and the location of anganwadi centre.

- There is no significant difference between the mothers whose children were attending anganwadi located in urban area and rural area with regard to child rights knowledge. There is no significant difference between mothers whose children are attending anganwadi located in rural area and urban slum with regard to their child rights knowledge. There is significant difference in knowledge between mothers whose children were attending anganwadi located in urban area and urban slum.

- The mothers of children attending anganwadi in rural area differed significantly with regard to their child rights attitudes with the mothers of children attending anganwadi in urban slum and urban area whereas the mothers of children attending anganwadi in urban slum and urban area did not differ significantly in their child rights attitudes.

- There is significant difference in participation or mothers of children attending anganwadi in urban, urban slum and rural areas. However Duncan multiple range test shows insignificant difference between pairs of urban slum and rural, rural and urban, urban slum and urban.

- There was no significant difference between mother's educational status with regard to their child rights knowledge, attitudes and practise. But significant difference was found between the educational status of mothers and their participation in anganwadi activities, though the mothers did not differ significantly in their child rights knowledge, attitudes and practises on the basis of their educational status, significant difference was seen for participation in anganwadi activities. This shows that education of mothers had an influence on their participation in anganwadi activities.

- The mothers who were illiterate, high school educated and primary school educated did not differ significantly in their participation in anganwadi activities, similarly the mothers who were high school educated, primary school educated and college educated did not differ significantly in their participation. Like-wise the mothers who were primary school educated, college educated and literates did not differ in their participation in anganwadi activities. But there is significant difference between mothers who were illiterates and college educated high school educated and literates and also illiterate and literate mothers.

- Mothers did not differ significantly with regard to their occupation and child rights knowledge and practises. But significant difference was found between occupation and child rights attitudes and participation in anganwadi activities. This shows that occupation of mothers had an influence on their child rights attitudes and their participation in anganwadi activities. As significant difference was found between occupation and child rights attitudes of mothers and also between occupation and participation of mothers in anganwadi activities. Duncan test was employed to examine the difference between groups of mothers with regard to their child rights attitudes and participation.
- There is no significant difference between the housewives and others (Employed in Private sector, Government sector and Business) with regard to child rights attitudes. But these two groups of mothers differed significantly with the daily wage earners. The ANOVA shows that there is effect of different groups of occupation on mothers' participation.

  However Duncan test shows insignificant difference between pairs; daily wage earners and others, housewives and others, daily wage earners and housewives with respect to participation.
- The mothers of anganwadi children did not differ on their family size and their child rights knowledge, attitudes, practise and participation in anganwadi centres activities. It indicates that the family size may not have an influence on the participation of mothers and their child rights.
- There was no significant difference between mothers belonging to less than Rs.12,000 and 12,001 to 18,000 with regard to child rights knowledge, attitudes, practise and participation in anganwadi activities. It indicates that the family income may not have an influence on mother's child

rights knowledge, attitude, practise and participation in anganwadi activities.

- ❖ The mothers of anganwadi children did not differ significantly with regard to their family types and their child rights knowledge, attitude, practise and participation in anganwadi activities.
- ❖ The mothers did not differ significantly on their child rights knowledge. But significant difference was found between the two groups of mothers for child rights attitudes, practises and participation. This shows that the type of management had an influence on the mothers child rights attitudes, practises and participation in anganwadi activities.
- ❖ There was no association between the age of the mothers and their child rights knowledge, attitudes, practises and participation in anganwadi activities. Similar results were also found in ANOVA test that is, the mothers did not differ either between groups or with the groups with regard to their age and child rights knowledge, attitudes, practises and participation is anganwadi activities. It indicates that the age had no influence on child rights knowledge, attitudes, practises and participation of mothers in this study
- ❖ The location of anganwadi is significantly associated with child rights knowledge, attitudes and participation in anganwadi activities. The location of anganwadi was not significantly associated with the child rights practises. It shows that location of anganwadi may have an influence on child rights knowledge, attitudes and participation of mothers.
- ❖ There is an association between the annual income of mothers and their child rights knowledge. But no association found between the annual income of mothers and their child rights attitudes, practises and participation in anganwadi activities.

- There is no association found between the family type and child rights knowledge, attitudes, practises and participation of mothers in anganwadi activities.
- The type of management showed significant association with the child rights attitudes, practises and participation of mothers. There was no association found between the type of management and child rights knowledge of mothers. This shows that the type of management had an influence on child rights attitudes, practises of mothers and also on their participation in anganwadi activities.
- With regard to nutritional status (weight for age), majority of children in the age group 2 to 3 years and 4 to 5 years were normal. Around 14 per cent and 3 per cent of children in the age group of 2 to 3 years had mild and moderate malnutrition respectively. Similarly 15 per cent and 8 per cent of children in the age group of 4 to 5 years had mild and moderate malnutrition respectively. None of the children found to have grade-III and grade-IV malnutrition. This may be attributed to the nutritional services of anganwadi centres.
- A 79 per cent of children in the age group of 2-3 years and 61 per cent of children in the age group of 4-5 years were found to be normal. Around 21 per cent of children in the age group of 2-3 years and 39 per cent of children in the age group of 4 to 5 years found to be stunted, that is their percentage heights for age of NCHS median values were less than two standard deviation (<2 SD). This shows that though majority of children had normal heights for their age, considerable percentage of children showed stunted growth.
- Majority of the children fell in the category of normal. Whereas 19 per cent of children aged

between 2-3 years and 25 per cent of children aged between 4-5 years had grade-I malnutrition as their MUAC values were between 12.5 to 13.5 cms.

- The ratings for nutritional supplements indicate that 35 per cent of anganwadi centres were rated as very good, 55 per cent of anganwadi centres were rated as good and only 10 per cent of anganwadi centres were rated as average.

- Health check-up was rated as very good in 45 per cent of centres, as good in 30 per cent of centres and as average in 25 per cent of centres. This indicates that the health check-up, which is to be done at least once in three days is not done regularly in the anganwadi centres under study.

- The monthly monitoring reports should include vital statistics *viz.*, Birth rate, still birth rate, infant mortality rate, under five mortality rate, maternal mortality rate, number of pregnant and lactating women in the anganwadi area. This responsibility of anganwadi workers was rated as very good (70%) and good (30%).

- Deworming tablets are provided to children once a year, the deworming of children was rated as very good in 90 per cent of centres and good in 10 per cent of centres.

- One of the prime duties of the anganwadi workers is to monitor the growth of children through monthly assessment of nutritional status. This service of anganwadi was rated as very good in all the anganwadi centres and good in 10 per cent of anganwadi centres.

- The supplementary nutrition to children in anganwadi centres was rated as very good in all the twenty anganwadi centres.

- The supplementary nutrition given to pregnant and lactating women provides 500 K.Cals of energy and

20-25 g of protein per day. All the anganwadi centres under study distribute the supplementary nutrition regularly to the pregnant and lactating women enrolled. Hence this service of anganwadi were rated as very good for all the anganwadi centres under study.

- Supply of nutritional supplements *viz.*, iron folic acid tablets and vitamin-A for pregnant women and nursing mothers along with nutritional counselling was included in the package of services of ICDS. Only iron folic acid (IFA) was distributed to women as and when the supply was received. This service of ICDS was rated as very good (5%) and good (95%) centres.

- Health and nutrition education to adolescent girls and mothers in anganwadi centres were rated as very good in 20 per cent, good in 35 per cent, average in 15 per cent, poor in 20 per cent and very poor in 10 per cent of anganwadi centres under study.

- The anganwadi workers role in promotion of breast feeding in their anganwadi area was rated as very good in 35 per cent and good in 65 per cent.

- The ratings for the preschool education programme was very good in 15 per cent, good in 30 per cent, average in 30 per cent, poor in 15 and very poor in 10 per cent centres.

- The ICDS services for HIV/AIDs infected mothers and children were rated as very good in 80 per cent and good in 20 per cent.

- The health, nutrition and education services provided under ICDS programme at the anganwadi centres were assessed for their quality in selected anganwadi centres, which showed that immunisation and supplementary nutrition to children and mothers were rated as very good for all twenty centres understudy. Only the health and nutrition education services to women and adolescent girls and pre-school education programme to children found to be poor and very poor in 30 per cent and 35 per cent of centres respectively. The remaining 9 services *viz.*, health check-up, vital statistics, nutritional supplements, deworming, nutritional status assessment, screening of HIV/AIDS were rated as very good to average.

The hypothesis formulated for the study were compared with the study findings and the outcome is as follows:

Hypothesis 1: "The coverage of child rights in ICDS programme is in adequate" is accepted.

Hypothesis 2, 4, 6: The results in table 4.24 indicate that the mean knowledge, attitudes and practise scores of anganwadi workers of government and NGO ICDS projects were not low but were well above the average. Hence the following hypothesis were rejected.

Hypothesis 2: The child rights knowledge of anganwadi workers is low.

Hypothesis 4: The attitudes of anganwadi workers towards child rights are low.

Hypothesis 6: The practise of child rights by anganwadi workers is not adequate.

Hypothesis 3, 5, 7: The results in the table 4.11.1 indicate that the mean knowledge, attitudes and practise scores of mothers of anganwadi children attending government and NGO ICDS projects were not low but were well above the average. Hence the following hypotheses were rejected.

Hypothesis 3: The child rights knowledge of mothers of anganwadi children is low.

Hypothesis 5: The attitudes of mothers of anganwadi children towards child rights are low.

Hypothesis 7: The practise of child rights by mothers of anganwadi children is not adequate.

Hypothesis 8: Hence the hypothesis 8 "The child rights component is not covered in the anganwadi workers training programme of ICDS" is rejected as the anganwadi workers indicated the sources of knowing about child rights as ICDS.

Hypothesis 9: The participation of mothers in the ICDS programme is found to be passive. Majority of mothers of children attending government managed ICDS programme (63 per cent) was low, around 31 per cent of mothers' participation was moderate and only 6 per cent showed high participation. Among the mothers of children attending NGO managed ICDS project 59 per cent showed low participation, 37 per cent moderate participation only 4 per cent showed high participation. This allows to accept the hypothesis 9. "The participation of mothers in the ICDS programme is not adequate". Efforts should be made to improve the participation of mothers in the ICDS programme.

Hypothesis 10: Part of the hypothesis No.10 "There is no relationship between personal and service profile of anganwadi workers and their knowledge, attitude and practise on child rights is rejected". As there was significance difference between the anganwadi workers having 11-15 years of service and other groups with regard to child rights practises, the hypothesis is rejected.

Hypothesis 11: "There is no relationship between personal and family profile of the mothers and their knowledge, attitude and practise on child rights and participation in anganwadi activities" is rejected as:

- **(a) Age:** The mother's age had no influence on knowledge, attitude and practise of child rights and also on their participation in anganwadi centers' activities.
- **(b) Location of Anganwadi Centre:** The mothers significantly differed in their child rights knowledge, attitudes and participation with regard to location of anganwadi centre, but did not differ significantly

with regard to their child rights practises and location of anganwadi centre.

(c) **The Educational Status:** There was no significant difference between mother's educational status with regard to child right knowledge, attitude and practise. But significant difference was found between the educational status of mothers and their participation in anganwadi activities.

(d) **Occupation of Mothers:** Occupation of mothers had an influence on their attitudes on participation in anganwadi activities but had no influence on their child right knowledge and practises.

(e) **Family Size and Family Type:** Family size and Family Type of the mothers had no influence on their child rights knowledge, attitudes and practise and participation in anganwadi centre's activities.

Thus, among the variables related to personal and family profile of mothers' only age, family size and type did not have an influence on the child rights knowledge, attitudes and practise of the sample. Hence the hypothesis 11 is rejected.

Hypothesis 12: There is no difference between mothers of children attending anganwadi centers run by government organisations and non governmental organisations management with regard to their child rights knowledge, attitude and practise.

The type of management had an association with the child rights attitudes, practise and participation of mothers, but had no significant association with the child right knowledge of mothers, hence hypothesis 12 is rejected.

Hypothesis 13: There is no relationship between child rights knowledge, attitude and practise of anganwadi workers and mothers. The hypothesis 13 is accepted as there is no relationship between mothers and anganwadi workers with regard to their child rights knowledge, attitudes and practises.

5

Summary and Conclusion

Children are considered as a gift of God by all cultures around the world. India's commitment to the cause of children is as old as its civilisation. Ancient texts like vedas, epics and religious scriptures provided the details of upbringing children and prescribed the roles and responsibilities of parents, families and societies towards children. These ancient texts are highly valued and respected by majority of Indians. Yet they are commented and criticised for the discrimination shown towards female children, indigenous populations, socially backward and the poor. The discrimination was prominent in accessing resources, education, health and nutrition. Over the years as a result of several social movements notable reforms were brought to eliminate discriminations and legislations were made to effect the reforms. (Pandey, 1993)

The convention on the rights of the child speaks of four sets of civil, political, social, economic and cultural rights of every child. They are: The right to survival, the right to protection, the right to development and the right to participation (UNICEF, 1997).

This conviction, expressed as the convention on the rights entered into international law on 2 September 1990, nine months after the convention's adoption by the United Nations General Assembly. Since then the convention has been ratified (as of mid-September 1996) by all countries except the Cook Islands, Oman, Somalia, Switzerland, the United

Arab Emirates and the United States, making it the most widely ratified Human Rights treaty in history.

The convention has produced a profound change that is already beginning to have substantive effects on the world's attitude towards its children. Once a country ratifies, it is obliged in law to undertake all appropriate measures to assist parents and other responsible parties in fulfilling their obligations to children under the convention. Now, 96 per cent of the world's children live in states that are legally obligated to protect child rights.

A statement of child rights is a statement of adult responsibilities. It is the responsibility of all adults, of governments and the international community, to create and maintain the circumstances in which families themselves can protect the rights of the child. Child rights needs to be understood by one and all, for which the information on child rights should be made available in all languages in the form of booklets, pamphlets, brochures, handouts etc. Any attempt to help children to utilise rights requires education of adults on child rights.

Child rights education demands appraisal of existing levels of knowledge, attitudes and practises of child rights by various sections of people and the stake holders of child welfare and development programmes. Basing on these appraisals need based child rights education programmes have to be developed using appropriate participatory methodologies. Such programmes receive greater attention, participation and commitment from the people for whom it is intended.

Several child welfare programmes launched at different intervals highlight the priority and importance of young child's right to survival and development, which is the responsibility of the State. National policy on children (NPC) 1974 directed the "State to provide adequate services to children, both before and after birth and throughout the period of growth – to ensure their full physical, mental and social development". A study team constituted by the planning commission in 1972 suggested comprehensive plan of action to meet the needs of children. As a result of the recommendation of the study team, along with the national policy on children in 1974, the Integrated Child Development Services (ICDS) project was started in 1975. In the initial stages ICDS was implemented in 33 selected community development blocks. Young children are most vulnerable, because the foundation for the life long learning and human development is laid in the early years, therefore the ICDS Programme has been designed to promote and facilitate total development of the child, through different components *viz.*, health, nutrition, preschool education etc. (Lakshmi Devi, 1998)

Basic ICDS services include supplementary nutrition, immunisation, health check-ups, nutrition and health education, referral services and pre-school education. These services are provided through a vast network of ICDS centres, better known as "anganwadis". Each anganwadi is managed by an anganwadi worker (AWW), assisted by an anganwadi helper (AH). An anganwadi is supposed to cover a population of about 1,000 persons – roughly 200 families. The coverage of ICDS has steadily expanded since its inception in 1975. Currently, the programme is operational in almost every block, and the country has more than seven lakh anganwadis (AWs). However, the effective coverage of ICDS remains quite limited: barely one-fourth of all children under six are covered under the supplementary nutrition component. (Dreze, 2006)

ICDS aims at providing basic needs to the children of India. Basic needs of children have been included in the UN declaration of child rights as rights of children. So the needs of children have become the rights of children, fulfillment of which is a responsibility of families, societies, and the State. Hence it is become necessary to assess the child welfare programmes in view of child rights and their coverage. As ICDS is the largest and chief child development programme in India, the investigator made an attempt to study the reflection of child rights especially the health, nutrition and education rights in the ICDS programme.

Statement of the Problem

Reflection of child rights in the Integrated Child Development Services (ICDS) Programme.

Objectives of the Study

1. To assess the coverage of child rights in the ICDS programme.
2. To assess the knowledge of anganwadi workers and mothers on child rights.
3. To assess the attitudes of anganwadi workers and mothers towards child rights.
4. To assess the practise of child rights by the anganwadi workers and mothers.
5. To assess the coverage of child rights component in the anganwadi workers training programme.
6. To assess the participation of mothers in the ICDS programme.
7. To know the relationship between the personal and service profile of anganwadi workers and their knowledge, attitudes and practise of child rights.
8. To know the relationship between personal and family profile of the mothers of anganwadi children on their knowledge, attitude and practise of child rights.
9. To know the difference between urban and rural anganwadi workers and mothers with regard to their knowledge, attitude, practise on child rights and participation.

Hypotheses

1. The coverage of child rights in ICDS programme is inadequate

2. The child rights knowledge of anganwadi workers is low
3. The child rights knowledge of mothers of anganwadi children is low
4. The attitudes of anganwadi workers towards child rights is low.
5. The attitudes of mothers of anganwadi children towards child rights is low.
6. The practise of child rights by anganwadi workers is not adequate.
7. The practise of child rights by mothers of anganwadi children is not adequate.
8. The child rights component is not covered in the anganwadi workers training programme.
9. The participation of mothers in the ICDS programme is not adequate.
10. There is no relationship between personal and service profile of anganwadi workers and their knowledge, attitude and practise on child rights.
11. There is no relationship between personal and family profile of mothers and their knowledge, attitude and practise on child rights and participation anganwadi activities.
12. There is no difference between anganwadi workers of government organisation and non-governmental organisation managed ICDS projects with regard to their knowledge, attitude and practise on child rights.
13. There is no difference between mothers of children attending anganwadi centres run by government organisation and non-governmental organisations management with regard to their child rights knowledge, attitude and practise.
14. There is no relationship between child rights knowledge, attitudes, practise of anganwadi workers and mothers.

METHODOLOGY

Research Design

To facilitate the implementation of research project, a research design was developed after the review of relevant literature and visits to the ICDS projects. The research design indicates the various steps in the research project envisaged by the researcher. It serves as a blue print for execution of research work planned.

Selection of the Sample

Integrated child development service projects are implemented by the government and non-governmental organisations and they are located in urban, rural and tribal areas. In order to study; the influence of management, the location of anganwadi and place residence of sample which were also included as independent variables in the study, the ICDS projects functioning under the management of government and non-government organisations and were located in neighbouring mandals were selected for the study.

Out of 21 ICDS projects in Chittoor district, the ICDS project functioning under government management in Puttur, Ramachandrapuram and Vadamalapeta mandals and the neighbouring ICDS project functioning under a reputed non-governmental organisation called Rastriya Seva Sanstha (RASS) in Tirupati urban and rural mandals were selected for the study. From each ICDS project hundred anganwadi workers, working in hundred anganwadi centres were selected as respondents for the study. Thus two hundred anganwadi workers were selected for the study. For the selection of mothers of anganwadi children, ten anganwadi centers were selected, from the hundred anganwadi centers of each ICDS project. Further from each anganwadi center ten mothers were selected, thus hundred mothers were selected as respondents from each ICDS project. Finally the sample comprised of two hundred mothers of anganwadi children and two hundred anganwadi workers, out of which hundred anganwadi workers and mothers were drawn from government run ICDS project and the remaining hundred mothers and hundred anganwadi workers were drawn from ICDS project functioning under non-governmental organisation management.

In order to examine the ICDS services especially health, nutrition and early childhood education/preschool education services, rendered to the children of anganwadi centres, ten anganwadi centres from each ICDS project were selected and from each anganwadi centre ten children were selected. Thus the sample comprised of 100 anganwadi children from each ICDS project that is 200 anganwadi children from the two ICDS projects were selected. All the two hundred children selected are the children of mothers who are respondents of the study.

Selection of Variables

In this study the child rights knowledge, attitudes, practises, ICDS services, participation of mothers are the dependent variables. The major independent variables are age, educational status, marital status, place of residence, type of family, family income, size of family, access to public facilities, location of the anganwadi, length of service, training received and sources of knowing child rights information.

Tools for Assessment of Variables

In order to assess independent and dependent variables included in the study the following tools were developed: 1. Child rights knowledge scale; 2. Child rights attitudinal scale; 3. Child rights practise scale for mothers; 4. Child rights practise scale for anganwadi workers; 5. Questionnaire for anganwadi workers; 6. Questionnaire for mothers of anganwadi children; 7. Checklist on health, nutrition and preschool education services.

The child rights approach and perspective are new areas in research. Hence there were no tools or scales available on child rights assessment. A need is therefore felt for the development of appropriate tools to assess child rights knowledge, attitudes and practise and also their reflection in the existing ICDS programme.

Statistical Techniques

The scores for each tool administered with sample selected were calculated. The total scores obtained by each of two hundred anganwadi workers and two hundred mothers of anganwadi children on all the variables included in the study were computed. The data were carefully analysed by employing appropriate statistical techniques.

An Overview of Results and Discussion

The study on "Reflection of Child Rights in the ICDS Programme" carried out on anganwadi workers, mothers of anganwadi children and children, reveal that ICDS is performing crucial functions in the study area. The data collected on personal and service profile of anganwadi workers indicate that majority (80.5%) of anganwadi workers were not trained and not received ICDS information during the study period. Only a small percentage of anganwadi workers were adequately satisfied with their work performance (job satisfaction). Majority of anganwadi workers were spreading messages about ICDS services regularly. The data on the facilities available in anganwadi centres reveal that 64.5 per cent of anganwadi centres had water facility, 54.5 per cent of anganwadi centres were located in pucca buildings, only 34 per cent of centres had toilet facilities, all the anganwadi centres do not have the basic facilities and amenities to run the programme effectively. There is a greater need to co-ordinate and converge other programmes and services at the local level to equip the anganwadi centres with the basic facilities. Among the anganwadi workers' only 85.8 per cent indicated the ICDS as their source of knowing about child rights.

The personal and family profile of mothers under study shows that majority of mothers were housewives and had income below poverty line. A 45 per cent of the mothers' understudy did not have a ration card and 85 per cent of them had family sizes of 5-8 members. A 55.5 per cent of the mothers belonged to nuclear – two parent families and a 83 per cent of the mothers had 2 to 4 children which reflects the living conditions of the mothers of anganwadi children. ICDS services are beneficial to all children and mothers irrespective of their socio-economic status. The concept that children from well to do families have better health and nutritional status is a myth. The health, nutrition, educational status of children mostly depends on several factors, one of them being mothers' and family's capabilities to provide for them. ICDS in its package of services encompasses, these aspects, hence ICDS needs to be universalised for all irrespective of their socio-economic status.

The data on the mothers accessibility to public facilities indicate that 99 per cent of them have access to primary health centres and whole of them to anganwadi centre services. A 5.5 per cent of the mothers rated anganwadi services as nominal. The water facilities for their families were also rated as average. The Municipal and Panchayat services were not available to 55.5 per cent and for those it is available rated these services as nominal. A 23 per cent of mothers did not have access to civil supplies and this services was rated as average. The electricity is available to all and primary school education is available to 99 per cent. The non-formal education services were accessible to 67.5 per cent.

The law and order services were accessible to only 33 per cent of the mothers. The accessibility to public facilities influence the quality of life of the people. Poor access to these facilities deteriorate the living conditions and also affects the mothers' and families' capabilities to fulfil the children's needs and rights.

The child rights knowledge, attitudes and practises of anganwadi workers were assessed with the help of the tools developed for the purpose. The relationship between the independent variables *viz.*, age, educational status, marital status, place of residence, type of management, job experience, length of service, trainings and refresher trainings received by the anganwadi worker were also examined with the help of statistical techniques *viz.,* ANOVA, Duncan multiple range test, Pearson correlation, chi-square and t-tests. The results indicate that the anganwadi workers did not differ in their child rights knowledge, attitudes and practises with regard to their age, educational status, marital status and place of residence.

The anganwadi workers showed significant difference with regard to child rights practise and job experience. There is significant difference between the anganwadi workers having 11-15 years of service and other groups with regard to child rights practises. Though the anganwadi workers did not differ significantly in their child rights knowledge, practises with regard to trainings received, significant difference for the child rights attitudes and the trainings received was found. The anganwadi workers' belonging to government and non-governmental organisation ICDS projects did not differ significantly on their child rights attitudes and practises, but differed significantly with regard to their child rights knowledge. Thus the ANOVA test results reveal that the anganwadi workers did not differ in their child rights knowledge, attitudes and practises with regard to most of the independent variables, significant difference was found for job experience and child rights practises, length of service and child rights practises, trainings received and child rights attitudes, type of management and child rights knowledge. This reflects that some of the independent variables had an influence on some of the dependent variable under study.

The association between the independent variables and child rights knowledge, attitudes and practises of anganwadi workers were examined which showed that the age of the anganwadi workers had significant association with their child rights attitudes, but not with their child rights knowledge and practises. There was no association between the educational status and child rights knowledge, attitudes and practises of anganwadi workers. Similarly the place of residence of anganwadi workers was not significantly associated with their child rights knowledge, attitudes and practises. The anganwadi workers' child rights knowledge and practises were not associated significantly with the type of management but showed a significant association with the child rights attitudes. This shows that only the child rights attitudes of the anganwadi workers was significantly associated with the independent variable *viz.*, age and type of management. Attitudes play an important role in delivery of ICDS services. Hence it is necessary undertake appropriate activities to change the attitudes of anganwadi workers in the training and refresher programmes in order to fulfill the rights of children through ICDS.

The data on child rights knowledge, attitudes, practises and participation of mothers in anganwadi activities were analysed and examined for the relationship between the independent and dependent variables under study. The results showed that the mothers of anganwadi children did not vary in their child rights knowledge, but varied in their child rights attitudes and child rights practises. The mothers participation in anganwadi activities showed significant negative correlation with their child rights knowledge and positive correlation with their child rights attitudes and showed no correlation with their child rights attitudes. No significant correlation was found between child rights knowledge, attitudes and practises of mothers. This shows that the mothers child rights knowledge was inversely related to their participation but directly related to their child rights practises. Practises in general include skills, adequate skills lead to confidence and efficiency in the work. The ICDS programme should include strengthening the mothers' skills and equipping the adolescent girls who are on the threshold of marriage and motherhood of with the skills in childcare and management, in order to fulfill the rights of children in the areas of health, nutrition, education and others.

The results of ANOVA test indicates that the mothers under study did not differ in their child rights knowledge, attitudes and practises with regard to their age. The mothers differed in their child rights knowledge with regard to location of anganwadi that is the significant difference was found between mothers whose children were attending anganwadis located in urban area and urban slum. In contrary, for the child rights attitudes there was no difference between mothers whose children were attending anganwadis in urban areas and urban slum but the mothers whose children attending anganwadi in remote area differed significantly in their child rights attitudes with the mothers of children attending anganwadis in urban slum and urban area.

Though the mothers did not significantly differ with regard to their educational status and child rights knowledge, attitudes and practise, significant difference was found between the educational status of mothers and their participation in anganwadi activities. The mothers did not differ significantly with regard to their occupation and child rights knowledge and practises, but significant difference was found between occupation and child rights attitudes and participation in anganwadi activities. Interestingly the mothers did not differ in their child rights knowledge, attitudes, practises and participation, with regard to their family type, family size, annual income and type of ICDS management. Thus the results indicate that there is a relationship between independent variables *viz.*, age of the mothers, location of anganwadi centres, educational status, occupation and some of the dependent variables *viz.*, child rights knowledge, attitude and participation in anganwadi activities.

The relationship between the mothers personal and family profile and child rights knowledge, attitudes, practises and participation was further studied using chi square test. The results revealed that there was no association between the age of the mothers and their child rights knowledge, attitudes, practises and participation in anganwadi activities. In contrary, the location of anganwadi centre was significantly associated with the child rights knowledge, attitudes and participation but did not show an association with child rights pracitses. The mothers' family type did not show an association with their child rights knowledge, attitudes, practises and participation. Interestingly the mothers' child rights attitudes, practises and participation had significant association with the type of ICDS management but did not show an association with their child rights knowledge. Thus only the type of ICDS management and location of anganwadi centre found to have an influence on some of the dependent variables *viz.*, child rights knowledge, attitude, practise and participation.

Though the nutritional status of children attending anganwadi centre under study found to be normal, there is every need to monitor their growth and development with more efficiency.

The assessment of the quality of health, nutrition and education services delivered at anganwadi centres understudy showed that immunisation and supplementary nutrition to children and mothers were rated as very good for all twenty centres under study. Only the health and nutrition education services to women and adolescent girls and preschool education programme was found to be poor and very poor in 30 per cent and 35 per cent of centres respectively. The remaining seven services *viz.*, Health check-ups, Vital statistics, Nutritional supplements, Deworming, Nutritional status assessment, Screening of HIV/AIDS were rated as very good to average.

CONCLUSION

ICDS as a largest and nation-wide programme can address the needs of children under six, from rights perspective. The study results also indicate that the existing ICDS programme reflects the health nutrition and educational rights of children under six, though not adequately. In order to strengthen the ICDS programme there is every need to make the anganwadi centres functional in every habitation and throughout the country. The basic premise of the demand for universalisation of ICDS is that all children have a right to health, nutrition, preschool education and related opportunities. The anganwadi is the institutional medium to protect these rights or at least to bring them within the realm of possibility. All children irrespective of their socio-economic status should avail ICDS services, which means that all the adolescent girls and mothers also become stakeholders of ICDS. The ICDS has enormous potential as a institutionalised service to fulfill the needs and rights of Indias' children and their care givers, for which the programme has to be revisited, strengthened in all aspects, at all levels.

Implications of the Study

- All the anganwadi centres do not have the basic facilities and amenities to run the programme effectively. There is a greater need to co-ordinate and converge other programmes and services at the local level to equip the anganwadi centres with the basic facilities.

- The concept that children from well to do families have better health and nutritional status is a myth. The health, nutrition, educational status of children mostly depends on several factors, one of them being mothers' and family's capabilities to provide for them. ICDS in its package of services encompasses, these aspects, hence ICDS needs to be universalised for all irrespective of their socio-economic status.

- Poor access to public facilities deteriorate the living conditions and also affects the mothers' and families' capabilities to fulfil the children's needs and rights. Hence empowering the participants of ICDS to avail the public facilities for fulfilling their child rights and also their own human rights need to be considered.

- It is necessary to undertake appropriate activities to change the attitudes of anganwadi workers in the training and refresher programmes in order to fulfill the rights of children through ICDS.

- The ICDS programme should include strengthening the mothers' skills and equipping the adolescent girls who are on the threshold of marriage and motherhood of with the skills in childcare and management, in order to fulfill the rights of children in the areas of health, nutrition, education and others.
- Though the nutritional status of children attending anganwadi centre under study found to be normal, there is every need to monitor their growth and development with more efficiency.
- The basic premise of the demand for universalisation of ICDS is that all children have a right to health, nutrition, preschool education and related opportunities. The anganwadi is the institutional medium to protect these rights or at least to bring them within the realm of possibility.
- All children irrespective of their socio-economic status should avail ICDS services, which means that all the adolescent girls and mothers also become stakeholders of ICDS.
- The ICDS has enormous potential as an institutionalised service to fulfill the needs and rights of Indias' children and their care givers, for which the programme has to be revisited, strengthened in all aspects, at all levels.

References

Akhan, S.L. 1996. Rights of Unborn Child. The Journal of Social Defence, Vol.XXXVIII (125), New Delhi.

Alikhan, M. 1980. Sociological Aspects of Child Development: A Study of Rural Karnataka. Published by Concept Publishing Company, New Delhi, pp. 205-206.

Arora, G.L. 1995. Child Centered Education for Learning Without Burden. Published by Krishnna Publishing Company, I Edition, New Delhi, pp. 137-151.

Arvindrani, D.N. 1990. Family and Child Welfare. Published by Ashish Publishing House, New Delhi.

Bahaj. 1995. Turning Point for all Nations: A Statement on the Occasion of the 50th Anniversary of the United Nations.

Bajaj, C.P. and Gupta, P.N. 1984. Elements of Statistics. Published by R.Chand and Co, III Edition, New Delhi.

Bakshi, S.R. and Kiranbala. 2000. Child Welfare and Development. Published by Deep and Deep Publications, New Delhi, pp. 28-29.

Basotia, G.R. 1999. Research Methodology. Published by Mangal Deep Publications, Jaipur, p. 125.

Bhanti, R. 1991. Welfare of Women and Children. Published by Himanshu Publications, Udaipur, pp. 77-80, 209.

Boyle, G.J. and Langley, P.D. 1989. Elementary Statistical Methods. Published by Oxford Publications, New Delhi, pp. 49-50.

Brenner, B. 1970. Cited by Laxmi Devi (1998) Encyclopaedia of Child and Family Welfare. Published by Anmol Publications, Vol. 5, New Delhi, p. 111.

Carol, S. and Barbour, N. 1990. Early Childhood Education an Introduction. Published by Marill Publishing Company, II Edition, London.

Chandra Sekhar, B. 2002. Women Empowerment. Published by Lakshmi Publications, Hyderabad, pp. 74-48.

Chandra, J. 1993. Women and Child: A Paradigm for Rural Development. Published by Rawat Publications, New Delhi, pp. 37-39.

Chaplin, J.P. 1985. Dictionary of Psychology. Published by Dell Publishing Company, New York, p. 78.

Chaturvedi, T.N. 1979. Administration for Child Welfare. Published by Indian Institute of Public Administration, New Delhi, pp. 169-176.

Chowdary, D.P. 1985. Child Welfare Development. Published by Atma Ram and Sons, New Delhi, pp. 313-327.

Chowdary, D.P. 1985. Child Welfare Development. Published by Atma Ram and Sons, New Delhi, pp. 340-343.

Chowdary, D.P. 1993. Hand Book of Social Welfare. Published by Atma Ram and Sons, New Delhi, p. 13.

Chowdhry, P.D. 1995. Hand book of Social Welfare. Published by Atma Ram and Sons, New Delhi, p. 16.

Compton, R.B. 1980. Introduction to Social Welfare and Social Work. Published by Dorsey Press, New York.

Deogaohkar, S.G. 1980. Administration for Rural Development in India. Published by Concept Publishing Company, New Delhi.

Desai, M., Montiern, A. and Narayan, L. 1998. Child Rights. The Indian Journal of Social Work, Part-I, Vol. 59.

Devi, L. 1998. Child and Family Welfare. Published by Anmol Publications, New Delhi, pp. 306-309.

Devi, L. 1998. Encyclopaedia of Child and Family Welfare. Published by Anmol Publications, Vol. 5, New Delhi, pp. 111, 366.

Devi, L. 1998. Encyclopaedia of Child and Family Welfare: Health, Nutrition and Early Childhood Education. Published by Anmol Publications, Vol. 2, New Delhi, p. 354.

Devi, L. 1999. Policies and Programmes Related to Child Development. Published by Anmol Publications, New Delhi, pp. 384-386.

Donald Mc Burney, H. 1998. Research Methods. Published by Cole Publishers Company, 4th Edition.

Dreze and Sen. 2004. Universalisation with Quality: An Agenda for ICDS. Report Prepared for the National Advisory Council, www.righttofoodindia.org.

Dreze, J. 2006. Universalition with Quality ICDS in a Rights Perspective. Economic and Political Weekly, August 26.

Dubowitz, H. and Depanfilis, D. 2000. Handbook for Child Protection Practice. Published by Sage Publications, New Delhi.

Dutta, P.K. 1993. Scope of Health Systems Research in Child Survival and Safe Motherhood Programme. Indian Journal of Maternal Child Health.

Duvall, E.M. 1977. Marriage and Family Development. Published by J.B. Publishers, Lippincott, Philadelphia.

Edward, W.M., Bruce King, M. and Gorden Bear. 1993. Statistical Reasoning in Psychology and Education. Published by Johnwiley and Sons, III Edition, Canada, pp. 378-430.

Eshleman, Jr. 1974. The Family: An Introduction. Published by Allyn and Bacon Inc, Boston.

Ganguly, E. 2005. Says a Child Who Speaks for My Rights? HAQ Centre for Child Rights, New Delhi, p. 9.

Gard, S. and Ghosh, S. 2006. Cited by Dreze, J. (2006) Universalisation with Quality ICDS in a Rights Perspective. Economic and Political Weekly, August 26.

Genecole, M. 1999. Cited by Wal, S. (1999). International Encyclopaedia of Child Development Priorities for 21st Century. Published by Sarup and Sons, New Delhi, pp. 29-31, 61-69.

Ghosh, S. 1997. Integrated Child Development Programme. Indian Paediatrics 34, pp. 911-18.

Ghosh, S. 2002. Integrated Child Development Programme. The National Medical Journal of India, 15, No. 2. (Supplement) pp. 14-16.

Ghosh, S. 2004. Child Malnutrition. Economics and Political Weekly, Oct. 2.

Ghosh, S. and Shah, D. 2004. Nutritional Problems in Urban Slum Children. Indian Paediatrics 41, pp. 682-96.

Goel, S.L. 1980. Health Care Administration Policymaking and Planning. Published by Sterling Publishers, New Delhi, p. 203.

Goonesekere, S. 1998. Children, Law and Justice: A South Asian Perspective. Published by Sage Publications, New Delhi, pp. 25-27.

Gopal, K.K. 1997. Statistical Tests. Published by Sage Publications, New Delhi, p. 28.

Gore, M.S. 1985. Social Aspects of Development. Published by Rawat Publications, Jaipur.

Government of India. 2006. Cited by Dreze, J. (2006) Universalisation with Quality ICDS in a Rights Perspective. Economic and Political Weekly, August 26.

Govinda, R. 2002. India Education Report: A Profile of Basic Education. Published by Oxford University Press, New Delhi, pp. 47-198.

Graham, I. 1999. There's No Such Thing as Reflection. The British Journal of Social Work, Published by Oxford University, Vol. 29(4), pp. 513-523.

Grant, J.P. 1989. The State of the World's Children. Published by Oxford University Press, New Delhi.

Guenzel, P.J., Berkmans and Cannel. 1983. Research in Education. Published in Prentice Hall International, Englewood Cliffs.

Gupta, A. 2001. Governing Population: The ICDS Service Programme in India. Published by Duke University Press, Durham, pp. 65-96.

Gupta, A. 2003. Status of Infant and Young Child Feeding : A National Report of Quantitative Study. Breastfeeding Promotion Network of India.

Gupta, A., Jon E Rode. 2004. Infant and Young Child Undernutrition. Economic and Political Weekly, December 4.

Gupta, S. 1996. Rights of the Child Workers. Published by Ministry of Social Justice and Empowerment, Vol. XXXVIII (124), New Delhi, pp. 1-3.

Hays, W.L. 1981. Statistics. Published by CBS College Publications, III Edition, New Delhi.

Hegarty, S. and Alur, M. 2002. Education and Children with Special Needs. Published by Sage Publications, New Delhi, pp.57-59.

Henry, E.G. and Wood Worth, R.S. 1966. ...... Published by Vakils Bebbur and Simons Ltd, Bombay, pp. 95-100.

Hoover, H. 1998. Cited by Pramila Pandit Barooah, 1999 Handbook of Child. Published by Concept Publishing Company, New Delhi.

ICDS. 1986. Manual on the Integrated Management Information System. Published by Department of Women Welfare, Ministry of Human Resource Development, 1st Edition, New Delhi, p. 7.

ICDS. 1988. Monitoring and Continuing Education System. Published by Central Technical Committee on Health and Nutrition, AIIMS, New Delhi, p. 18.

ICDS. 1990. Manual on ICDS. Published by Central Technical Committee, Department of Women and Child Development, AIIMS, New Delhi, pp. 7-13.

Iyer, K.S. 1998. Human Rights Vibrant Issue. Published by Satishgarg Publishers, New Delhi, p. 116.

Jain, S.N. 1979. Children and the Law. Published by the Indian Law Institute, New Delhi, pp. 42-43.

Jha, R. 1998. Rights of the Child: An Assessment. The Journal of Indian Bar Review, Vol XXV (4).

John, W.S. 1999. Lifespan Development. Published by McGraw Hill Publications, Seventh Edition, New Delhi, p. 18.

Joshi, S. 1996. Child Survival Health and Social Work Intervention. Published by Concept Publishing Company, New Delhi, pp. 65-67.

Kapil Pradhan, R. 2002. ICDS Scheme: A Programme for Holistic Development of Children in India. Indian Journal of Paediatrition, AIIMS, New Delhi.

Kapil Pradhan, R. 2002. ICDS Scheme and its Impact on Nutritional Status of Children in India and Recent Initiatives. www.righttofoodindia.org/ICDS.

Kapur, M. 1995. Mental Health and Indian Children. Published by Sage Publications, New Delhi.

Khanna, S.K. 1998. Children and Human Rights. Published by Common Wealth Publishers, I Edition, p. 25.

Khosla, R., Manu and Kaul, R. 1997. Time Management by Anganwadi Workers. Published by NIPCCD, New Delhi, pp. 1-37.

Kumar, A. 2005. Childcare and Protection. Published by Anmol Publications Ltd, New Delhi, p. 518.

Kumar, H. 1998. Children at the Edge of the Margin. The Journal of Contemporary Social Work, Published by Department of Social Work, Vol. XV, pp. 31-33.

Kumar, R. 2002. Child Development in India: Health Welfare and Management. Published by Ashish Publishing House, Volume-I, New Delhi, pp. 157-163.

Kurtz, K.A. 1979. Statistical Methods of Educational Psychology. Published by Narosa Publishing House, New York, pp. 46, 362, 392.

Lal, S. and Sachar, R.K. 1993. Present and Future of ICDS. Indian Journal of Maternal Child Health, pp. 19-24.

Leela, B.C. 1979. Child Welfare. Published by McGraw Hill Book Company, II Edition, New York, p. 185.

Mahadevan, K. 1990. Policies and Strategies for Child Survival: Experience from Asia. Published by B.R. Publishing Corporation, New Delhi, pp. 375-379.

Mahadevan, K. 1990. Policies and Strategies for Child Survival. Published by B.R.Publishing Corporation, New Delhi, pp. 375-389.

Mahtab, S.B., Pralhad Rao, N. and Vinodini Reddy. 1996. Testbook of Human Nutrition. Published by Oxford and IBH Publishers Ltd, New Delhi, p. 227.

Mandal, B.B. 1991. Child and Action Plan for Development. Published by Mittal Publications, New Delhi, pp.15, 18-19, 25, 89-90.

Mangal, S.K. 2002. Statistics in Psychology and Education. Published by Prentice Hall India Private Limited, II Edition, New Delhi.

Manjuvani, E. 2000. Influence of Home and School Environment on Mental Health of Children. Published by Discovery Publishing House, New Delhi, p. 2.

Manohar. 1979. Children in India Critical Issues in Human Development. Published by Manohar Publications, New Delhi.

Marchant, A.K. 1997. Tomorrow Belongs to Children. Journal of Social Change, Vo1. 27, pp. 90-102.

Matterson. 1990. Cited by Laxmi Devi Child and Family Welfare. Published by Anmol Publications, New Delhi.

Meherdale, A. 1997. Law and Child Labour : A Case for Protecting Children's Rights. The Journal of Social Change, Vol. 27(33), pp. 132-146.

Mehta, P.L. 1996. Child Labour and the Law. Published by Deep and Deep Publications, New Delhi.

Michael, J.G., Barrie, M.M., John, M.K. and Lenore, A. 2005. Public Health and Nutrition. Published by Backwell Science, UK, p. 232.

Misra, R., Chatterjee, R. and Sujatha Rao. 2003. India Health Report. Published by Oxford University Press, New Delhi, p. 41.

Mohanty, J. 1994. Education for All. Published by Deep and Deep Publications, New Delhi, pp. 45-60.

Mohanty, J. 1998. Child Development and Education Today Literature, Art, Media and Materials. Published by Deep and Deep Publications, New Delhi, p. 366.

Mohanty, J. 1998. Child Development and Education Today Literature, Art, Media and Materials. Published by Deep and Deep Publications, New Delhi, pp. 35-37.

Mohsin, S.M. 1990. Attitude Concept for Motion and Change, The Attitude Object. Published by Wiley Eastern Limited, New Delhi, pp. 19-28.

Munro, E. 1996. Avoidable and Unavoidable Mistakes in Child Protection Work. The British Journal of Social Work, Published by Oxford University Press, Vol. 26(6), pp. 793-797.

Murthy, L.S.N., Kumar, K. and Nagendranath. 1993. Technical Bulletin Management of Community Participation in ICDS. Published by NIPCCD, New Delhi, pp.1-14.

Muthuswamy. 2000. Rights of the Children. The Journal of Social Welfare, Vol.46(10), pp. 15-17.

Naik, S.V. 1999. Planning, Research Evaluation. The Journal of Social Welfare, Published by Department of Women and Child Development, Vol.46 (5), New Delhi, p. 4.

Narayana, K.S. and Pushpa Rani, P. 2000. The Working Child. The Journal of Social Welfare, Vol. 47(8), pp. 7-13.

Naswa, S. 1998. ICDS Towards Universalisation. The Journal of Social Welfare, p. 3-4.

National Family Health Survey. 1999. Cited by Rajiv Misra. India Health Report. Published by Oxford University Press, New Delhi, p. 41.

National Seminar on Gender Statistics. 2004. Proceedings of the National Seminar on Gender Statistics and Data. Published by Central Statistical Organisation, p. 117.

Nayanatara, S. and Kumar, U. 1998. Integrated Child Development Services. Published by Ashish Publishing House, New Delhi, pp. 2-3.

NIPCCD. 1994. Statistics on Children in India. Published by National Institute of Public Cooperation and Child Development, New Delhi, pp. 138-139.

NIPCCD. 2004. Orientation Course on Nutrition Health Education. Published by NIPCCD, New Delhi, pp. 1-13.

Paisley, W.J. and Butler, M. 1983. Knowledge Utilisation Systems in Education. Published by Sage Publications, 1st Edition, New Delhi, pp. 262-263.

Pandey, V.P. 1999. International Perspectives on Human Rights. Published by Mohit Publications, New Delhi, p. 204.

Phillips, W.S.K. 1994. Street Children in India. Published by Rawat Publications, Jaipur, p. 176.

Pimpley, P.N. and Singh, K.P. 1989. Social Development Process and Consequences. Published by Rawat Publications, New Delhi, pp. 226-229.

Prabhu, R.D. 2001. Child Development and Nutrition Management. Published by Book Enclave, Jaipur, pp. 198-210.

Prakash Srivastava, G.N. 1994. Advanced Research Methodology. Published by Radha Publications, New Delhi, p. 77.

Pramila Pandit, B. 1992. Handbook on Child with Historical Background. Published by Concept Publishing Company, New Delhi.

Pramila Pandit, B. 1998. Handbook on Child with Historical Background. Published by Concept Publishing Company, New Delhi, pp. 195-217.

Pramila Pandit, B. 1999. Handbook on Child with Historical Background. Published by Concept Publishing Company, New Delhi, pp. 195-199.

Puri, S. 2004. Child Development and Welfare Services. Published by Pointer Publishers, India, pp. 90-95.

Puri, S. 2004. Child Development and Welfare Services. Published by Pointer Publishers, India, pp. 90-95.

Ramaswamy, G. 1981. The Child and the Law. Published by Andhra Pradesh Judicial Academy, Khairatabad, Hyderabad, pp. 4-7.

Ramchandraiah. 1998. Indian Bar Review. Published by The Bar Council of India Trust, Vol. XXV(4).

Rao, D.B. 1997. Care the Child. Published by Discovery Publishing House, 1st Edition, New Delhi, pp. 54-172.

Rao, D.B. 1997. Care the Child. Published by Discovery Publishing House, Volume-1, New Delhi, pp. 9-26.

Rao, E.N. 1986. Strategy for Integrated Rural Development. Published by B.R. Publishing Company, New Delhi.

Rao, P.K. 1983. Child Constitution and Reality in India: A Social Legal Study. The Journal of Kurukshetra, Vol. No. 8 & 9.

Raul, J. 1999. Encyclopaedic Dictionary of Child Development. Published by Anmol Publications, New Delhi, p. 100.

Ray, G.L. and Mondal, S. 1999. Research Methods in Social Sciences and Extension Education. Published by Nayaprakash Publishers, Calcutta, pp. 177-185.

Reddy, A.R. 1995. Health Care Services Management. Published by Delta Publishing House, Hyderabad.

Richard Levin, I. and David Rubin, S. 1999. Statistics for Management. Published by Prentice Hall of India Private Limited, 7th Edition, New Delhi, pp. 19-20, 793-794.

Robert, M.G. 1984. Longman Dictionary of Psychology and Psychiatry. Published by Longman, New York, p. 139.

Sachdev, A.V.S., Neeru Gandhi, T., Tandon, B.N. and Krishnamurthy, K.S. 1998. Integrated Child Development Services Scheme and Nutritional Status of Indian Children, Published by Central Technical Committee, Department of Women and Child Development, New Delhi.

Sarada, D. 1999. Family Life Education for Adolescent Girls. Published by Discovery Publishing House, New Delhi, p. 52.

Sarada, D. 2006. Participation of Mother in ICDS Programme. Journal of Contemporary Social Work, Published by Department of Social Work, Lucknow, p. 3.

Saraswathi, T.S. and Kaur, B. 1993. Human Development and Family Studies in India and Agenda for Research and Policy. Published by Sage Publications, New Delhi, pp. 223-253.

Saraswathi, T.S. and Kaur, B. 1993. Human Development and Family Studies in India, Published by Sage Publications, 1st Edition, New Delhi, pp. 252-253.

Saxena, N.C. and Sankaran, N.R. 2004. Cited by Vimala Ramachandran (2005). Reflection on the ICDS Programme, www.india_seminar.com.

Sethi, D.P. 1998. ICDS Involvement of Community Essential. The Journal of Social Welfare, Published by Department of Women and Child Development, New Delhi, pp. 9-12.

Sharma, A. and Gupta, S. 1993. Impact of ICDS on Health and Nutritional Status of Children, Journal of Maternal Child Health, Vol. XXIII.

Sharma, A. and Sood, N. 1989. Approach and Strategies of Child Development in India. Published by NIPCCD, New Delhi, p. 59-61.

Sharma, S.R. 1994. Statistical Methods in Educational Research. Published by Anmol Publications, 1st Edition, New Delhi, pp. 110-111.

Sharma, U. 1996. Development of Child in India. Published by Agarwal Printers, Vol.II, Jaipur, pp. 1-4.

Sharma. S.R. and Kaushik, V. 1994. Child Development. Published by Anmol Publications, New Delhi, pp. 90-91.

Siddiqui, H.Y. 1990. Social Welfare in India. Published by Hanam Publications, New Delhi.

Singh Seghal, B.P. 1999. Human Rights in India. Published by Deep and Deep Publications, New Delhi.

Singh, D. 1995. Child Development Issues, Policies and Programmes. Published by Kanishka Publishers, Volume-3, New Delhi, pp. 339-341.

Singh, D. 1995. Child Development Issues, Policies and Programmes. Published by Kanishka Publishers, New Delhi, pp. 1-10.

Singh, D. 1999. New Dimensions in Child Education and Learning Processes. Published by Kanishka Publishers, New Delhi, p. 160.

Singh, K.K. 1995. Report on Exchange Visit of the Instructors of Middle Level Training Centres of ICDS. Published by NIPCCD, New Delhi.

Sinha, D. 2004. Caring for Children. www.righttofoodindia.org

Sinha, M.K. 1999. Rights of the Child. Published by Manak Publications, New Delhi, p. 81.

Sinha, S. 2006. Infant Survival—A Political Challenge. Economics and Political Weekly, August 26.

Sita, R. 1992. Welfare Services. Published by Northern Book Centre, New Delhi.

Sonawat, R. and Porichha, T. 2000. Scale to Measure the Quality of Early Childhood and Educational Programmes (ECCE) in the City of Mumbai. Journal of Perks Pectines in Social Work, Vol. XV(2), p. 1116.

Sravana., Bhadra and Saka. 1995. ICDS—Nurturing the Budding Human Resource. The Journal of Kurukshetra, Vol. XLIII (11), pp. 110-111.

Srivastava, P.A. 1968. On Bringing up Weak and Slow Learning Children: Research Findings and Know-how. Published by the Learning Laboratory, New Delhi.

SRS. 1999. Cited by Rajiv Misra (2003) Indian Health Report. Published by Oxford University Press, New Delhi, p. 41.

Subhangani Joshi, A. 1997. Nutrition and Dietetics, Published by Tata McGraw Hill Publishing Company Limited, New Delhi.

Swaminathan, M. 1974. Food and Nutrition. Published by the Bangalore Publishing Co. Ltd, Vol. 2, Bangalore.

Swaminathan, M. 1987. Food Science. Published by the Bangalore Printing and Publishing Co. Ltd, Bangalore.

Tandon, R.K. 1999. Organising Childcare Services. Published by Rajat Publications, New Delhi, pp. 4-7.

Tandon, Ramachandran and Bhatnagar. 1981. Cited by Akhil Gupta (2001). Governing Population: The ICDS Service Programme in India. Published by Duke University Press, Durham, pp. 65-96.

Tharker, B.N. 1988. Sociology of Rural Development. Published by Classical Publishing Company, New Delhi.

UNICEF. 1989. The State of the World's Children. Published by Oxford University Press, New York, pp. 60-63.

UNICEF. 1992. The State of the World's Children. Published by Oxford University Press, New York, pp. 6-9, 15-17.

UNICEF. 1993. Promotion of Sanitation in Anganwadi. Published by UNICEF, pp. 1-3.

UNICEF. 1993. The State of the World's Children. Published by Oxford University Press, New York, p. 12.

UNICEF. 1995. The Continuing Revolution for Children. Published by UNICEF, New Delhi.

UNICEF. 1997. The State of the World's Children. Published by Oxford University Press, UK, pp. 9-14.

UNICEF. 1997. The State of Worlds' Children. Published by Oxford University Press, London, UK.

Vanuaria, V. and Kapoor, M. 1998. ICDS Health Awareness of Anganwadi Workers. The Journal of Social Welfare, pp. 16-17.

Varma, M.S. 1994. Social Welfare Services for Children in India. Published by Hanam Publications, New Delhi.

Varma, S.K. 1998. Rights of the Child. Journal of the Indian Law Institute, Vol. 41(1).

Varma., Mathur., Agarwal., Goyle and Singh. 1996. Child Nutrition Problems and Prospects. Published by Shree Publications, Vol.II, Jaipur, p. 199.

Vasundhara, M.K. and Harish, B.N. 1993. Nutrition and Health Education through ICDS. Indian Journal of Maternal Child Health, pp. 25-26.

Vimala, R. 2004. Analysis of Positive Deviance in the ICDS Programme in Rajasthan and Uttar Pradesh, World Bank, New Delhi.

Vimala, R. 2004. Reflection on the ICDS Programme. Seminar, No. 546, www.india_seminar.com.

Wal, S. 1999. International Encyclopaedia of Child Development Priorities for 21st Century. Published by Sarup and Sons, New Delhi, pp. 29-31, 61-69.

Ward, W.M., Bruce King, M. and Gordon Dear. 1993. Statistical Reasoning in Psychology and Education. Published by Johnwiley and Sons, III Edition, Singapore.

Weiner. 1991. The Child and the State in India. Published by Oxford University Press, Calcutta.

Index

D

E

❑❑❑

2. The [illegible]
3. The child [illegible] children [illegible]
4. The [illegible] is low. [illegible]
5. The [illegible] child [illegible]
6. [illegible]
7. [illegible]
8. [illegible]
9. [illegible]
10. There is [illegible]
11. [illegible]
12. There is [illegible]